The Bills of Exchange Act, 1882 (45 & 46 Vict. c. 61) : with explanatory notes and decisions, and also an appendix / by Aviet Agabeg and William F. Barry.

Aviet Agabeg

The Making of Modern Law collection of legal archives constitutes a genuine revolution in historical legal research because it opens up a wealth of rare and previously inaccessible sources in legal, constitutional, administrative, political, cultural, intellectual, and social history. This unique collection consists of three extensive archives that provide insight into more than 300 years of American and British history. These collections include:

Legal Treatises, 1800-1926: over 20,000 legal treatises provide a comprehensive collection in legal history, business and economics, politics and government.

Trials, 1600-1926: nearly 10,000 titles reveal the drama of famous, infamous, and obscure courtroom cases in America and the British Empire across three centuries.

Primary Sources, 1620-1926: includes reports, statutes and regulations in American history, including early state codes, municipal ordinances, constitutional conventions and compilations, and law dictionaries.

These archives provide a unique research tool for tracking the development of our modern legal system and how it has affected our culture, government, business – nearly every aspect of our everyday life. For the first time, these high-quality digital scans of original works are available via print-on-demand, making them readily accessible to libraries, students, independent scholars, and readers of all ages.

old books. new life.

The BiblioLife Network

This project was made possible in part by the BiblioLife Network (BLN), a project aimed at addressing some of the huge challenges facing book preservationists around the world. The BLN includes libraries, library networks, archives, subject matter experts, online communities and library service providers. We believe every book ever published should be available as a high-quality print reproduction; printed on-demand anywhere in the world. This insures the ongoing accessibility of the content and helps generate sustainable revenue for the libraries and organizations that work to preserve these important materials.

The following book is in the "public domain" and represents an authentic reproduction of the text as printed by the original publisher. While we have attempted to accurately maintain the integrity of the original work, there are sometimes problems with the original work or the micro-film from which the books were digitized. This can result in minor errors in reproduction. Possible imperfections include missing and blurred pages, poor pictures, markings and other reproduction issues beyond our control. Because this work is culturally important, we have made it available as part of our commitment to protecting, preserving, and promoting the world's literature.

GUIDE TO FOLD-OUTS MAPS and OVERSIZED IMAGES

The book you are reading was digitized from microfilm captured over the past thirty to forty years. Years after the creation of the original microfilm, the book was converted to digital files and made available in an online database.

In an online database, page images do not need to conform to the size restrictions found in a printed book. When converting these images back into a printed bound book, the page sizes are standardized in ways that maintain the detail of the original. For large images, such as fold-out maps, the original page image is split into two or more pages

Guidelines used to determine how to split the page image follows:

• Some images are split vertically; large images require vertical and horizontal splits.
• For horizontal splits, the content is split left to right.
• For vertical splits, the content is split from top to bottom.
• For both vertical and horizontal splits, the image is processed from top left to bottom right.

THE

BILLS OF EXCHANGE ACT,

1882

(45 & 46 Vict. c 61).

WITH

EXPLANATORY NOTES AND DECISIONS,

AND ALSO

AN APPENDIX.

BY

AVIET AGABEG AND WILLIAM F. BARRY,

OF THE INNER TEMPLE, ESQUIRES, BARRISTERS-AT-LAW.

LONDON:

WILLIAM CLOWES AND SONS, LIMITED,

27, FLEET STREET.

1884.

LONDON
PRINTED BY WILLIAM CLOWES AND SONS, Limited,
STAMFORD STREET AND CHARING CROSS.

Rec'd Nov 29 1898

PREFACE.

THE codification of that important branch of the law which relates to bills of exchange, promissory notes and cheques, cannot fail to be of the utmost value to the mercantile community.

The Authors have ventured to publish this work, containing the above-mentioned code with explanatory notes of decisions, &c., showing what the law was and is, in the hope that such work may be of use both to the legal profession and to the mercantile community.

Many recent Irish and American decisions have been embodied herein, as well as an Act of the Council of the Viceroy of India (which will be found in the Appendix), passed in 1881, and containing provisions similar to those of the English Statute or Code.

In the margin of the English Act is given a reference to the corresponding section of the Indian Act, and *vice versâ ;* so that the reader by perusing either Act may be able to know the law of both countries. .

As this work contains an Abstract of Enactments, a List of Contents has been considered superfluous.

In conclusion, the Authors beg to acknowledge their great indebtedness to the following works, viz., the late

Mr. Justice Byles' Treatise on the Law of Bills of Exchange; Chalmers' Digest of the Law of Bills of Exchange; Chitty on Bills and Notes; Story on Bills and Notes; Parsons on Bills; Grant's Treatise on the Law relating to Bankers and Banking Companies; Walker's Treatise on Banking Law.

A. A.
W. F. B.

Temple,
   March, 1884.

INDEX OF CASES.

BILLS OF EXCHANGE ACT, 1882.

45 & 46 VICT. c. 61.

—◦◦◦—

ABSTRACT OF THE ENACTMENTS.

PART I.

PRELIMINARY.

1. Short title.
2. Interpretation of terms

PART II.

BILLS OF EXCHANGE

Form and Interpretation.

3. Bills of exchange defined.
4. Inland and foreign bills.
5. Effect where different parties to bill are same person.
6. Address to drawee.
7. Certainty required as to payee.
8. What bills are negotiable.
9. Sum payable.
10 Bill payable on demand
11. Bill payable at a future time.
12. Omission of date in bill payable after date.
13. Ante-dating and post-dating
14. Computation of time of payment.
15. Case of need.
16. Optional stipulations by drawer or indorser.
17. Definition and requisites of acceptance.
18. Time for acceptance.
19. General and qualified acceptances.
20. Inchoate instruments.
21. Delivery.

B

ζſ

PART IV.

PROMISSORY NOTES.

PART V.

SUPPLEMENTARY.

An Act to codify the law relating to Bills of Exchange, Cheques, and Promissory Notes.

Be it enacted by the Queen's most Excellent Majesty, by and with the advice and consent of the Lords Spiritual and Temporal, and Commons in this present Parliament assembled, and by the authority of the same, as follows :

PART I.

PRELIMINARY.

SS 1, 2.

1.—This Act may be cited as the Bills of Exchange Act, 1882.   Short title.

2.—In this Act, unless the context otherwise requires,   Interpretation of terms.
" Acceptance " (*a*) means an acceptance completed by delivery or notification.

" Action " includes counter-claim (*b*) and set-off. (*c*)

" Banker " (*d*) includes a body of persons whether in-   Ind Act, s. 3. corporated or not who carry on the business of banking.

" Bankrupt " (*e*) includes any person whose estate is vested in a trustee or assignee under the law for the time being in force relating to bankruptcy.

" Bearer " means the person in possession of a bill or note which is payable to bearer.

" Bill " means bill of exchange (*f*) and " note " means a promissory note (*g*).

" Delivery " (*h*) means transfer of possession, actual or   Ind Act, s. 14. constructive, from one person to another.

" Holder " (*j*) means the payee or indorsee of a bill or   Ind Act, s 8. note who is in possession of it, or the bearer thereof.

" Indorsement " (*k*) means an indorsement completed by delivery.

" Issue " (*l*) means the first delivery of a bill or note, complete in form to a person who takes it as a holder.

" Person " includes a body of persons whether incorporated or not.

" Value " means valuable consideration (*m*).

" Written " includes printed, and " writing " includes print.

(*a*) By sect. 17 of this Act the acceptance of a bill of exchange is defined to be " the signification by the drawee of his assent to the order of the drawer." And by the present (the 2nd) section an acceptance is defined to be an acceptance completed by delivery or notification as indeed it has been held to be hitherto, *Smith* v. *McClure*, 5 East, 476; also *In re Hayward*, L. R. 6 Ch. Ap. 546; 40 L. J. Bank. 49; and before delivery the acceptance may be obliterated, *Cox* v. *Troy*, 5 B. & Ald. 474; 1 D. & Ry. 38; therefore the cause of action does not arise until such delivery, *Chapman* v. *Cottrell*, 34 L. J. Ex. 186. See also note (*z*) to sect. 17 and subsects. (1) & (2) of sect. 21, and the notes thereto. As a bill of exchange, according to the definition given in the 3rd section of this Act, is an unconditional order in writing, addressed by one person to another, signed by the person giving it (i.e. the drawer) requiring the person to whom it is addressed *to pay* on demand or at a fixed or determinable future time a *sum certain in money* to or to the order of a specified person or to bearer; so the acceptance of a bill of exchange, which is the signification by the drawee of his assent to the order of the drawer, must be an engagement not only to pay the bill when due, but also to pay it in money. And such engagement, assent or acceptance must be in writing on the bill and signed by the drawee; and now the mere signature of the drawee without additional words is sufficient; see sect. 17 of this Act and sub-sects. (1) and (2) thereof and the notes to the same.

(*b*) As to counter-claim and set-off *vide* Judicature Act of 1873 (36 & 37 Vict. c. 66), sect. 24, sub-sect. 3, and also Order XIX., rule 3.

(*c*) As to set-off, see 2 Geo. 2, c. 22, s. 13, and the decisions thereon.

(*d*) By s. 45 of 33 & 34 Vict. c. 97, the term banker is defined to mean and include any corporation, society, partnership, and persons and every individual person carrying on the business of banking in the United Kingdom. " The ordinary relation between banker and customer is this: the customer opens an account with the banker by paying a sum of money into the bank, the banker undertaking to hold himself liable for the payment of a like sum to the customer's use, either paying interest on the money or not, as the course of business of the bank or the special arrangements between the banker and the individual customer may be, and also agreeing to honour or cash any cheques, or orders for the payment of any sums of money, which the customer may send to him, during business hours, to the extent of the sum deposited. A less ordinary, but still a not uncommon, relation between banker and customer is, that the banker makes advances to the customer or allows him to overdraw his account, charging interest on the advances, and in most cases requiring a deposit of securities, or obtaining the guarantee of some third person, for the repayment of such advances, with interest; and whilst such accommodation continues the former relation of the parties is of course inverted. But neither of these relations partakes of a fiduciary character, nor bears analogy to the relation between principal and factor or agent, who is a quasi trustee for the principal with respect to the particular matter for which he was appointed factor or agent. Therefore money paid into a bank ceases altogether to be the money of the person paying it; it is the money of the banker, who is bound to return an equivalent by paying a similar sum to that deposited with him when he is asked for it. To all intents it is the money of the banker to do as he may please with; though it is true that, in a popular sense, it is spoken of as 'My money at my banker's,' 'My balance at my banker's;' and though no one can doubt that in ordinary language the term 'ready money' includes the speaker's balance at his banker's." *Vide* Grant's Law of Bankers and Banking Companies (4th edition), pp. 1 and 2.

(*e*) All persons capable of making a binding contract are liable to be made bankrupt. Married women therefore who are competent to be petitioning creditors are amenable to bankruptcy. As to what married women are competent to be petitioning creditors see *Roche & Hazlitt's* Bankruptcy (2nd Edition), pp. 357 & 358. As to adjudication in bankruptcy see section 20 of the Bankruptcy Act of 1883 (46 & 47 Vic. c. 52). As to the definition of "commencement of bankruptcy" see sect. 43 of the Bankruptcy Act of 1883. As to appointment of trustee and the vesting and division of the property of the bankrupt, see section 54 of the Bankruptcy Act of 1883. By section 168 of the Act of 1883 "Trustee" means the trustee in bankruptcy of a debtor's estate.

(*f*) By sub sect. (1) of sect. 3 of this Act a bill of exchange is defined to be an unconditional order in writing addressed by one person to another, signed by the person giving it, requiring the person to whom it is addressed to pay on demand or at a fixed or determinable future time a sum certain in money to, or to the order of, a specified person or to bearer. See further that sub-section and also sub-sects. (3) & (4) of sect. 3 and the subdivisions thereof, and the notes to the same respectively.

(*g*) By sub-sect. (1) of sect. 83 of this Act a promissory note is defined to be an unconditional promise in writing made by one person to another, signed by the maker, engaging to pay, on demand

or at a fixed or determinable future time, a sum certain in money,
to, or to the order of, a specified person, or to bearer. See further that
sub-section as well as sub-sects. (2), (3), & (4) of sect. 83, and all the
notes to the same respectively.

(*h*) Delivery has always been necessary to complete an acceptance
or indorsement, *Smith* v. *McClure*, 5 East, 476, *Cox* v. *Troy*, 5 B. &
Ald. 474; *Chapman* v. *Cottrell*, 34 L. J. Ex. 186, *In re Hayward*,
L. R 6 Ch. Ap. 546; 40 L. J. Bankr. 49. See also note (*z*) to
sect. 17, and note (*z*) to sub-sect. (1) of sect. 21.

(*j*) Holder has been defined to be "any one in actual or constructive possession of the bill and entitled at law to recover or receive its
contents from the parties to it." Byles on Bills (13th Edition), p. 2.
As to who can sue upon a bill, see sect. 38. It is doubtful whether
such words as "entitled at law to recover or receive its contents" are
any longer necessary to the definition of holder. It is submitted that
they are not, inasmuch as by the definition given by this section a
holder means "the payee or the indorsee or the bearer of a bill or note
who also is in possession of it."

(*k*) As to delivery see note (*h*) hereto. An indorsement is
generally though not necessarily made by the signature of the
indorser on the back of the bill. Such signature may however be put
in any part of the bill. An indorser of a bill is in the position of a
surety for the acceptor, and as such upon payment to a discounter of
the amount due on the bill after its dishonour by the acceptor, is
entitled to the benefit of the securities deposited by the acceptor with
the discounter, whether at the time of his indorsement he knew of the
deposit of those securities or not, *Duncan Fox & Co.* v. *North and
South Wales Bank*, 6 App. Cas. 1, 50 L. J. Ch. D. 355; 43 L. T.
N. S. 706; 29 W. R. 763.

(*l*) A bill of exchange is not issued till in the hands of the party
entitled to demand the money, till then it may be altered without
rendering a fresh stamp necessary, *Ex parte Bignold, in re Brereton*,
2 Mont. & Ayr. 650; 1 Deac. 712.

(*m*) The rules relating to the consideration of a bill or note are in
general the same as those which relate to the consideration of any
other simple contract, see sect. 27, sub-sect. (*a*). A consideration has been defined to be "either some detriment to the plaintiff,
sustained for the sake or at the instance of the defendant, or some
benefit to the defendant moving from the plaintiff," see Addison on
Contracts (7th Edition by Mr Justice Cave), p. 7; see also *Sowerby*
v. *Butcher*, 2 Cr. & M. 368; *Hulse* v. *Hulse*, 17 C. B. 711.

PART II.

BILLS OF EXCHANGE.

Form and Interpretation.

3.—(1.) A bill of exchange (z) is an unconditional (y) ordei in writing, addressed (x) by one person to another, signed (w) by the person giving it, (v) requiring (t) the person (s) to whom it is addressed to pay on demand (r) or at a fixed or determinable future time, (q) a sum certain (p) in money, (o) to or to the order of a specified person (n) or to bearer (m).

(2.) An instrument which does not comply with these conditions, or which orders any act to be done in addition to the payment of money, is not a bill of exchange (l).

(3.) An order to pay out of a particular fund (k) is not unconditional within the meaning of this section ; but an unqualified order to pay, coupled with (a) an indication (j) of a particular fund out of which the drawee is to reimburse himself or a particular account (h) to be debited with the amount, or (b) a statement of the transaction (g) which gives rise to the bill, is unconditional.

(4.) A bill is not invalid by reason :—

    (a.) That it is not dated; (f).

    (b.) That it does not specify the value given, or that any value has been given ; (e).

    (c.) That it does not specify the place where it is drawn, or the place where it is payable (d).

(z) The definition here given of a bill of exchange is the same as that given prior to this Act, *Vide* Chalmers' Digest of the Law of Bills of Exchange (2nd Edition); Byles on Bills (13th Edition), p. 1. As to the definition of a promissory note, see sub-sect. (1) of sect. 83 of this Act. By sub-sect. (1) of sect. 89 of this Act, the provisions of this Act relating to bills of exchange, are with a few exceptions, equally applicable to promissory notes. There is no particular form or language necessary to make a document a valid bill of exchange, any words will do, provided they embrace the different points of the definition given by this section. The following is a common form of a bill of exchange, viz.:

LONDON, 1st *January*, 1883.

£100. 0s. 0d.

Three months after date pay to our order the sum of one hundred pounds. Value received.

To Messrs. JONES BROTHERS.

J. SMITH & SON.

(*y*) Before this Act too it was held that the order must be to pay absolutely, in other words, the payment must not be made to depend on a contingency, Story on Bills, s. 46; *Palmer* v. *Pratt*, 9 Moore, 358; 2 Bing. 185; *Carlos* v. *Fancourt*, 5 T. R. 482; *Kingston* v. *Long*, 4 Doug. 9; *Lovell* v. *Hill*, 6 C. & P. 238; *Richardson* v. *Martyr*, 25 L. T. 64; it must not be payable out of another person's fund, *Dawkes* v. *De Lorane*, 3 Wils. 209; *Clarke* v. *Percival*, 2 B. & Ad. 660; *Robins* v. *May*, 11 A. & E. 213; but see *Ellison* v. *Collingridge*, 9 C. B. 570. The following document was held not to be a promissory note, viz.: "We promise to pay on the death of George Hindshaw, provided he leaves either of us sufficient to pay the said sum, or if we otherwise shall be able to pay it," *Roberts* v. *Peake*, 1 Burr. 323. The makers of a joint and several note signed on the back of it a memorandum in these words: "The within note is taken for security of all such balances as James Marriott may happen to owe to Thomas Leeds & Co., not extending further than the within-named sum of £200; but this note is to be in force for six months, and no money is liable to be called for sooner in any case." It was held that in the hands of the payee the document was an agreement, and not a promissory note; but that in the hands of a *bonâ fide* holder who received it as a promissory note, it might possibly be considered as such, *Leeds* v. *Lancashire*, 2 Camp. 205; see also *Haussoullier* v. *Hartsinck*, 7 T. R. 733. In *Pearson* v. *Garrett*, 4 Mod. 242, it was held that an action brought by the payee of a note by which the maker promised to pay him sixty guineas within two months after the maker shall have married such a person, cannot be sustained, for such a note was not within the custom of merchants. It has been also decided that a promissory note to pay money so many days after the defendant should marry is not a negotiable note within that statute, *Beardsley* v. *Baldwin*, 2 Stra. 1151. Any promise, order, or undertaking, therefore, which is dependent on any such contingency, is not a promissory note or bill of exchange. For the same reason a note promising to pay "on the sale or produce, immediately when sold, of the White Hart, St. Albans, Herts, and the goods, &c., value received," was held not to be a promissory note within the statute 3 & 4 Anne, c. 9, *Hill* v. *Halford*, 2 B. & P. 413; but see *Dixon* v. *Nutall*, 6 C. & P. 320. A promise to pay £50 "at such period of time that my circumstances will admit without detriment to myself or family," is not a note; *Ex parte Tootell*, 4 Ves. 372. "At 12 months date I promise to pay Messrs. R. F. & Co. £500, to be held by them as collateral security for any moneys now owing to them by B., which they may be unable to recover on realizing the securities they now hold, and others which may be placed in their hands by him," is not a note; *Robins* v. *May*, 11 A. & E. 213. In *Ayrey* v. *Fearnsides*, 4 M. & W. 168, a document whereby the defendants promised to pay the plaintiffs or order the sum of £13 0s. 0d. for value received, with interest at £5 per cent. and all fines according to rules, was held not to be a promissory note. A promise to pay a certain sum by instalments, but it was declared that "all installed payments thereupon from and after the decease of the plaintiff should cease," is not a note; *Worley* v. *Harrison*, 3 A. &. E. 669. In *Shenton* v. *James*, 5 Q. B. 199, the following document was held not to be a promissory note, viz.: "On demand I promise to pay W. S. £50 in consideration of foregoing and forbearing an action in the Queen's Bench for damages ascertained by consent to amount to that sum by reason of the injury sustained by his wife in respect of my liability for non-repair of a footway." An order for a sum payable ninety days after sight or when realised was held not to be a bill of exchange, *Alexander* v. *Thomas*, 16 Q. B. 333. In *Drury* v. *Macaulay*, 16 M. & W. 146, the following document was held not to be a promissory note: "*Drury* v. *Vaughan*. In consideration of W. Drury not taking any further proceedings in the above actions, I hereby undertake with the said W. Drury that I will pay him £3 5s. 0d. every quarter of a year from this day until the whole of the principal money now due from Messrs. J. & T. Vaughan to Mr. Drury, £26 1s. 0d., with lawful interest, be paid and satisfied; the first of such quarterly payments to become due on the 30th October next. It is understood that this undertaking is not to be a release or discharge of the note signed by Messrs. Vaughan to the said W. Drury on the 9th March, 1840, but as an additional security for the above-mentioned amount now due on such note, with the interest." The following document was also held not to be a promissory note. "Nine months after date I promise to pay to the secretary for the time being of the Indian Laudable and Mutual Assurance Society or order, Company's rupees twenty thousand, with interest at the rate of six per cent. per annum. And I hereby deposit in his hands twenty two Union Bank shares, as particularised at foot, by way of pledge or security for the due payment of the said sum of Company's rupees twenty thousand, as aforesaid; and in default thereof, hereby authorize the secretary for the time being, forthwith, either by private or public sale, absolutely to

sell or dispose of the said twenty-two Union Bank shares so deposited
with him; and out of the proceeds of sale to reimburse himself the
said loan of Company's rupees twenty thousand, and interest thereon
as aforesaid, he rendering to me any surplus which may be forth-
coming from such sale. And I hereby promise and undertake to make
good whatever, if anything, may be wanting over and above the
proceeds of such sale, to make up the full amount of the said loan of
Company's rupees twenty thousand, and interest as aforesaid," *Storm*
v. *Stirling*, 3 E. & B. 832, affirmed by the Court of Exchequer Chamber,
6 E. & B. 333. See further as to this point sect. 83, note (*b*). It has
been held also that if the contingency or event on the happening of
which a promise or an order to pay is made or given, must inevitably
happen, the document is a good bill or note. Thus a promise to pay
within two months after a king's ship is paid off, was held to be a good
promissory note, *Evans* v. *Underwood*, 1 Wils. 262; see also *Andrews*
v. *Franklin*, 1 Stra. 24; see these cases discussed in a note on p. 334
of 1 Sel. N. P. 13th ed., see sect. 11, subs. 2. So in *Roffey* v. *Greenwell*, 10 A. & E. 222, a promise on behalf of oneself and executors to
pay F. H. or her executors one year after his death was held to be a
good promissory note; see also *Cooke* v. *Colehan*, 2 Stra. 1217;
Sackett v. *Palmer*, 25 Barb. 179; a note of hand, however, payable to
an infant, when he shall come of age, specifying the day, is a good
note, *Goss* v. *Nelson*, 1 Burr. 226. A bill or note may be made
payable by instalments, *Worley* v. *Harrison*, 3. A. & E. 669; *Oridge*
v. *Sherborne*, 11 M. & W. 374; and it may also provide that on
default of one instalment the whole shall become payable on demand,
Carlon v. *Kenealey*, 12 M. & W. 139; *Cook* v. *Horne*, 29 L. T. N. S.
369; the time for the payment of the instalments must be stated in it,
Moffat v. *Edwards*, C. & M. 16. As is frequently the case a bill may
be directed to be paid "as per advice" or "without further advice."
See Chitty on Bills (9th Edition), 162.

(*x*) See *Gray* v. *Milner*, 8 Taunt. 739, *Miller* v. *Thompson*,
3 M. & G. 576; *Davis* v. *Clarke*, 6 Q. B. 16; see also *Polhill* v.
Walter, 3 B. & Ad. 114; *Jackson* v. *Hudson*, 2 Camp. 447; and
Reynolds v. *Peto*, 11 Ex. 418.

(*w*) In *Geary* v. *Physic*, 5 B. & C. 234, it was held that an indorsement written with pencil is valid. In that case Abbott, C.J., in
giving judgment said: "There is no authority for saying that where
the law requires a contract to be in writing, that writing must be in
ink. The passage cited from Lord Coke shews that a deed must be
written on paper or parchment, but it does not show that it must be
written in ink. That being so, I am of opinion that an indorsement
on a bill of exchange may be by writing in pencil." It follows that
any signature to a negotiable instrument may be written with pencil;
and such signature may be made by a mark, *George* v. *Surrey*, 1 M. &
M. 516. An instrument in the form of a bill of exchange, addressed

to and accepted by the defendant, but without the names of either a payee or drawer, is neither a bill of exchange nor a promissory note, but only an inchoate instrument. *McCall* v. *Taylor,* 19 C B. N. S. 301; 34 L. J. C. P. 365; see also *Ex parte Hayward, In re Hayward,* L. R. 6 Ch. 546; 40 L J. Bankr. 49. Without the drawer's signature an instrument in all other respects complete as a bill, and signed even by the acceptor, is not a bill of exchange, *Stoessiger* v. *South Eastern Railway Company,* 3 E. & B. 557; as to inchoate instruments and the power of filling them in, see sect. 20.

(*v*) The person giving the order is the drawer. As to the necessity for the signature of the drawer see the last note.   Ind Act, s 7

(*t*) No precise words are requisite for the order or promise to pay, *Morris* v. *Lee,* 2 Ld. Raym. 1397; 1 Stra. 629; the question is whether it imports a promise; *Brooks* v. *Elkins,* 2 M. & W. 74. In *Brown* v. *De Winton,* 6 C. B. at p. 376, it is said that though no precise form is requisite, the instrument ought to have the essentials of a contract. See also *Peto* v. *Reynolds,* 9. Ex. at p. 416. But a *request* is not sufficient, *Little* v. *Slackford,* 1 M & M. 171.

(*s*) The person to whom it is addressed is the drawee of the instrument. By sub-sect. (1) of sect. 6 of this Act the drawee must be named or otherwise indicated in a bill with reasonable certainty. See further that sect. and the notes thereto. By sub-sect. (1) of sect. 5 of this Act a bill may be drawn payable to, or to the order of the drawer. By the sub-section just referred to, a bill may be drawn payable to or to the order of the drawee. See further that sub-section and the notes thereto.   Ind. Act, s. 7.

(*r*) The time of payment is generally stated in the bill or note, which, however, must be made payable at a time determinable, or on an event which must happen at some time or other, see sect. 11, subs. 2, also *Andrews* v. *Franklin,* 1 Stra. 24; *Cooke* v. *Colehan,* 2 Stra. 1217; *Roffey* v. *Greenwell,* 10 A. & E. 222; *Pearson* v. *Garret,* 4 Mod. 242; *Evans* v. *Underwood,* 1 Wils. 262; *Goss* v. *Nelson,* 1 Burr. 226, *Ex parte Tootell,* 4 Ves. 372; *Clayton* v. *Gosling,* 5 B. & C. 360; see also notes (*y*) hereto. A bill or note which is payable to bearer generally, that is to say, on which no time of payment is specified, is payable on demand, as is now provided by division (*b*) of sub-sect. (1) of sect. 10 of this Act, which see, as also the notes thereto.

(*q*) By section 11 of this Act a bill is payable at a determinable future time within the meaning of this Act which is expressed to be payable: (1) At a fixed period after date or sight; (2.) On or at a fixed period after the occurrence of a specified event which is certain to happen. See that section and the notes thereto. See also note (*y*) hereto.

(*p*) The amount of the bill or note must be a sum certain. Thus in *Bolton* v. *Dugdale,* 4 B & Ad 619, the following document was held not to be a promissory note, viz.: " Received and borrowed

of A. B. £30 which I promise to pay with interest at the rate of
£5 per cent. I also promise to pay the demands of the sick club at
H. in part of interest, and the remaining stock and interest to be
paid on demand to the said A. B;" nor a document by which the
party promises to pay a sum certain, and all such other sums as by
reference to his books he owed, *Smith* v. *Nightingale*, 2 Stark. 375;
but see *Leeds* v. *Lancashire*, 2 Camp. 205; *Jones* v. *Simpson*, 2 B. &
C. 318. In *Ayrey* v. *Fearnsides*, 4 M. & W. 168, it was held that a
document whereby one promised to pay a sum certain and all fines
according to rule was not a promissory note. As to bills and notes
payable with interest, see *Warrington* v. *Early*, 2 E. & B. 763; *Ayrey*
v. *Fearnsides*, *supra*; and as to such instruments payable by instalments, see *Origde* v. *Sherborne*, 11 M. & W. 374; *Carlon* v. *Kenealy*,
12 M. & W. 139; 13 L. J. Ex. 64; see also *Worley* v. *Harrison*, 3 A.
& E. 669; Story on Notes, s. 28. But the rate of the interest payable
on the bill or note must be fixed. Thus an instrument whereby the
maker promises to pay £400 with "bank interest" is not a promissory
note, *Tennent* v. *Crawford*, Court of Sess. Cas., 4th series, Vol. 5,
p. 433. As to interest see division (*b*) of sub-sect. (1) of sect. 57 of
this Act and the notes thereto; see also sect. 9 of this Act and the
sub-sections thereof and the notes thereto.

(*o*) Bills and notes must be for the payment of money only; thus
an acceptance to pay by another bill is no acceptance, *Russell* v.
Phillips, 14 Q. B. 891, 19 L. J. Q. B. 227; *Petit* v. *Benson*, Comb.
452; *Davies* v. *Wilkinson*, 10 A. & E. 98. As to promissory notes
containing a pledge of security, see sect. 83, subs. 3.

(*n*) A specified person, *i.e.* the payee; he need not be named, but must be
a person who is capable of being ascertained when the bill is drawn,
Gray v. *Milner*, 8 Taunt. 739; and the payee must not be uncertain,
see *Storm* v. *Stirling*, 6 E. & B. 333. And now by sub-sect. (1) of
sect. 7 of this Act, where a bill is not payable to bearer, the payee must
be named or otherwise indicated therein with reasonable certainty.
See sub-sects. (1) and (2) of sect. 7 of this Act, and the notes
thereto. As to extrinsic evidence for identifying the payee, see *Soares*
v. *Glyn*, 8 Q. B. 24. By sub-sect. (4) of sect. 8, a bill is payable
to order which is expressed to be so payable, or which is expressed to
be payable to a particular person, and does not contain words prohibiting transfer or indicating an intention that it should not be transferable
So that it would follow from the sub-section just referred to that if a bill
be payable to a particular person, it is payable to his order and is
therefore negotiable, thus setting aside the decisions wherein it was
held that unless a bill or note be payable to order or to bearer, it is not
negotiable, *Hill* v. *Lewis*, 1 Salk. 133; *Smith* v. *Kendall*, 6 T. R. 123;
Plimley v. *Westley*, 2 Bing. N. C. 251. If a bill be payable to the
order of a particular person, it is payable to him or his order at his
option; sect. 8, subs. 5; *Smith* v. *McClure*, 5 East, 476. It has been
held that the addition of the words "or order" does not render the

instrument invalid, *Kershaw* v. *Cox*, 3 Esp. 246. As to the negotiation of bills payable to order see subsect. (3) of sect. 31 of this Act and the notes thereto. It has been held that a bill made payable to the order of —— may be filled up by anyone who came regularly to the possession of it with his own name; *Cruchley* v. *Clarance*, 2 M. & S. 90; *Crutchley* v. *Mann*, 5 Taunt. 529; even after the acceptor's death, *Carter* v. *White*, 20 Ch. D. 228; see also *Hatch* v. *Searles*, 2 Sm. & G. 147.

    (*m*) As to the definition of "bearer" see sect. 2. By sub-sect. (3) of sect. 7 of this Act, where the payee is a fictitious or non-existing person, the bill may be treated as payable to bearer. See that sub-section and the notes thereto; see also the last preceding note (*n*) hereto. As to the negotiation of bills payable to bearer see sub-sect. (2) of sect. 31 of this Act and the notes thereto.

    (*l*) As to instruments requiring or ordering any act to be done in addition to the payment of money, see note (*o*) hereto. It has been held that if an instrument is so ambiguous that it is doubtful whether it is a bill of exchange or promissory note, it may be treated as either, *Edis* v. *Bury*, 6 B. & C. 433; *Block* v. *Bell*, 1 Moo. & Rob. 149; *Shuttleworth* v. *Stephens*, 1 Camp. 407; *Allan* v. *Mawson*, 4 Camp. 115; *Fielder* v. *Marshall*, 9 C. B. N. S. 606; *Lloyd* v. *Oliver*, 18 Q. B. 471, *Forbes* v. *Marshall*, 11 Ex. 166; audit is so provided by sect. 17 of the Indian Act. See also 1 Parsons on Bills, 63. A bill drawn by a bank at one place on a branch bank at another place may be declared on as a note; *Miller* v. *Thomson*, 3 M. & G. 576. As to coupons and letters of credit, see Byles on Bills (13th edition), 99.

    (*k*) It has been long settled that an instrument, though in the form of a bill or note, but made payable out of a particular fund, is not a bill or note, *Dawkes* v. *Delorane*, 3 Wils. 207; *Stevens* v. *Hill*, 5 Esp. 247; nor is a promise to pay, but "if the agent does not sell enough in one year, one more is granted;" *Miller* v. *Poage*, 41 Amer. Rep 82; nor if it state that the amount is directed by an order of the Court to be paid to the order of the drawers, *Russell* v. *Powell*, 14 M. & W. 418; nor if the bill be accepted for A. B. of Leghorn, to pay as remitted from thence at usance; *Banbury* v. *Lisset*, 2 Stra. 1211; nor if it be payable on the sale or produce of a house when sold, *Hill* v. *Halford*, 2 B. & P. 413.

    (*j*) An instrument containing simply an indication of a particular fund out of which the money is to come is a bill of exchange, *Haussoullier* v. *Hartsinck*, 7 T. R. 733, where the promise was to pay £50, "being a portion of value as under deposited in security for the payment hereof."

    (*h*) As for instance, pay to Messrs. Griffin, Morris, Griffin & Morris, or order, on account of moneys advanced by me for the Isle of Man Slate and Flag Company, Ld., *Griffin* v. *Weatherby*, L. R. 3 Q. B. 753. As to a bill expressed on the face of it to be "against cotton per *Sultan*," see *Inman* v. *Clare*, Johnson, 769. As to a bill accepted subject to the delivery of shipping documents, see *Banner v. Johnston,* L. R. 5 H. L. 157.

(*g*) Thus in *Dixon v. Nuttall,* 6 C. & P. 320, the following document was held to be a good promissory note, viz.: "I promise to pay to Mary Ann Dixon or bearer, on demand, the sum of £16 at sight by given up clothes and papers." Again an instrument reciting the fact that real security has been given is a good note, *Fancourt v. Thorne,* 9 Q. B. 312; see also *Haussoullier v. Hartsinck,* 7 T. R. 733.

(*f*) A date never was considered necessary; and if the date is omitted, it is considered as dated on the day on which it was made, which is shewn by parol evidence, *Davis v. Jones,* 17 C. B. 625; 25 L. J. C. P. 91; *Giles v. Bourne,* 6 M. & S. 73; Story on Bills, sect. 37; see also sect. 12 of this Act and the notes thereto. Where, however, the instrument is dated, the date on it is *prima facie* evidence of the time when the instrument was made, *Malpas v. Clements,* 19 L. J. Q. B. 435; *Laws v. Rand,* 3 C. B. N. S. 442; *Anderson v. Weston,* 6 Bing. N. C. 296; 8 Scott, 583; *Potez v. Glossop,* 2 Ex. 195. And now it is so provided by subsect. (1) of sect. 13 of this Act; see that sub-section and the notes thereto. Before this Act there was an exception to this rule, viz. a bill, dated on a Sunday, see *Begbie v. Levy,* 1 C. & J. 180. But this exception is now removed by sub-sect. (2) of sect. 13 of this Act. As to ante-dated or post-dated instruments, see *Passmore v. North,* 13 East, 517; *Austin v. Bunyard,* 34 L. J. Q. B. 217; 11 Jur. N. S. 874; 12 L. T. N. S. 452; *Forster v. Mackreth,* L. R. 2 Ex. 163; 36 L. J. Ex. 94; *Bull v. O'Sullivan,* L. R. 6 Q. B. 209; 40 L. J. Q. B. 141; *Gatty v. Fry,* 2 Ex. D. 265; 46 L. J. Ex. 605; 36 L. T. N. S. 182. And so it is now provided by subsect. (2) of sect. 13 of this Act, which see.

(*e*) The consideration of a bill of exchange and promissory note is presumed till the contrary appear; see sections 27–30 (both inclusive) of this Act and the notes thereto. Before this Act it had been settled that the words "value received" are not essential to constitute a bill; *White v. Ledwick,* 4 Doug. 247; *Hatch v. Trayes,* 11 A. & E. 702. Where a bill or a note states that it is for value received parol evidence is admissible to shew the want of the consideration, *Thomson v. Clubley,* 1 M. & W. 212; *Abbott v. Henricks,* 2 Scott, N. R. 183; but not to show a different consideration to that stated, *Ridout v. Bristow,* 1 Cr & J. 231; *Nelson v. Serle,* 4 M. & W. 795; *Abrey v. Crux,* L. R. 5 C. P. 37; *Hill v. Wilson,* 42 L. J. Ch. 817. But the consideration of a bill or note must not be future or executory, as it thus becomes conditional, *Drury v. Macaulay,* 16 M. & W. 146.

(*d*) "It never has been necessary to specify on a bill or note the name of the place where it is drawn or made, nor the place where it is made payable; although of course both the places are frequently specified." See Chalmers' Digest of the Law of Bills of Exchange (2nd edition) p. 24; and Byles on Bills (13th Edition) p. 79.

4.—(1.) An inland bill is a bill which is or on the face of it purports to be (*a*) both drawn and payable within the British Islands, or (*b*) drawn within the British Islands upon some person resident therein (*z*). Any other bill is a foreign bill.

For the purposes of this Act " British Islands " mean any part of the United Kingdom of Great Britain and Ireland, the Islands of Man, Guernsey, Jersey, Alderney, and Sark, and islands adjacent to any of them being part of the dominions of Her Majesty (*y*).

(2.) Unless the contrary appear on the face of the bill the holder may treat it as an inland bill (*x*).

(*z*) This is the same as the definition in sect. 7 of the 19 & 20 Vict. c. 97, which is as follows: " Every bill of exchange or promissory note drawn or made in any part of the United Kingdom of Great Britain and Ireland, the Islands of Man, Guernsey, Jersey, Alderney, and Sark, and the islands adjacent to any of them, being part of the dominions of Her Majesty, and payable in or drawn upon any person resident in any part of the said United Kingdom and Islands, shall be deemed to be an inland bill."

(*y*) It will be seen that the local limits specified herein are the same as the local limits in sect. 7 of the 19 & 20 Vict. c 97, above cited, see the last preceding note hereto.

(*z*) " The statute (*i.e.* 55 Geo. III. c 184) *primâ facie* intends that inland bills are such as are not drawn payable abroad," per Lord Abinger in *Amner* v. *Clarke*, 2 B. & Ad. 471. In the course of the arguments in that case his lordship remarked. " It (*i.e.* the same statute) defines an inland bill by saying what a foreign bill is, and all others are taken to be inland bills." See also *Armani* v. *Castrique*, 13 M. & W. 443. As to what is an Inland instrument in India, see sec. 11 of the Indian Act.

Effect where
different
parties to bill
are the same
person

Ind. Act, s. 13.

5.—(1.) A bill may be drawn payable to, or to the order of, the drawer (*a*) ; or it may be drawn payable to, or to the order of, the drawee (*b*).

(2.) Where in a bill drawer and drawee are the same person (*c*), or where the drawee is a fictitious (*d*) person or a person not having a capacity to contract (*e*), the holder may treat the instrument, at his option, either as a bill of exchange or as a promissory note (*f*).

(*a*) The drawer is the person who gives the order or direction ; see note (*v*) to subsect. (1) of sect. 3 of this Act. As to a bill drawn

C

SS. 5, 6.

Effect where
different
parties to bill
are the same
person.

Ind. Act, s. 42.

payable to the drawer or his order, see *Butler* v. *Crips*, 1 Salk. 130. As to the negotiation of bills payable to order see subsect. (3) of sect. 31 of this Act, and the notes thereto. Where a bill is drawn payable to the drawer's order it is payable to himself without alleging any order made, *Smith* v. *McClure*, 5 East, 476. Where a bill is drawn in the name of a fictitious person payable to the order of the drawer, the acceptor is considered as undertaking to pay to the order of the person who signed as the drawer, *Cooper* v. *Meyer*, 10 B. & C. 468; see also 1 Parsons on Bills, 32; *Beeman* v. *Duck*, 11 M. & W. 251.

(*b*) The drawee is the person on or to whom the order or direction is given, and on his acceptance he becomes and is known as the acceptor, and is then presumed to be the principal debtor on the bill. As regards acceptance see sect. 2 and sub-sect. (1) & (2) of sect. 17 of this Act and the notes thereto. Where a bill is drawn by the drawer on himself it is considered a promissory note, *Roach* v. *Ostler*, 1 M. & R. 120; *Williams* v *Ayers*, 3 ap. Cas. at p. 142. So also where a bill is drawn by a bank at one place on a branch bank at another place, it may be treated as a promissory note, *Miller* v. *Thomson*, 3 M. & G. 576.

(*c*) As regards the drawer and drawee being the same person, see *Roach* v. *Ostler*, 1 M. & R. 120; also *Miller* v. *Thomson*, 3 M. & G. 576; *Williams* v. *Ayers*, 3 Ap Cas. at p. 142, see also note (*v*) to sect. 50 of this Act.

(*d*) As to fictitious parties, it has been held that where a bill is drawn in the name of a fictitious person, payable to the order of the drawer, the acceptor is considered as undertaking to pay to the order of the person who signed as the drawer, *Cooper* v. *Meyer*, 10 B. & C. 468; see also *Beeman* v *Duck*, 11 M. & W. 251. Where the bill was made payable to a fictitious or non-existing person, it was held to be payable to bearer, *Phillips* v. *Im-Thurn*, L. R 1 C. P. 464, following *Minet* v. *Gibson*, 3 T. R. 481; and overruling *Bennett* v *Farnell*, 1 Camp. 130 and *Were* v. *Taylor*, cited in 1 Camp. 131; see also *Tatlock* v. *Harris*, 3 T. R. 174, *Vere* v. *Lewis*, 3 T. R. 182; Story on Bills, s. 56

(*e*) As regards the capacity to contract, see subsects (1) & (2) of sect. 22 of this Act and the notes thereto.

(*f*) As to promissory notes see sects. 83–89 of this Act and the sub-sections of the same and notes thereto.

Address to
drawee.

6.—(1.) The drawee must be named or otherwise indicated in a bill with reasonable certainty (*a*).

(2.) A bill may be addressed to two or more drawees, whether they are partners or not, but an order addressed to two drawees in the alternative or to two or more drawees in succession is not a bill of exchange (*b*).

(*a*) As to a bill not addressed to any one see *Reynolds* v. *Peto*,
11 Ex. 418 Where a bill was made payable at No. 1 Wilmot Street, ——————
opposite the Lamb, "Bethnal Green, London," without being addressed
to any person, and the defendant who resided there accepted it, he was
held liable upon the instrument as a bill of exchange, *Gray* v. *Milner*,
8 Taunt. 739; 3 Moore, 90. In *Peto* v. *Reynolds*, 9 Ex. at p. 416,
Alderson, B., says that "*Gray* v. *Milner* may be thus explained · that
a bill of exchange, made payable at a particular house or place, is
meant to be addressed to the person who resides at that place or
house." *In R.* v. *Curry*, 2 Moody's C C. 218, the instrument was
held not to be a bill, apparently on the ground that it was not
addressed to anyone. In *Shuttleworth* v. *Stephens*, 1 Camp. 407, an
instrument had the word "*at*" instead of the word "*to*" preceding
the name of the drawees, it was held that it was a bill of exchange or
that it might be considered a promissory note at the option of the
holder; so also an instrument which appears on common observation
to be a bill of exchange may be treated as such, although words be
introduced into it for the purpose of deception which might make it a
promissory note, *Allan* v. *Mawson*, 4 Camp. 115.

(*b*) As to a bill addressed to one man and accepted by another, see
Davis v. *Clarke*, 13 L. J Q B. 305; 6 Q B. 16. "There is no
authority," said Lord Denman, in his judgment in this case, "either in
the English law or the general law merchant, for holding a party to
be liable as acceptor upon a bill addressed to another" See also
Polhill v. *Walter*, 3 B. & Ad. 114; *Jackson* v. *Hudson*, 2 Camp 447.
"Save in the case of acceptances for honour or per procuration, no one
can become a party to a bill quâ acceptor who is not a proper draw ee,
or in other words an addressee," per Lord Watson in *Steele* v.
McKinlay, 5 Ap. Cas. at p 779 A bill addressed to the M. Co was
accepted by F. M. "for M Co. and self;" Held, that F. M. was not
liable as acceptor, *Malcolmson* v. *Malcolmson*, 1 L. R. Ir. 228

7.—(1.) Where a bill is not payable to bearer, the
payee must be named or otherwise indicated therein with
reasonable certainty (*a*).

(2.) A bill may be made payable to two or more
payees jointly (*b*), or it may be made payable in the
alternative to one of two, or one or some of several (*c*)
payees. A bill may also be made payable to the holder
of an office for the time being (*d*).

(3.) Where the payee is a fictitious or non-existing
person the bill may be treated as payable to bearer (*e*).

(*a*) In *Yates* v. *Nash*, 8 C B N S. 581, 29 L J C P. 306, it was
held that to constitute a valid bill of exchange, the payee must be a

person who is capable of being ascertained at the time the instrument is drawn. It has also been held that there must be a payee ascertained by name or designation, per Jervis, C. J., in *Cowie* v. *Stirling*, 6 E. & B. 333; see also *Reynolds* v. *Peto*, 11 Ex. 418; *Gray* v. *Milner*, 8 Taunt. 739. Where the name is spelt wrong, or the payee wrongly designated, the payee may indorse the bill as therein described, adding, if he think fit, his proper signature; sect. 32, subs. 4. So where a note was made payable "to trustees" without naming them, that was sufficient; *Holmes* v. *Jaques*, L. R. 1. Q. B. 376; *Megginson* v. *Harper*, 2 Cr. & M. 822; see also *Soares* v. *Glyn*, 8 Q. B. 24. Where a man and his son are of the same name, the instrument is payable to the father, unless the contrary is shown, *Sweeting* v. *Fowler*, 1 Stark. 106. If a bill or note be made payable to a specified person, the words "to his order" may with the consent of the parties be added without rendering the instrument invalid, *Kershaw* v *Cox*, 3 Esp. 246.

(*b*) See *Megginson* v. *Harper*, 2 Cr & M. 322; *Holmes* v. *Jaques*, L. R. 1 Q. B. 376.

(*c*) In *Watson* v. *Evans*, 32 L. J. Ex. 137, 1 H. & C. 662, it was decided that the following instrument was a promissory note, and that the three persons mentioned therein could jointly maintain an action thereon, viz.: "On demand we jointly and severally promise to pay to Messrs. Joseph Watson, Thomas Southern, and Daniel Mayer, or to their order, or the major part of them, the sum of one hundred pounds, &c., &c."

(*d*) In *Robertson* v. *Sheward*, 1 M. & G. 511; 1 Scott N. R. 419, an instrument payable to the manager of the National Provincial Bank of England was held to be a good note, see also *Megginson* v *Harper*, 2 Cr & M. 322, cited in note (*a*) to this section. But in *Yates* v. *Nash*, 29 L. J. C. P. 306; 8 C. B. N. S. 581, an instrument drawn payable to the treasurer for the time being of the Commercial Travellers' Benevolent Institution was held not to be a bill of exchange. But this decision and that in *Cowie* v. *Sterling*, 6 E. & B 333, would seem to be now overruled by this subsection of this section, under which a bill or a note may be made payable to the holder of an office for the time being.

(*e*) As to such a bill see *Minet* v. *Gibson*, 3 T. R. 481, *Tatlock* v. *Harris*, 3 T. R. 174; *Vere* v. *Lewis*, 3 T. R. 182; see also sub-sect. 3 of sect. 8 of this Act and the notes thereto. As regards fictitious payees, it was once held that where a bill is drawn payable to a fictitious person or his order, it is neither in effect payable to the order of the drawer nor to bearer, *Bennett* v. *Farnell*, 1 Camp. 130. But in *Minet* v. *Gibson*, 3 T. R. 481, it was held that where at the time of the acceptance the payee is known to be a fictitious person, the bill is really payable to bearer; and this was followed in a later case, where knowledge was held immaterial, as a bill payable to a fictitious payee is payable to bearer; *Phillips* v. *Im-Thurm*, L. R. 1 C. P. 463;

35 L. J. C. P. 220. Where a bill was drawn payable to a person for money belonging to him and was indorsed to such person and who, at the time of such indorsement was, but was not known to be dead, it is competent to the administrator to elect to take the bill as payment, *Murray* v. *The East India Company,* 5 B. & Ald. 204.

SS. 7, 8
———
Certainty
required as to
payee.

8. (1.) When a bill contains words prohibiting transfer, or indicating an intention that it should not be transferable, it is valid as between the parties thereto, but it is not negotiable (*a*).

What bills are
negotiable.

(2.) A negotiable bill may be payable either to order or to bearer (*b*).

(3.) A bill is payable to bearer which is expressed to be so payable, or on which the only or last indorsement is an indorsement in blank (*c*).

(4.) A bill is payable to order which is expressed to be so payable, or which is expressed to be payable to a particular person, and does not contain words prohibiting transfer or indicating an intention that it should not be transferable (*d*).

(5.) Where a bill, either originally or by indorsement, is expressed to be payable to the order of a specified person, and not to him or his order, it is nevertheless payable to him or his order at his option (*e*).

(*a*) It has hitherto been held that a bill or note is not negotiable which is payable neither to order nor to bearer, *Smith* v *Kendall,* 6 T. R. 123; *Plimley* v. *Westley,* 2 Bing. N. C. 251; where in 1 Hodges, 325, it is said that an indorsee can only sue the maker on a negotiable note   These decisions would seem to be overruled by this, and the fourth sub-section of this section.

(*b*) If the bill or note be made payable to order, it is assignable by indorsement; but as is provided by section 2 of this Act the indorsement must be completed by delivery. If the bill or note be made payable to bearer, it is assignable by mere delivery. It has been held that the addition, after issue, of the words "to his order" with the consent of the parties to a bill or note will not render the instrument invalid, *Kershaw* v. *Cox,* 3 Esp. 246.

(*c*) See *Minet* v. *Gibson,* 3 T. R. 481; *Phillips* v. *Im-Thurn,* L. R. 1 C. P. 463.

(*d*) See note (*a*) to this section and note (*n*) to section 3 of this Act.

(*e*) Where a bill was made payable to the drawer's order, it was held to be payable to himself, *Smith* v. *McClure,* 5 East, 476.

9.—(1.) The sum payable by a bill is a sum certain (z) within the meaning of this Act, although it is required to be paid.

(*a*) With interest (*y*).

(*b*) By stated instalments (*x*).

(*c*) By stated instalments, with a provision that upon default in payment of any instalment the whole shall become due (*w*).

(*d*) According to an indicated rate of exchange, or according to a rate of exchange to be ascertained as directed by the bill (*v*).

(2.) Where the sum payable is expressed in words, and also in figures, and there is a discrepancy between the two, the sum denoted by the words is the amount payable (*t*).

(3) Where a bill is expressed to be payable with interest, unless the instrument otherwise provides, interest runs from the date of the bill (*s*), and if the bill is undated, from the issue thereof (*r*).

(*z*) See note (*p*) to sect 3 of this Act.

(*y*) As to bills payable with interest, see *Warrington* v. *Early*, 2 E. & B. 763, *Ayrey* v. *Fearnsides*, 4 M. & W. 168; *Bolton* v. *Dugdale*, 4 B. & Ad 619. And the rate of interest must be fixed, see *Tennent* v. *Crawford*, Court of Sess. Cas., 4th Series, Vol. V, p. 433.

(*x*) As to bills payable by instalments see *Worley* v. *Harrison*, 3 A. & E. 669, and *Oridge* v. *Sherborne*, 11 M. & W. 374.

(*w*) In *Carlon* v. *Kenealy*, 12 M. & W. 139, an instrument stipulating the amount to be payable by instalments, with a proviso that on default of one instalment the whole amount of the balance remaining unpaid should become due, was held to be a good promissory note; see also *Moffat* v. *Edwards*, C. & M. 16; *Cooke* v. *Horne*, 29 L. T. N. S. 369.

(*v*) " Foreign bills are commonly drawn at one, two, or more usances, or, as it is sometimes expressed, at single, double, treble, or half-usance. Usance signifies the usage of the countries between which bills are drawn with respect to the time of payment. If a foreign bill be drawn, payable at sight, or at a certain period after sight, the acceptor will be liable to pay according to the course of exchange at the time of acceptance, unless the drawer express that it is payable according to the course of exchange at the time it was drawn "*en espèces de ce jour*," Byles on Bills (13th edition), 82; see also *Pollard* v. *Herries*, 3 B. & P. 335.

SS. 9, 10.

Sums payable

(*t*) It was so laid down in *Sanderson* v. *Piper*, 5 Bing. N. C. 425; 7 Scott, 408; see also *Garrard* v. *Lewis*, 10 Q. B. D. 30; 47 L. T. N. S. 408; 31 W. R. 475, where it was held that the marginal figures are not an essential part of a bill of exchange; although such figures will assist any omission in the body, *Elliot's Case*, 2 East, P. C. 951; or ambiguity, *Hutley* v. *Marshall*, 46 L. T. N. S. 186. See also sect. 73 of this Act and note (*a*) thereto.

(*s*) So laid down in *Doman* v *Dibden*, Ry. & Moo. N. P. C. 381; *Ruffey* v. *Greenwell*, 10 A & E. 222. In *Keene* v. *Keene*, 3 C. B N. S 144, the Court refused to interfere with the Master, who had allowed 10 per cent.; the amount specified in the bill, against the drawer. The bill, it seems, ought to be produced, *Fryer* v. *Brown*, R. & M. 145; *Hutton* v. *Ward*, 15 Q. B. 26.

(*r*) This is new. "Issue" is, in the second section of this Act, defined to be "the first delivery of a bill or note, complete in form, to a person who takes it as a holder."

Bill payable on demand

Ind Act, s 19

10.—(1.) A bill is payable on demand (*z*).

   (*a*) Which is expressed to be payable on demand, or at sight, or on presentation (*y*).

   (*b*) In which no time for payment is expressed (*x*).

(2.) Where a bill is accepted or indorsed when it is overdue, it shall as regards the acceptor who so accepts, or any indorser who so indorses it, be deemed a bill payable on demand (*w*).

(*z*) "In strict law no demand is necessary against an acceptor, but in practice a demand is usual, and ought to be made before proceedings are instituted, and it might make a material difference in the costs, if a solvent acceptor, against whom proceedings are instituted without a demand, promptly applies to the Court, *McIntosh* v. *Haydon*, Ry. & Moo. N. P C. 362 (per Abbott, L. C. J); see also *Brush* v. *Barrett*, 82 N. Y. Rep. 400.

(*y*) It is so provided in sect. 2 of 34 & 35 Vict. c 74, which is as follows. "Every bill of exchange or promissory note, drawn after this Act comes into operation and purporting to be payable at sight or on presentation, shall bear the same stamp, and shall, for all purposes whatsoever, be deemed to be a bill of exchange or promissory note payable on demand, any law or custom to the contrary notwithstanding." This statute is repealed by this present Act

(*x*) So decided in *Whitlock* v. *Underwood*, 3 Dowl. & R. 356, 2 B. & C. 157.

(*w*) A bill or note assigned in due time on the day of payment is to be considered as assigned before it is due, Byles on Bills (13th edition), p. 170, and Byles on Bills (6th American edition), 269. The

SS. 10, 11

Bill payable on demand.

mdorsee of an overdue bill or note takes it subject to all its equities, *In re European Bank,* L. R. 5 Ch. Ap. 362. As to the question whether prior want of consideration is such an equity, in *Ex parte Swan,* L. R. 6 Eq. 344, Malins, V.C, gave an elaborate judgment, reviewing all the authorities (pp. 358–362), and shewing that until 1808, it was held (*Ex parte Lambert,* 13 Ves. 179; *Brown v. Davies,* 3 T. R. 180; *Tinson v. Francis,* 1 Camp. 19) that such want of consideration was such an equity, but thatt it is not so now. As to the authorities since 1808, Malins, V.C, says, at p. 360:—"These authorities" (*Charles* v. *Marsden,* 1 Taunt. 224; *Sturtevant* v. *Ford,* 4 M. & G. 101; *Stein* v. *Yglesias,* 1 C. M. & R. 565; *Oulds* v. *Harrison,* 10 Ex. 572, 578) "have settled the law that an indorsee of a bill of exchange for value after its dishonour, has as good a title against the acceptor as if it had been indorsed to him before maturity, unless there is an equity attaching to the bill itself; and they also show that a right of set-off as between acceptor and drawer is not an equity attached to the bill, which can be enforced against the indorsee; . . . *Burrough* v. *Moss,* 10 B. & C. 558, is a remarkably strong application of the rule that a set-off as between drawer and acceptor cannot be pleaded against the holder who became so after its dishonour." See also *Holmes* v. *Kidd,* 3 H. & N. 891, as to what an equity attached to the bill is. As to when a bill payable on demand is overdue, see sect. 36, sub-s. 3.

Bill payable at a future time

11. A bill is payable at a determinable future time (*a*) **within the meaning of this Act which is expressed to be payable.**

(1.) At a fixed period (*b*) **after date or sight** (*c*).

Ind. Act, s 5.

(2.) On or at a fixed period after the occurrence of a specified event which is certain to happen (*d*)**, though the time of happening may be uncertain.**

An instrument expressed to be payable on a contingency (*e*) **is not a bill, and the happening of the event does not cure the defect** (*f*)**.**

(*a*) See notes (*y*) and (*q*) to section 3 of this Act.

(*b*) The time or event must come or happen, *Cooke* v. *Colehan,* 2 Stra. 1217; *Roffey* v. *Greenwell,* 10 A. & E. 222, *Evans* v. *Underwood,* 1 Wils. 262; *Goss* v. *Nelson,* 1 Burr. 226; *Clayton* v. *Gosling,* 5 B & C. 360; *Sackett* v. *Palmer,* 26 Barb. 179. So also a bill or note may be made payable by instalments, *Worley* v. *Harrison,* 3 A & E. 669; *Oridge* v. *Sherborne,* 11 M. & W. 374. Also with a proviso that on default of one instalment the whole shall become payable on demand, *Carlon* v. *Kenealy,* 12 M. & W. 139; *Cooke* v. *Horne,* 29 L T. N. S. 369; *Moffat* v. *Edwards,* C. & M. 16.

(c) After sight means after acceptance, sect. 39, sub-sect. 1 of this Act; *Campbell* v. *French*, 6 T. R. at p. 212.

(d) See *Andrews* v *Franklin*, 1 Stra. 24; *Carlos* v. *Fancourt*, 5 T. R. 482; and the cases mentioned in note (b) hereto.

(e) See notes (y) (q) and (p) to sect 3 of this Act It has been held that unless the contingency is on the face of the instrument it is not void, *Richards* v. *Richards*, 2 B. & Ad. 447.

(f) So held in *Hill* v. *Halford*, 2 B. & P. 413, see also Chitty on Bills (9th Edition), pp. 135 & 144.

12.—Where a bill expressed to be payable at a fixed period after date is issued undated, or where the acceptance of a bill payable at a fixed period after sight is undated, any holder may insert therein the true date of issue or acceptance, and the bill shall be payable accordingly (a).

Provided that (1) where the holder in good faith and by mistake inserts a wrong date, and (2) in every case where a wrong date is inserted, if the bill subsequently comes into the hands of a holder in due course the bill shall not be avoided thereby; but shall operate and be payable as if the date so inserted had been the true date (b).

(a) If there be no date on a bill or note, it has been held that it will be considered as dated at the time it was drawn or made, *Giles* v. *Bourne*, 6 M & S. 73; Story on Bills, s. 37; and parol evidence is admissible to show such date, *Davis* v. *Jones*, 17 C. B. 625; 25 L. J. C. P. 91.

(b) See *Way* v. *Hearne*, 32 L. J. C. P. 34.

13.—(1.) Where a bill or an acceptance or any indorsement on a bill is dated, the date shall, unless the contrary be proved, be deemed to be the true date of the drawing, acceptance, or indorsement, as the case may be (a).

(2.) A bill is not invalid by reason only that it is ante-dated or post-dated (b), or that it bears date on a Sunday (c).

(a) This is a rule of evidence, *Malpas* v. *Clements*, 19 L. J. Q. B. 435; *Laws* v *Rand*, 3 C. B. N S. 442; *Anderson* v. *Weston*, 6 Bing. N. C. 296, *Potez* v. *Glossop*, 2 Ex. 195; and note (f) to sect. 3 of

Side notes: SS. 11, 12, 13. Bill payable at a future time. Omission of date in bill payable after date. Ante-dating and post-dating Ind. Act. s 118, sub s (6).

SS. 13, 14.

Ante-dating and post-dating.

this Act. See note (c) hereto for what was formerly an exception to this rule.

(b) As to antedated and postdated instruments see *Passmore* v. *North*, 13 East, 517; *Austin* v. *Banyard*, 34 L. J. 217, *Forster* v. *Mackreth*, L. R. 2 Ex. 163; 36 L. J. Ex. 94; *Bull* v. *O'Sullivan*, L. R 6 Q. B. 209; 40 L. J. Q B 141, *Gatty* v *Foy*, 2 Ex. D. 265. As to cheques see note (a) to sect. 73 of this Act.

(c) Before this Act a bill or note dated on a Sunday was presumed not to have been issued on that day, *Begbie* v. *Levy*, 1 Cr. & J. 180.

Computation of time of payment.

Ind Act, s 22

14. Where a bill is not payable on demand (z) the day on which it falls due is determined as follows :

(1.) Three days, called days of grace (y), are, in every case where the bill itself does not otherwise provide, added to the time of payment as fixed by the bill, and the bill is due and payable on the last day of grace. Provided that :

Ind Act, s 25

(a) When the last day of grace falls on Sunday, Christmas Day, Good Friday, or a day appointed by the Royal proclamation as a public fast or thanksgiving day, the bill is, except in the case hereinafter provided for, due and payable on the preceding business day (w).

Ind Act, s 25

34 & 35 Vic c 17

(b) When the last day of grace is a bank holiday (other than Christmas Day or Good Friday) under the Bank Holiday Acts 1871, and Acts amending or extending it, or when the last day of grace is a Sunday and the second day of grace is a Bank holiday, the bill is due and payable on the succeeding business day (v).

Ind Act, s 24

(2.) Where a bill is payable at a fixed period after date, after sight, or after the happening of a specified event, the time of payment is determined by excluding the day from which the time is to begin to run, and by including the day of payment (t).

Ind Act, s 23.

(3.) Where a bill is payable at a fixed period after sight the time begins to run from the date of the acceptance if the bill be accepted, and from the date of noting or protest if the bill be noted or protested for non-acceptance or for non-delivery (s).

(4.) The term "month" in a bill means calendar month (r).

(z) Days of grace have been also allowed on promissory notes, *vide Brown* v. *Harraden*, 4 T. R. 148. But not, as also provided in this section, on bills or notes payable on demand. As we have seen before, a bill payable at sight is a bill payable on demand. In *Oridge* v. *Sherborne*, 11 M & W. 374, it was held that the maker of a note is entitled to the days of grace upon the falling due of each instalment; see also *Gaskin* v. *Davis*, 2 F. & F. 294.

(y) So called because they were formerly allowed the drawee as a favour, but they have long since been recognised as a right, vide Byles on Bills (13th edition), pp. 209 and 210, where a table of the days of grace in different countries is given, taken from Mr. Kyds' work on Bills

In India they have three days of grace; see sect 22 of the Indian Act It has been held that a demand for payment before the expiration of the days of grace is premature, *Wiffen* v. *Roberts*, 1 Esp 261 The parties to a bill contract for the payment of it according to the existing law of the country in which it is to be paid, per Cockburn, C. J , in *Rouquette* v *Overman*, L. R 10 Q. B. 525.

(w) See 39 & 40 Geo. 3, c. 42, and 7 & 8 Geo. 4 c. 15 In a recent case the plaintiff in the action sued on a promissory note dated the 11th March, 1874, and payable three months after date. The third day of grace was the 14th day of June, 1874, which was a Sunday The action was commenced on the 14th day of June, 1880, which was a Monday It was held that the claim was barred by the Statute of Limitations, *Morris* v *Richards*, 45 L T. N S. 210. As to a bill falling due on a public holiday in India, see sect. 25 of the Indian Act.

(v) This is practically the same as the provisions of section 1 of the Bank Holidays Act (34 Vict. c. 17) by which all bills of exchange and promissory notes which are due and payable on any Bank Holiday shall be payable on the next following day. There seems to be an omission in the present sub-sect of a case where the last day of grace is a Sunday, and the second day of grace a Christmas Day. In such a case it would seem that the bill is payable on the first day of grace

(t) See *Coleman* v. *Sayer*, 1 Barnard, 303 , and *Campbell* v. *French*, 6 T R 212

(s) See *Campbell* v. *French*, supra.

(r) So held as to bills and notes, *Cockell* v. *Gray*, 3 B & B. 186; months usually denote at law lunar months, *Simpson* v. *Margitson*, 11 Q. B. 23. As to the meaning of the word "calendar month," and as to its length, see *Migotti* v *Colville*, 4 C. P. D. 233, 48 L. J. C P. 695 , 10 L T. N. S. 717 , 27 W. R. 741

Case of need.

Ind. Act, s. 7

15.—The drawer of a bill and any indorser may insert therein the name of a person to whom the holder may resort in case of need, that is to say, in case the bill is dishonoured by non-acceptance or non-payment. Such person is called the referee (*a*) in case of need. It is in the option of the holder to resort to the referee in case of need or not as he may think fit (*b*).

(*a*) "The referee, in case of need, is more properly an original alternative drawee than an acceptor for honour." Byles on Bills (11th edition), p. 262. See 1 Parsons on Bills, 64 ; see also the judgment of Lord Lyndhurst, C. B., in *Leonard* v. *Wilson*, 2 Cr. & M. 589.

(*b*) It seems that the words "in case of need" in an indorsement mean, "in case it is necessary to resort to the indorser ;" and it has been held that the naming a referee in case of need, assuming that it constitutes such referee agent of the indorser for payment, does not constitute him the indorser's agent for notice of dishonour generally, and therefore notice to him of dishonour by the acceptor is not notice to the indorser, *In re Leeds Banking Company, Ex parte Prange*, L. R. 1 Eq. 1, 35 L. J Ch. 33.

Optional stipulations by drawer or indorser.

Ind. Act, s. 52.

16.—The drawer of a bill, and any indorser, may insert therein an express stipulation (*a*).

(1.) Negativing or limiting his own liability to the holder (*a*).

(2.) Waiving as regards himself some or all of the holder's duties (*b*).

(*a*) This does at first sight seem inconsistent with the definition of a bill of exchange given in sect. 3 (1) and (2). But on a careful consideration it will be found that it is not so. A bill of exchange is still unconditional even though it contains a stipulation on the part of the drawer negativing or limiting his own liability to the holder. Any stipulation to this effect cannot affect the order from the drawer to the drawee. Again as to promissory notes, an express stipulation inserted in a promissory note by the first indorser thereof (who corresponds with the drawer of a bill), negativing or limiting his liability, will not make the promise of the maker conditional. Nor is this section altogether new, for even before this Act a bill could be indorsed with a written or a verbal agreement between an indorser and his immediate indorsee that the latter will not look to the former for payment, *Pike* v. *Street*, 1 M. & M. 226, *Thompson* v. *Clubley*, 1 M. & W. 212. So also it was held that if the indorsement is unqualified, the indorsee is liable, *Goupy* v. *Harden*, 7 Taunt 159. So also it was held that when an indorsement is made and taken "without recourse," every liability that would otherwise exist is excluded and no action can be maintained upon it, *Dumont* v. *Williamson*, 17 L. T. N. S 71.

(b) As to such waiver, see *Leonard* v. *Wilson*, 2 Cr. & M 589, *Phipson* v. *Kneller*, 4 Camp. 285.

SS. 16, 17

Optional stipulations by drawer or indorser.

17.—(1.) The acceptance (z) of a bill is the signification by the drawee of his assent to the order of the drawer.

Definition and requisites of acceptance.

(2.) An acceptance (y) is invalid unless it complies with the following conditions, namely·

Ind Act, s 7

> (a.) It must be written on the bill and signed by the drawee (x). The mere signature of the drawee without additional words is sufficient (w).
>
> (b) It must not express that the drawee will perform his promise by any other means than the payment of money (v).

(z) This is the same definition that has existed before this Act, vide Byles on Bills (13th edition), p. 187, Chalmers' Digest of the Law of Bills of Exchange (2nd edition), p 32. "What is an acceptance but an engagement to pay the bill when due," per Lawrence, J, in *Clarke* v. *Cock*, 4 East, 72. See also note (z) to sect. 54 of this Act. As to liability before acceptance see *Frith* v. *Forbes*, 32 L. J. Ch. 10 As provided in sect. 2 of this Act, it has been held that delivery is necessary to complete acceptance, see the cases in note (a) to that section. See further sub-sects. (1) & (2) sect 21 of this Act and the notes thereto.

(y) As to what has before this Act been considered in form a sufficient acceptance, the result of the old cases may be stated thus·— Any form of words which intimates that the drawer intends to pay is a sufficient acceptance; that is, anything in writing, and signed by the party, *Smith* v. *Vertue*, 9 C. B. N. S. at p. 227 (per Byles, J). See also notes (x) and (w) hereto.

(x) This is virtually the same as the provisions as to acceptance contained in section 6 of the 19 & 20 Vict. c. 97, by which an acceptance had to be written on the bill (which was done by writing the word "accepted" across the face of it) and signed by the drawee, who after he has put his signature is called the acceptor. And in a recent case it was held that a bill of exchange was not sufficiently accepted to satisfy the 19 & 20 Vict. c. 97, s. 6, if the drawee merely wrote his name across the face of it, and there were no words amounting to a statement that the bill was accepted, *Hindhaugh* v. *Blakey*, 47 L J Q. B. D 345; L. R. 3 C. P. D 136. But the legislature altered this

SS. 17, 18.

Definition and requisites of acceptance

state of the law by 41 & 42 Vict. c. 13, sect. 1 of which, like the latter part of this sub-section, provided that an acceptance was not insufficient by reason of such acceptance consisting merely of the signature of the drawee written on such bill. Under the last-named statute it was held that the signature of a person across the back of a bill is not an acceptance but an indorsement, *Steele v. McKinlay,* 5 Ap Cas 754; 43 L. T. N. S. 358; 29 W R. 17 As to proof of an acceptance, see *Scard v Jackson,* 24 W. R. 159.

(*w*) This is the same as section 1 of 41 Vict c. 13, which see.

(*v*) Thus it has been held that the acceptance of a bill must be to pay in money, and that an acceptance to pay by another bill is no acceptance. *Russell* v. *Phillips,* 14 Q. B. 891, 19 L J Q B. 297.

Time for acceptance

18.—A bill may be accepted—

(1.) Before it has been signed by the drawer (*a*), or while otherwise incomplete (*b*).

(2.) When it is overdue (*c*), or after it has been dishonoured by a previous refusal to accept (*d*), or by non-payment (*e*).

(3.) When a bill payable after sight is dishonoured by non-acceptance, and the drawee subsequently accepts it, the holder, in the absence of any different agreement, is entitled to have the bill accepted as of the date of first presentment to the drawee for acceptance (*f*).

(*a*) In *Schultz v Astley,* 2 Bing N. C 544; 2 Scott, 815, 7 C. & P. 99, it was decided that it is no objection to the validity of a bill of exchange that the acceptance and indorsement are written before the bill is drawn, notwithstanding the indorsement is made by a stranger to the acceptor, and this even though the bill be antedated, *Armfield v Allport,* 27 L. J Ex. 42

(*b*) But as we have already seen, no liability exists before the delivery or issue of the bill, *In re Hayward,* L. R. 6 Ch. Ap. 546, 40 L J. Bankr. 49; sect. 21, sub-sect. 1.

(*c*) Thus it has been held that an acceptance of a bill after the time appointed for its payment is a general acceptance to pay it on demand, *Jackson v Pigott,* 1 Ld. Raym. 364, *Mutford v. Walcot,* 1 Ld. Raym. 574, 1 Salk. 129 See also sub-sect. (2) of sect. 10 of this Act, and the notes thereto.

(*d*) So held before this Act, *Wynne v Raikes,* 5 East, 514, see further as to acceptance and payment for honour, sects. 65, 66, 67, and 68 of this Act.

(e) See note (c) to this section.

(f) As to what the practice on this point was before the Act, see Chalmers' Digest of the Law of Bills of Exchange (2nd edition), p 34. Where a bill of exchange, payable after sight, having been presented for acceptance and refused, and duly protested, was eight days afterwards accepted by a third person for the honour of the drawer, and when at maturity, according to that acceptance, was presented for payment both to the drawee and the acceptor for honour, it was held that these presentments for payment were made at a proper time, and that a protest for non-payment by the drawee was unnecessary, *Williams* v. *Germaine,* 7 B. & C. 468.

19.—(1.) An acceptance is either (a) general or (b) qualified.

(2) A general acceptance assents without qualification to the order of the drawer. A qualified acceptance in express terms varies the effect of the bill as drawn (z).

In particular an acceptance is qualified which is—

(a) conditional (y), that is to say, which makes payment by the acceptor dependent on the fulfilment of a condition therein stated.

(b) partial (x), that is to say an acceptance to pay part only of the amount for which the bill is drawn.

(c) local (w), that is to say, an acceptance to pay only at a particular specified place.

An acceptance to pay at a particular place is a general acceptance, unless it expressly states that the bill is to be paid there only and not elsewhere (v).

(d) qualified as to time (t).

(e) the acceptance of some one or more of the drawees but not of all.

(z) Such have hitherto been the definitions of general and qualified, see Byles on Bills (13th edition), 195 and 196, Chalmers' Digest of the Law of Bills of Exchange (2nd edition), p. 37. Parol evidence cannot be admitted to vary the legal effect of a bill or note, *Woodbridge* v *Spooner,* 3 B. & Ald. 233; *Abrey* v. *Crux,* L R. 5 C. P. 37, *Stott* v. *Fairlamb,* 52 L. J. Q B. 420, 48 L J N. S 584; on app. 49 L T N. S at p. 526; *Martin* v. *Cole,* 14 Otto Sup. Ct. M. S. 30. But as between immediate parties, a written agreement may vary or control its legal effect, *Bowerbank* v *Monteiro,* 4 Taunt. 844. But a *subsequent* written agreement must have a consideration to support it; *McManus* v. *Bark,* L. R. 5 Ex. 65, 39 L. J. Ex. 65.

(*y*) *Sproat* v. *Matthews,* 1 T. R. 182. For instances of conditional acceptances, see *Smith* v. *Abbott,* 2 Stra. 1152; *Banbury* v. *Lissett,* 2 Stra. 1211; and other cases collected in Story on Bills, sect. 239. "An acceptance is general when it imports an absolute acceptance precisely in conformity to the tenour of the bill itself It is conditional or qualified when it contains any qualification, limitation, or condition different from what is expressed on the face of the bill, or from what the law implies upon a general acceptance." Story on Bills, sect. 239, where the cases are collected A conditional acceptance becomes absolute when the condition has been performed, per *Gibbs,* C. J., in *Miln* v. *Prest,* 4 Camp. 393; per *Park,* J., in *Mendizabal* v. *Machado,* 6 C. & P. 218, *Smith* v. *Vertue,* 9 C. B. N. S. at pp. 225, 227, 30 L. J. C. P. 56.

(*x*) The same as hitherto, see *Wegersloffe* v *Keene,* 1 Stra. 214.

(*w*) See *Rowe* v. *Young,* 2 Bligh H. L. 391 and the following note (*v*).

(*v*) This is the same as the provisions of sect. 1 of the 1 & 2 Geo 4, c. 78, which is, however, repealed by this Act.

(*t*) An acceptance to pay at a time subsequent to that appointed by the drawer was held to be a partial or varying acceptance, *Walker* v. *Atwood,* 11 Mod. 190.

20.—(1.) Where a simple signature on a blank stamped paper is delivered by the signer in order that it may be converted into a bill, it operates as a *primâ facie* authority to fill it up as a complete bill for any amount the stamp will cover, using the signature for that of the drawer (*a*), or the acceptor (*b*), or an indorser (*c*); and, in like manner, when a bill is wanting in any material particular, the person in possession of it has a *primâ facie* authority to fill up the omission in any way he thinks fit (*d*).

(2) In order that any such instrument when completed may be enforceable against any person who became a party thereto prior to its completion, it must be filled up within a reasonable time (*e*) and strictly in accordance with the authority (*f*) given. Reasonable time for this purpose is a question of fact (*g*).

Provided that if any such instrument after completion is negotiated to a holder in due course it shall be valid and effectual for all purposes in his hands, and he may enforce it as if it had been filled up within a reasonable time and strictly in accordance with the authority given (*h*).

(*a*) Where a person sent a bill to the defendant with a blank space for the drawer's name, and the defendant after accepting it returned the bill to the sender, who, before the bill became due, transferred it for value to the plaintiff, who inserted his own name as drawer, and sued the defendant, it was held that the plaintiff had authority to insert his own name as drawer and could recover, *Harvey* v. *Cane*, 34 L. T. N. S. 64. See also *Scard* v. *Jackson*, 34 L. T. N. S. 65 Again, where A., being member of a partnership consisting of several individuals, drew a bill in the partnership firm, and also indorsed it in the partnership firm, and gave it to a clerk to be filled up for the use of the partnership as the exigencies of business might require, after A.'s death and after the surviving partners had assumed a new firm, the clerk filled up the bill, inserting a date prior to A.'s death, and put it in circulation. It was held that the surviving partners were liable, *Usher* v. *Dauncey*, 4 Camp. 97. See also *Carter* v. *White*, 51 L. J Ch. D. 465.

(*b*) An acceptance in blank was considered sufficient to charge the acceptor where the bill was afterwards drawn in pursuance of his authority, *Leslie* v. *Hastings*, 1 Moo. & Rob. 119. See also *Molloy* v. *Delves*, 4 C. & P. 492; *Schultz* v. *Astley*, 2 Bing. N. C. 544; *Ingham* v. *Primrose*, 7 C. B. N. S. 82.

(*c*) Thus in *Russel* v. *Langstaffe*, 2 Doug. 514, it was held that an indorsement on a blank note or cheque will afterwards bind the indorser for any sum and time of payment which the person to whom he entrusts the note chooses to insert in it. See also *Snaith* v. *Mingay*, 1 M. & S. 87.

(*d*) Thus a bill made payable to the order of   may be filled up by any bearer who can show that he came regularly to the possession of it, with his own name; *Crutchley* v. *Mann*, 5 Taunt. 529.

(*e*) So laid down in *Montague* v. *Perkins*, 22 L. J. C. P. 187, following *Mulhall* v. *Neville*, 8 Ex. 391; *Temple* v. *Pullen*, 22 L. J. Ex. 151; 8 Ex 389. But the fact that the bill was not filled up within a reasonable time will not affect the rights of a *bonâ fide* holder, per Jervis, C J., in *Montague* v. *Perkins*, *supra* In a recent case it was held that the drawer's name might be filled in in the blank space left for that purpose even after the acceptor's death; *Carter* v. *White*, 20 Ch. D. 225; 51 L. J Ch. D. 465; 46 L. T. N. S. 236; 30 W R 466, following *In re Duffy*, 5 L. R Ir. 92.

(*f*) In *Armfield* v. *Armport*, 27 L. J. Ex. 42, it was held that the authority given by a blank acceptance to fill it up for the amount which the stamp will cover, is not lost merely because the drawer by mistake antedates the instrument a whole year, even although it is

D

made payable some time after date, and if the period has in fact
elapsed from the time of the completion of the instrument, an action
may be maintained on it.   And in a recent case it was held that a
person to whom an acceptance, blank as to drawer's name, is delivered
for value, can complete the bill by filling in his own name as drawer
even after the acceptor's death; *Carter* v. *White, supra.* See also
note (*e*) hereto.   But where a partner fraudulently accepts in his firm's
name a bill with the drawer's name blank and a holder for value, but
not a *bonâ fide* holder for value, fills in his name as drawer, he cannot
recover against the firm; *Hogarth* v. *Latham*, 3 Q. B. D. 643, 39 L
T. N. S 75; 47 L. J. Q. B. D. 339; see also *Awde* v. *Dixon*, 6 Ex.
869.   But see, *Chemung Canal Bank* v. *Bradner*, 44 New York Rep.
680, where, however, the holder was a *bonâ fide* holder, and was held
entitled to recover.   In a recent case it was held that a person who
accepts a bill which has figures for the amount in the margin, but a
blank in the body of it for such amount, holds out the person to whom
it is entrusted as having authority to fill in the bill as he pleases within
the limits of the stamp, and that no alteration of such marginal figures
however fraudulent vitiates the bill as a bill for the full amount inserted
in the body when in the hands of a *bonâ fide* holder for value without
notice, *Garrard* v. *Lewis*, 10 Q. B. D. 30; 47 L. T. N. S. 408;
31 W. R. 475. The holder of a bill may convert a blank into a special
indorsement, *Clark* v. *Piggott*, 1 Salk. 126; *Hirschfield* v. *Smith*, L R.
1 C. P. at p. 353.

(*g*) So laid down in *Temple* v. *Pullen*, 8 Ex. 389; 22 L. J. Ex. 151
(per Pollock L. C. B.)

(*h*) So laid down by Stuart V.-C. in *Hatch* v. *Searles*, 2 Sm. & G.
152   It has been held that when a bill is accepted in blank for the
purpose of being negotiated, and is afterwards filled in with the name
and signature of a person as drawer and indorser, the acceptor cannot
as against a *bonâ fide* indorsee for value adduce evidence to show that
either the drawing or indorsement is a forgery, *London and South
Western Bank* v. *Wentworth*, 5 Ex. D. 96; 49 L. J. Q. B. D. 657·
See also *Putnam* v. *Sullivan*. 4 Mass. 45; *Nance* v. *Lary*, 5 Alabama,
370.

**21.—(1.) Every contract on a bill, whether it be the
drawer's, the acceptor's (*z*), or an indorser's (*y*), is incomplete and revocable, until delivery (*x*) of the instrument**
in order to give effect thereto (*w*).

**Provided that where an acceptance is written on a bill
and the drawee gives notice to or according to the
directions of the person entitled to the bill that he has
accepted it, the acceptance then becomes complete and
irrevocable (*v*).**

(2.) As between immediate parties, and as regards a remote party other than a holder in due course (*t*) the delivery— S. 21.
Delivery.

- (*a*) in order to be effectual must be made either by or under the authority (*s*) of the party drawing, accepting, or indorsing, as the case may be;
- (*b*) may be shewn to have been conditional (*r*) or for a special purpose only (*q*), and not for the purpose of transferring the property in the bill.

But if the bill be in the hands of a holder in due course a valid delivery of the bill by all parties prior to him so as to make them liable to him is conclusively presumed. Ind. Act, s 118, sub-s (*a*)

(3.) Where a bill is no longer in the possession of a party who has signed it as drawer, acceptor, or indorser a valid and unconditional delivery by him is presumed, until the contrary is proved.

(*z*) Thus where a person having written his acceptance, changed his mind, and before the bill was delivered back to the holder, obliterated his acceptance, it was held that he was not bound as acceptor; his promise, however, is complete *unless* revoked; *Cox* v. *Troy*, 5. B. & Ald. 474; 1 D. & R. 38, as explained in *Wilde* v. *Sheridan*, 21 L. J. Q B. at p. 262. One purpose of the indorsement is to pass the property in the bill, and that purpose is not effected until actual or constructive delivery, *Wilde* v. *Sheridan, supra*; *Buckly* v. *Hann*, 5 Ex. 43; *Roff* v. *Miller*, 19 L. J. C. P. 278; see also the judgments in *Montague* v. *Perkins*, 22 L. J. C. P. 187; 1 Parsons on Bills, 48; and the cases cited in note (*a*) to sect. 2 of this Act, and note (*z*) to sect. 17 of this Act.

(*y*) See the last preceding note (*z*) hereto.

(*x*) Delivery is by sect. 2 defined to be "transfer of possession, actual or constructive, from one person to another" A transferor by delivery is not liable on the instrument, see sub-sect. (2) of sect. 58 of this Act and the notes thereto. But he is for the consideration, unless the holder of the instrument has been guilty of laches; *Camidge* v. *Allenby*, 6 B. & C. 373; *Rogers* v. *Langford*, 1 C. & M. 637; *Smith* v *Mercer*, L. R. 3 Ex. 51. As to constructive transfer of possession, see the cases in notes (*a*), (*b*), and (*c*) to sect. 20 (1) of this Act. As to delivery of a bill of exchange or promissory note as an escrow, see Byles on Bills, 13th ed 103 In *Vallett* v. *Parker*, 6 Wend. 615, it was held that it is no defence as against one who took the note before

SS. 21, 22.

Delivery

it was due and for value, and in good faith that it was delivered as an escrow, and was improperly put into circulation.

(*w*) It is submitted that, as any acceptance is revocable until delivery for value, where a person draws, accepts, or indorses a bill for the accommodation of another party thereto, he may, even after delivery to the person for whose accommodation it is, revoke the acceptance, provided he do so before the instrument gets into the hands of a *bonâ fide* holder for value.

(*v*) See *Grant* v. *Hunt*, 1 C. B. 44; 14 L. J. C. P. 106.

(*t*) A holder in due course is by sect. 29 (1) defined to be a holder who has taken a bill, complete and regular, on the face of it under the following conditions: (*a*) that he has become the holder of it before it was overdue, and without notice that it had been previously dishonoured, if such was the fact; (*b*) that he took the bill in good faith and for value, and that at the time the bill was negotiated to him he had no notice of any defect in the title of the person who negotiated it. See further that section and the notes thereto.

(*s*) The title of an innocent holder for value cannot be affected by an unauthorized delivery.

(*r*) The liability of an indorser to his immediate indorsee arises out of a contract between them, and this contract in no instance consists exclusively of the indorsement, but of that and also of the delivery to the indorsee, and of the intention with which the delivery was made and accepted, of which parol evidence is admissible, *Castrique* v. *Buttigieg*, 10 Moore, P. C. C. 94; see also *Bell* v. *Lord Ingestre*, 12 Q. B. 317; *Denton* v. *Peters*, L. R. 5 Q. B. 475.

(*q*) As for example, as an *escrow*, as to which, see also note (*x*) *supra*.

CAPACITY AND AUTHORITY OF PARTIES.

Capacity of parties.

·**22.**—(1.) Capacity (*a*) to incur liability as a party to a bill is coextensive with capacity to contract. (*b*) Provided that nothing in this section shall enable a corporation (*c*) to make itself liable as drawer, acceptor, or indorser of a bill, unless it is competent to it so to do under the law for the time being in force relating to corporations.

(2.) Where a bill is drawn or indorsed by an infant, minor, or corporation (*d*) having no capacity or power to incur liability on a bill, the drawing or indorsement entitles the holder to receive payment of the bill, and to enforce it against any other party thereto.

(*a*) "To constitute a binding agreement, there must exist the assent of the parties that a certain act shall be done or omitted. For the purpose of this assent, a person must be endowed with such a degree of reason and judgment as will enable him to comprehend the subject of negotiation. The assent, therefore, necessary to give validity to a contract necessarily presupposes a free, fair, and serious exercise of the reasoning faculty; or in other words, the power, both physical and moral, of deliberating upon and weighing the consequences of the engagement about to be entered into. So that if either of the parties to an engagement be absolutely deprived of the use of his understanding, or if he be deemed by law not to have attained to it, there can in such a case be no *aggregatio mentium*, and consequently no agreement which shall bind him. The rule of law therefore which requires the assent of the parties to a contract, assumes that such assenting parties shall be competent to contract. Accordingly a capacity to contract is absolutely necessary. The incompetency to contract is in some cases general and absolute; in other cases it is limited. In some cases the contract is void as against both the parties; in others, only the incompetent or protected party can shelter himself from liability upon it." Chitty on Contracts (11th edition), 134 and 135. Thus a contract with an idiot is void. But a contract with an infant or with a person not *compos mentis* was until lately voidable, except for necessaries. It has been held that a person *non compos mentis* is, like an infant, liable on contracts for necessaries and for monies proper for his protection and support, *Wentworth* v. *Tubb*, 1 Y. & C. Chan. Cas. 171; *Nelson* v. *Duncombe*, 9 Beav. 211. As to what are necessaries, see Chitty on Contracts, 11th ed. 139-155. But now by s. 1 of the Infants' Relief Act, 1874 (37 & 38 Vict c. 62) all contracts, whether by specialty or by simple contract, thereafter entered into by infants for the repayment of money lent or to be lent, or for goods supplied or to be supplied (other than contracts for necessaries) and all accounts stated with infants, shall be absolutely void; and by s. 2 no action can be brought on any ratification by a person after full age of any contract entered into during infancy. So also until recently contracts by married women, except for necessaries, were not binding on them. See as to such contracts Chitty on Contracts (11th Edit.), pp. 155-181. But now by sec. 1 of 45 & 46 Vict. c. 75, a married woman is capable of acquiring, holding, and disposing by will or otherwise of any real or personal property as her separate property, in the same manner as if she were a *feme sole*, without the intervention of any trustee. And by section 2, a married woman is capable of entering into and rendering herself liable in respect of and to the extent of her separate property on any contract, and of suing and being sued, either in contract or in tort or otherwise, in all respects as if she were a *feme sole*, and her husband need not be joined with her as plaintiff or defendant or be made a party to any action or other legal proceeding brought by or taken against her.

By the present section capacity to incur liability as a party to a bill is

coextensive with capacity to contract. An infant cannot accept a bill
of exchange even for necessaries; so held per Lord Mansfield, L. C. J.,
in *Williamson* v. *Watts*, 1 Camp. 552. At the foot of that case is the
following note: " I do not find any case in which it has been expressly
decided that an infant may not bind himself by a negotiable instrument for necessaries; and in *Williams* v. *Harrison*, Carth. 160, the
Court of King's Bench in the time of Lord Holt seem rather to have
been of opinion that he might, although not liable upon a bill of
exchange drawn in the course of trade. It is now settled, however,
that an account stated by an infant, even of monies due for necessaries,
is invalid, *Trueman* v. *Hurst*, 1 T. R. 40; *Bartlett* v. *Emery*, 1 T. R.
42 ; and it seems inevitably to follow that he cannot be bound by
his signature to a negotiable bill or note, as that not only *primâ facie*
admits the debt, but if valid, would render him liable to an action at
the suit of the indorsee, in which the amount of the original debt
could not be disputed. The old doctrine, that a single bill given by
an infant for necessaries is binding, though of no immediate practical
use, such an instrument being now as rare as a *statute staple*, seems to
afford an argument from analogy to shew that a promissory note given
by an infant for necessaries would be binding, if payable only to the
person who supplied them. Co. Litt. 172, a." In *Stevens* v. *Jackson*,
4 Camp. 164, it was held that a person is liable as acceptor of a bill of
exchange which was drawn while he was an infant, but was
accepted by him after he came of age. And in a recent case it was
also held that an action is maintainable by an indorsee for value,
against the acceptor of a bill of exchange, accepted by the latter
after attaining twenty-one years of age, for a debt contracted
during infancy, and after the passing of the Infants' Relief Act,
1874 (37 & 38 Vict. c. 62), though not in respect of necessaries.
The Belfast Banking Company v. *Doherty*, 4 L. R. Ir. 124. But
that as between the immediate parties to the bill the acceptance
would be a promise or ratification within the meaning of that Act,
upon which an action at the suit of the drawer would not lie. But it
has also been held that a person is not liable on a promissory note,
bearing interest made during infancy, though the money obtained
thereon was applied for necessaries, *Bateman* v. *Kingston*, 6 L. R. Ir.
328.

Again, a bill or note given by a person in favour of another exercising
undue influence over the former will not be enforced. Where a father,
whose son had forged his indorsement to a promissory note, was
appealed to to take upon himself a civil liability, with the knowledge
that unless he did so his son would be prosecuted and probably
convicted, even though that is not put forward as the motive for the
agreement, the father is not a free agent, and the agreement he makes
under such circumstances is not enforceable; *Williams* v. *Bayley*,
L. R. 1 H. L. 200. But where the holder of a bill says to a father,

"If you do not take upon yourself your sons debt, we must sue him for the amount," that is not undue pressure; *Williams* v. *Bayley, supra,* at p. 209. A threat to prosecute the debtor is not of itself illegal, and will not vitiate a subsequent agreement by the debtor himself to give security for the debt which he justly owes; *Flower* v. *Sadler,* 10 Q. B. D. at pp. 575, 576. But an agreement given by a third party on such a threat is not enforceable, being made without consideration; *Williams* v. *Bayley, supra; Flower* v. *Sadler, supra,* at pp. 575, 576. A bill or note given by a party in a complete state of drunkenness, unless it is given for actual necessaries, cannot be enforced against him; but it seems that he might ratify the transaction, when sober; *Gore* v. *Gibson,* 13 M. & W. 623; *Matthews* v. *Baxter,* L. R. 8 Ex. 132. But if the drunkenness was unknown to the other contracting party, and no advantage was taken of the person drunk, the contract might, perhaps, be enforceable; *Molton* v. *Camroux,* 4 Ex. 17. A bill or note drawn, accepted, or made, or indorsed by a lunatic, and who is known to be such at the time by the person in whose favour it is accepted, made, or indorsed, is utterly void; but where the lunacy was unknown to the other party, and no advantage was taken, especially if the parties cannot be placed in the same position, the bill may, perhaps, be enforced; *Molton* v. *Camroux,* 4 Ex. 17; *Sentence* v. *Poole,* 3 C. & P. 1. Also by an alien enemy; *Potts* v. *Bell,* 8 T. R. 548; *Griswold* v. *Waddington,* 16 Johns. R. 438; Story on Bills, s. 99; *Willison* v. *Patterson,* 7 Taunt. 439; 1 Moore, 133.

(*b*) Whatever of course a man may do by himself he may do by an agent, and the act of such agent is binding on him, the maxim of law being *quidquid facit per alium facit per se.* But an agent, unless expressly authorised in that behalf, cannot delegate his agency, the maxim being " *vicarius non vicarium habet,* or *delegatus non delegare potest.*" The ordinary personal disabilities, some of which are mentioned above, do not prevent such a person from acting as agent; 1 Parsons on Bills, 90.

(*c*) As a rule a corporation cannot contract except under seal. But this general rule admits of an exception in cases where the making of a certain description of contracts is necessary and incidental to the purposes for which the corporation was created—per Wightman, J., in *Clark* v. *Cuckfield Union,* 1 Bail Court Cases, 85 and 86. Thus in *Henderson* v. *The Australian Royal Mail Steam Navigation Company,* 5 E. & B. 409, it was held that a corporation, being a trading one and incorporated for a special purpose, was bound by a contract made in furtherance of the purpose of their incorporation, though not under seal. So also if a person be employed by a corporation, but not by a document under seal, and such person does the work for which he is employed, and such work is necessary and incidental to the purposes for which the corporation was created, he can recover from them the amount due for such work, *Haigh* v. *The Guardians of North Bierley Union*, E. B. & E. 873. It would seem to follow as the result of the authorities that where a corporation is established for trading purposes, the very object of which requires that it should have the power of issuing bills of exchange and promissory notes, e.g. in banking and trading corporations, or where expressly authorized by its charter, such a corporation has that power; per Lord Denman, C. J., in *Church* v. *Imperial Gas Light Company*, 6 A. & E. at p. 861; see also *Broughton* v. *Manchester Water Works Company*, 3 B. & Ald. 1; *Wells* v. *Kingston-upon-Hull*, L. B. 10 C. P. 402; 44 L. J. C. P. 257. Therefore a corporation cannot draw, accept or indorse a bill of exchange or be a party to a promissory note unless expressly or impliedly authorised to do so. But it is not competent to a company incorporated in the usual way for the formation and working of a railway to draw, accept, or indorse bills of exchange, *Bateman* v. *Mid-Wales Railway Company*, L. R. 1 C. P. 499. In another case a company was formed under the Companies Act, 1862, for the purpose of purchasing a concession from a foreign Government for the construction of a railway, and forming a *société anonyme* to make the railway. The memorandum stated that in order to attain their main object the Company might do in England or Peru, or elsewhere, whatever they thought incidental or conducive thereto. The articles gave the directors power to do all things and make all contracts which, in their judgment, were necessary and proper for the purpose of carrying into effect the object mentioned in the memorandum. It was held (by the Court of Appeal) that although the Companies Act, 1862, does not confer on all companies registered under it a power of issuing negotiable instruments, such a power exists only where, upon a fair construction of the memorandum and articles of association, it appears that it was intended to be conferred, and that such a power existed in that case, for that although it could not be inferred from the nature of the business of the company, it was conferred by the above general words in the memorandum and articles. *The Peruvian Railways Company* v. *Thames & Mersey Marine Insurance Company*, L. R. 2 Ch. Ap. 618.

(d) So held in *Smith* v. *Johnson*, 3 H. & N. 222; 27 L. J. Ex. 363.

23.—No person is liable as drawer (*a*), indorser (*b*), or acceptor (*c*) of a bill who has not signed (*d*) it as such: Provided that,

(1.) Where a person signs a bill in a trade or assumed name, he is liable thereon as if he had signed it in his own name (*e*);

(2.) The signature of the name of a firm is equivalent to the signature by the person so signing of the names of all persons liable as partners in that firm (*f*).

(*a*) See note (*v*) to sect. 3 of this Act

(*b*) See sect. 31, sub-sect. 3, and sect. 32, sub-sects. 1 and 2, of this Act, and the notes thereto.

(*c*) See sect. 17, sub-sect. 2 (*a*) of this Act, and the notes thereto.

(*d*) It has been long established that no one is liable on a bill unless he is a party to it, *Vincent* v. *Horlock*, 1 Camp, 442. Is it not an universal rule that a man who puts his name to a bill of exchange thereby makes himself personally liable? per Lord Ellenborough, in *Leadbitter* v. *Farrow*, 5 M. & S. 349; see also *Bult* v. *Morrell*, 12 A. & E. 745. Where two persons accepted a bill of exchange as managers of an association, it was held that they were personally liable, *Jones* v *Jackson*, 22 L. T. N. S. 828, following *Allen* v. *Miller*, 22 L. T. N. S. 825; and in which *Jenkins* v. *Morris*, 16 M & W. 877; *Nicholls* v. *Diamond*, 9 Ex. 154; 23 L J. Ex. 1, were referred to and approved of; see also *Price* v. *Taylor*, 2 L. T. N. S. 221, 5 H & N. 540; 29 L J. Ex. 331; so where the defendants as "Directors" jointly and severally promised to pay, it was held that the words jointly and severally were equivalent to jointly and personally, *Healey* v. *Story*, 3 Ex. 3; 18 L. J. Ex. 8; see also *Dutton* v. *Marsh*, L. R. 6 Q. B. 361, 40 L. J Q. B. 175; 24 L. T. N. S. 470; 19 W. R. 754. But under the Companies Act 1862 a bill of exchange shall be deemed to be accepted on behalf of any company under the Act if it is accepted by or on behalf or on account of the company by any person acting under its authority, see also *Okell* v. *Charles*, 34 L T. N. S. 822; *Herald* v. *Connah*, 34 L. T. N. S. 885; *Forbes* v. *Marshall*, 11 Ex. 166. But a bill, headed "office of B. Co." and concluding, "charge same to account of B. Co.; W. B., president, J. W., Secretary," is the bill of the Company, and not of the individuals signing, *Hitchcock* v. *Buchanan*, 15 Otto, Sup. Ct. U. S. 416.

(*e*) See *South Carolina Bank* v. *Case*, 8 B. & C. 427; 2 Man. & Ry. 459; *Wilde* v. *Keep*, 6 C. & P. 235; *Kirk* v. *Blurton*, 9 M. & W. 284, *Stephens* v. *Reynolds*, 5 H. & N. 513; *Edmunds* v. *Bushell*, L. R. 1 Q. B. 97.

(*f*) Thus in *Wells* v. *Masterman*, 2 Esp. 731, it was held that a bill drawn on a partnership and accepted by one of the partners, shall, even if for a separate debt of one of them, bind the partnership, if in the hands of a *bonâ fide* indorsee, without notice; see also *Stephens* v. *Reynolds*, 5 H. & N. 513. In a recent case it was held that where a signature to a bill is common to an individual and a firm of which the individual is a member, and when the individual carries on no business separate from the firm, there is a presumption that the bill is given for and is binding on the firm, *The Yorkshire Banking Company* v. *Beatson and another*, 5 C. P. D. 109, 49 L. J. Q B. D. 380.

Forged or
unauthorised
signature.

Ind Act, s. 41.

24.—Subject to the provisions of this Act, where a signature on a bill is forged (*a*) or placed thereon without the authority (*b*) of the person whose signature it purports to be, the forged or unauthorised signature is wholly inoperative, and no right to retain (*c*) the bill or to give a discharge therefor, or to enforce payment (*d*) thereof against any party thereto, can be acquired through or under that signature, unless the party against whom it is sought to retain or enforce payment of the bill is precluded from setting up the forgery or want of authority. Provided that nothing in this section shall affect the ratification of an unauthorised (*e*) signature not amounting to a forgery (*f*).

(*a*) Forgery has been defined to be the fraudulent making or alteration of a writing to the prejudice of another man's right, 4 Bl. Com. 247; it is forgery to make a deed fraudulently with a false date, when the date is a material part of the deed, *Reg.* v. *Ritson,* L. R. 1 C C R. 200. The general rule is that no title can be obtained through a forgery, per Tindal, C.J., in *Johnson* v. *Windle,* 3 Bing N. C. 229; 3 Scott, 608. There may, however, be negligence in the party whose signature on the bill is forged, which may make the case different; see note to sect. 74, title Forged and altered Cheques. In a recent case, where the defendant accepted a bill of exchange in blank, and the drawing and drawer's indorsements were afterwards forged by the person to whom the defendant gave the bill, and the plaintiffs took the bill without notice, it was held that the forgery of the drawing and indorsement did not prevent the defendant from being liable to the plaintiffs, *The London and South Western Bank* v. *Wentworth,* 5 Ex. D. 96; 49 L. J. Q. B. D. 657; 42 L T. N. S. 188; 28 W. R. 516. A forgery is incapable of ratification; see the proviso at the end of this section. A person who knows that a bank is relying upon his forged signature to a bill cannot lie by and not divulge the fact until he sees that the position of the bank is altered for the worse, *McKenzie* v. *British Linen Company,* 6 Ap. Cas. 82; 44 L. T. N. S. 431; 29 W. R. 477.

(*b*) Where a bill was presented for acceptance at the office of the drawee when he was absent, and A., who lived in the same house with the drawee, being assured by one of the payees that the bill was perfectly regular, and was induced to write on the bill an acceptance as by the procuration of the drawee, believing that the acceptance would be sanctioned and the bill paid by the latter, but the bill was dishonoured when due, the indorsee brought an action against the drawee, but was non-suited, *Polhill* v. *Walter,* 3 B. & Ad. 114. An agent "per procuration" is a specially appointed agent, but his authority is limited; as to such an agency see sect. 25, and the notes thereto. A power to receive all salary, and to recover, compound, and give discharges for the same; or a power to transact all business does not authorise the agent to negotiate bills, *Hogg* v. *Snaith*, 1 Taunt. 347; nor a power to demand or sue, *Murray* v. *East India Company*, 5 B. & Ald. 104; nor a power given by an executrix to act for her as such, *Gardner* v. *Baillie*, 6 T. R. 591, see also *Esdaile* v. *Lanauze*, 1 Y. & C. 394; and so it is provided by the Indian Act, s. 27. The manager of a farm who conducts all its business has no implied authority to issue bills in the name of his principal, *Davidson* v. *Stanley*, 2 M. & G. 721, see also *Hogarth* v. *Wherley*, L R. 10 C. P. 630; 44 L. J. C. P. 330; 32 L. T. N. S. 800. Where a principal is sued on the agent's bills, the agent having previously issued bills, it must be proved that the principal knew or might have known of it, *Davidson* v. *Stanley*, 2 M. & G. 721; see also *Llewelyn* v. *Winckworth*, 13 M. & W. 598; but an authority to draw does not give an authority to indorse, per Tindal, C. J., in *Prescott* v. *Flinn*, 9 Bing. 19. And so it is provided by the Indian Act, s. 27. An authority given to A. to draw bills in the name of B. may be exercised by the clerks of A., as it is given to be made use of in the common course of business; *Ex parte Sutton*, 2 Cox, Eq. Cas. 84. So where payment was made to an agent by cheque, the authority to receive payment is not of itself sufficient to authorise the agent to indorse his principal's name on the cheque, *Brush* v. *Barrett*, 82 N. Y. Rep. 400. One partner is generally the agent of his partner or partners in all partnership matters. If, therefore, a partnership be in trade, one partner can bind the firm by drawing, accepting or indorsing a bill or note, provided he does so in the name of the firm, *Norton* v. *Seymour*, 3 C. B. 792; *Stephens* v. *Reynolds*, 5 H. & N. 513, and for partnership purposes, *Browne* v. *Kidger*, 3 H. & N. at pp. 858, 859; *Dickenson* v. *Valpy*, 10 B. & C. at p. 140. In a recent case it has been held that a partner has no implied authority to bind his firm by issuing acceptances in blank, *Hogarth* v. *Latham*, 3 Q. B. D. 643; 47 L. J. Q. B. D. 339. An association, consisting of several firms, but that has no name, is not liable on bills drawn and accepted by the different firms, though for the purposes of this association, *In re Adansonia Fibre Company*, L. R. 9 Ch. 635; 43 L. J. Ch. 732; 31 L. T. N. S. 9; 22 W. R. 889; under an authority to indorse, a partner cannot indorse for his private purposes; *Garland* v. *Jacomb*, L. R. 8 Ex. 216; 28 L. T. N S. 877; 21 W. R. 868. Attorneys cannot bind their firms by bills, *Hedley* v. *Bainbridge*, 3 Q. B. 316. See also sect. 91.

(c) Thus where a bill is negotiated by means of a forgery of the name of the payee as indorser, it was held that a Court of Equity will restrain even a *bonâ fide* holder of the bill from suing the acceptor, and will direct the forged instrument to be delivered up to be cancelled.

§ 24.
———
Forged or unauthorised signature.

Ind Act, s. 27.

Esdaile v. *Lanauze*, 1 Y. & C. 394; in this case it was also held
that when the original indorsement of the payee's name on a bill is
a forgery, a real indorsement by the payee, after the bill has arrived at
maturity, will not give the holder any title. See also note (*a*) to this
section.

(*d*) So held in *Johnson* v. *Windle*, 3 Bing. N. C. at p. 229; see
also the cases cited in note (*a*) to this section.

(*e*) An agent's acts where he has acted without or has exceeded his
authority, are capable of ratification. Thus in *Ancona* v. *Marks*,
7 H. & N. 686, 31 L. J Ex. 163; it was held that an action may
be maintained by a person as the holder of a negotiable instrument, notwithstanding he has no real interest in it, and never
was the actual holder. If it has been indorsed and delivered to some
person professing to act as his agent, although without his knowledge,
and he subsequently adopts the acts of the assumed agent, that is
sufficient title, although such adoption is after action brought in his
name without his knowledge. So the acts of one partner can be
afterwards recognised or adopted by his co-partners, *Duncan* v.
Lowndes, 3 Camp. 478.

(*f*) A forgery cannot be ratified, *Brook* v. *Hook*, L. R. 6 Ex. 89;
40 L. J. Ex. 50, inasmuch as the act done is illegal and void; but if
the act had been only voidable, it might have been ratified.

**25. A signature by procuration operates as notice that
the agent has but a limited authority to sign (*a*), and
the principal is only bound by such signature if the
agent in so signing was acting within the actual limits of
his authority (*b*).**

(*a*) Before this Act, it was held that where a bill upon the face of it
purports to be accepted "per procuration," that circumstance is a
notice to whoever takes the bill that the acceptor has but a limited
authority; and the holder cannot maintain an action against the
principal if the authority has been exceeded, *Stagg* v. *Elliott*,
12 C. B. N. S. 373; see also the remarks in it of Willes, J., about
Smith v. *McGuire*, 3 H. & N. 554, where it was held that if a person
permits another to act as his general agent, he is bound by a contract
made by the agent, although the latter declares himself as acting " by
procuration " and has received special instructions which he exceeds.
The decision in *Stagg* v. *Elliott* followed that in *Alexander* v. *McKenzie*,
6 C. B. 766; 18 L. J. C. P. 94; see also *Attwood* v. *Munnings*,
7 B. & C. 278; *Smith* v. *Johnson*, 3 H. & N. 223, in the course of the
arguments in which Mr. Baron Bramwell put the following question :
If a partner signs the name of the firm the partnership is bound, but
if he signs " per proc.," does he not give notice that he is acting, not

under his general, but by virtue of some special authority? The answer given was this: "The doctrine laid down in *Alexander* v. *Mackenzie* (*supra*) and *Fearn* v. *Filica* (7 M. & G. 513), might apply to the cases of partners if it were shewn that a party who took the bill had notice of an agreement between the partners in contravention of which the bill had been indorsed."

(*b*) See the last preceding note (*a*) hereto.

26.—(1). Where a person signs a bill as drawer, indorser, or acceptor, and adds words to his signature, indicating that he signs for or on behalf of a principal, or in a representative character, he is not personally liable thereon (*a*); but the mere addition to his signature of words describing him as an agent, or as filling a representative character, does not exempt him from personal liability (*b*).

(2). In determining whether a signature on a bill is that of the principal or that of the agent by whose hand it is written, the construction most favourable to the validity of the instrument shall be adopted (*c*).

(*a*) This section seems to be suggested by the decision in *Alexander* v. *Sizer*, L. R. 4 Ex. 102, where a person who signed a note as secretary of a railway company was held not to be personally liable. "The true rule," said Byles J. in *Kelner* v. *Baxter*, L. R. 2 C. P 185, "is that stated by Mr. Thesiger, viz., that persons who contract as agents are generally personally responsible where there is no other person who is responsible as principal."

(*b*) Thus where a bill of exchange was accepted by the defendants as joint managers of the Royal Mutual Marine Association, they were held personally liable, and the introduction of the words "as managers" was considered immaterial, *Jones* v. *Jackson*, 22 L. T. N S. 828, following *Allen* v. *Miller*, 22 L. T. N. S. 825, and approving of *Jenkins* v. *Morris*, 16 M. & W. 877, and *Nicholls* v. *Diamond*, 9 Ex 154; 23 L. J. Ex. 1. As Mr. Justice Willes in *Kelner* v. *Baxter*, *supra*, said: Putting in the words "on behalf of, &c.," would operate no more than if a person should contract for a quantity of corn "on behalf of my horses." See also *Hitchcock* v. *Buchanan*, 15 Otto, Sup. Ct. U. S. 416. So also where a person signed a note as "trustee" of a building society, he was considered personally liable, *Price* v. *Taylor*, 2 L. T. N. S. 221; 5 H. & N. 540; 29 L J. Ex 331; see also note (*d*) to the 23rd section of this Act.

(*c*) Where an agent to a country bank, to whom plaintiff sent a sum of money, in order to procure a bill upon London, drew in his

SS. 26, 27.

Person signing as agent or in representative capacity.

own name for the amount upon the firm in London, the two firms being the same, it was held that the agent was liable as drawer, although the plaintiff knew that he was agent, and supposed that the bill was drawn by him as such, and on account of the country bank to which the agent paid over the money, *Leadbitter* v. *Farrow*, 5 M. & S. 345. Executors carried on their testator's trade in that character, and in the ordinary course of the business accepted a bill describing themselves in it simply as executors of their testator; it was held that neither the above circumstances, nor the form of the acceptance, relieved the estate of one of the executors, who died in the lifetime of the other, from the ordinary equitable liability on the bill, *Liverpool Bank* v. *Walker*, 4 De G. & J. 24; see also *Courtould* v. *Saunders*, 16 L. T. N. S. 562.

THE CONSIDERATIONS FOR A BILL.

Value and holder for value

27.—(1). Valuable consideration for a bill (z) may be constituted by—

(a). Any consideration sufficient to support a simple contract (y);

(b). An antecedent debt (x) or liability. Such a debt or liability is deemed valuable consideration, whether the bill is payable on demand or at a future time.

(2). Where value has at any time been given for a bill the holder is deemed to be holder for value as regards the acceptor and all parties to the bill who became parties prior to such time (w).

(3). Where the holder of a bill has a lien on it, arising either from contract or by implication of law, he is deemed to be a holder for value to the extent of the sum for which he has a lien (u).

(z) The consideration for bills of exchange and promissory notes, unlike the case of other contracts, is presumed till the contrary appears. See further sect. 30 of this Act, and sub-sections 1 and 2 thereof and the notes thereto; also sect. 29, sub-sect. 2, and the notes thereto.

(y) The consideration of a simple contract is thus defined in a work of high authority: "By the Common Law if anything is performed which the party is under no legal obligation to perform, or if anything is given or done at the request of the promisor, as the consideration or inducement for the promise whereby the promisor or party making the promise has obtained or secured for himself some benefit or advantage, or whereby the promisee or party to whom the promise has been made has sustained some trouble or loss, or suffered some injury or inconvenience, there is sufficient consideration to render the promise obligatory in law, and capable of sustaining an action." Addison on Contracts (7th Edition by Mr. Justice Cave), 7. Any loss or detriment, therefore, to the person to whom the promise is made, or gain to the person making the promise, is a good consideration. But not natural affection, *Holliday* v. *Atkinson*, 5 B. & C. 501; Story on Bills, sect. 181 Cross-acceptances have been considered good consideration for one another, *Burdon* v. *Benton*, 9 Q. B. 843; *King* v. *Phillips*, 12 M. & W 705; *Kent* v. *Lowen*, 1 Camp. 179 n. As to what is a sufficient consideration for a bill there has been a recent decision. In that case an agreement was, upon the dissolution of a partnership, entered into, which after reciting that one of the partners had brought £2000 into the business, provided that the other partner should pay him that sum within three years, with interest at £5 per cent., in full satisfaction of all his share in the stock, credits, and effects of the partnership, and should indemnity him against the debts of the partnership; subsequently a promissory note payable on demand for the same £2000 was given to the retiring partner, it was held by the Court of Appeal, overruling the decision of Denman J. (reported in 52 L. J. Q B. 420) that there was a good consideration for the note, *Stott* v. *Fairlamb*, 49 L. T. N. S. 525, following *Currie* v. *Misa*, L. R. to Ex. 153.

(*x*) Prior to this Act an antecedent or existing debt was always considered a good consideration for a bill or note, provided it were made payable at a future time, on the ground that a negotiable security given for such a purpose is a conditional payment of the debt, the condition being that the debt revives if the security is not realized, *Currie* v. *Misa*, L. R. 10 Ex. at p. 163; *Belshaw* v. *Bush*, 11 C. B. 191, *Watson* v. *Russell*, 3 B. & S. 34; 31 L. J. Q. B. 304; *Poirrier* v. *Morris*, 2 E. & B. 89; *In re Carew*, 31 Beav. 39, where a customer of certain bankers got them to discount bills at a time when his account was overdrawn, and the amount was simply carried to the credit of his account, it was held that the bankers became holders for value, though no money was paid. But until the decision given in *Currie* v. *Misa*, L. R. 10 Ex. 153, it was doubtful whether a pre-existing debt was a good consideration for a bill or note payable on demand. However, all doubt on this head has been removed by the latter part of this sub-section, which makes an antecedent debt a good consideration for all bills and notes whether payable on demand or at a future time. Where there exists a debt or liability in præsenti, payable in futuro, and a state of things exists which entitles the debtor to pay, the giving of a note payable on demand is a conditional payment, and there is consideration for it, *Stott* v. *Fairlamb*, 49 L. T. N. S. 525.

(*w*) See *Scott* v. *Lifford*, 1 Camp. 246, *Barber* v. *Richards*, 6 Ex. 63 If value has been given by an indorsee he can convey title to the

SS. 27, 28, 29.

Value and holder for value.

instrument by delivery, and erase his indorsement, *Fairclough* v. *Pavia*, 9 Ex. 690 ; Story on Bills, sect. 188.

(*u*) In *Hills* v. *Parker*, 14 L. T. N. S. 107, it was held that bills of exchange are not proper subjects of mortgage, and are *primâ facie* presumed to be given in part payment as they become due ; see *Re Boys*, L. R. 10 Eq. 467, where it was held that a promissory note given by principal and surety for a definite sum and payable on a fixed day is presumed to be given in consideration of an advance at the date of the note ; see also *Attenborough* v. *Clarke*, 27 L. J. Ex. 138.

Accommodation bill or party.
Ind. Act, s. 43.

28.—(1). An accommodation party to a bill is a person who has signed a bill as drawer, acceptor, or indorser, without receiving value therefor, and for the purpose of lending his name to some other person (*a*).

Ind. Act, s. 52.

(2). An accommodation party is liable on the bill to a holder for value ; and it is immaterial whether, when such holder took the bill, he knew such party to be an accommodation party or not (*b*).

(*a*) This has always been known as the definition of an accommodation party to a bill. See Chalmers' Digest of Bills, 2nd edition, 84 ; Byles on Bills (13th Edition), 131. For examples of what are or are not accommodation bills, see *Scott* v. *Lifford*, 1 Camp. 246 ; *Collott* v *Haigh*, 3 Camp. 281 ; *Sleigh* v. *Sleigh*, 5 Ex. 514 ; *Wilks* v. *Hornby*, 10 W. R. 742 ; *Ex parte Swan*, L. R. 6 Eq. 344 ; *Ex parte Cama, In re London, Bombay, and Mediterranean Bank*, L. R. 9 Ch. 686, 43 L. J. Chan. 683 ; 31 L. T. N. S. 234 ; 22 W. R. 809. The fact that the name of an acceptor is written across the stamp before the bill is drawn, does not of itself raise the inference that the bill was accepted for the accommodation of the drawer, *Harris* v. *Sterling*, 9 Ir. R. C. L. 198. A cross acceptance is a good consideration, Story on Bills, sect. 183 ; *Burdon* v. *Benton*, 9 Q. B. 843 ; 16 L. J. Q. B 353 ; see also *King* v. *Phillips*, 12 M. & W. 705.

(*b*) So held before this Act, see *Smith* v. *Knox*, 3 Esp. 47 ; *Scott* v. *Lifford supra* ; *Charles* v. *Marsden*, 1 Taunt. 224 ; but in *Parr* v. *Jewell*, 16 C. B. 684, it was held that it is a good defence by an indorsee against the acceptor of a bill of exchange that it was accepted for the accommodation of the drawer, without consideration, and that it was indorsed by the drawer after it had been paid by him at its maturity, Story on Bills, sect. 188.

Holder in due course

29.—(1). A holder in due course is a holder who has taken a bill, complete (*z*), and regular on the face of it, under the following conditions ; namely :

Ind. Act. s. 9

(*a*). That he became the holder of it before it

was overdue (*y*), and without notice that it had been previously dishononoured, if such was the fact :

S. 29.

Holder in due course.

(*b*). That he took the bill in good faith and for value (*x*), and that at the time the bill was negotiated to him, he had no notice of any defect (*w*) in the title of the person who negotiated it.

Ind. Act, s 9.

(2). In particular the title of a person who negotiates a bill is defective within the meaning of this Act, when he obtained the bill or the acceptance thereof by fraud (*v*), duress (*t*), or force and fear (*s*), or other unlawful means (*r*), or for an illegal consideration (*q*), or when he negotiates it in breach of faith (*p*), or under such circumstances as amount to a fraud (*o*).

Ind Act, s 58

(3). A holder (whether for value or not) who derives his title to a bill through a holder in due course, and who is not himself a party to any fraud or illegality affecting it, has all the rights of that holder in due course as regards the acceptor and all parties to the bill prior to that holder (*n*).

Ind. Act, s. 53

(*z*) Complete, i.e. complete by delivery. Where the holder is not the payee of the bill, it must be indorsed as well as delivered to him, unless it be payable to bearer, in which case mere delivery is sufficient. In *Whistler* v. *Forster*, 14 C. B. N. S. 248, it was held that one who receives a bill of exchange unindorsed (though for value) acquires no better title under it than the person from whom he receives it himself has.

(*y*) "The general rule of law," said Mr. Justice Willes in *Whistler* v. *Forster, supra,* p. 257, "is undoubted, that no one can transfer a better title than he himself possesses ; *nemo dat quod non habet.* To this there are some exceptions ; one of which arises out of the rules of the law-merchant as to negotiable instruments. These being part of the currency, are subject to the same rules as money ; and if such an instrument be transferred in good faith, for value before it is overdue, it becomes available in the hands of the holder, notwithstanding fraud which would have rendered it unavailable in the hands of a previous holder."

(*x*) Thus it has been long established that one who takes a negotiable security *bonâ fide*, that is giving value for it, and having no notice at the time that the party from whom he takes it has no title, is entitled to recover upon it, even although he may at the time have had the

E

means of knowledge of that fact, of which means he neglected to avail himself, *Raphael* v. *The Bank of England*, 17 C. B. 161; see also *Whistler* v. *Forster*, 14 C. B. N. S at 248. So in *Currie* v. *Misa*, L. R. 10 Ex. 153, it was held that the title of a creditor to a negotiable security given to him on account of a pre-existing debt, and received by him *bonâ fide* and without notice of any infirmity of title on the part of the debtor, is indefeasible. In *Ex parte Richdale, In re Palmer*, 19 Ch. D. 409; 51 L. J. Ch. D. 462; 46 L. T. N. S. 116; it was held that when a customer pays a cheque to his bankers with the intention that it shall be at once placed to his credit, and the bankers carry the amount to his credit accordingly, they become immediately holders of the cheque for value, even though the customer's account is not overdrawn.

(*w*) "Notice of any defect," i.e. *bonâ fide*, which was construed as "without knowledge," per Willes, J., in *Raphael* v. *The Bank of England*, 17 C. B. 174, again in *Oakeley* v. *Ooddeen*, 2 F. & F. 656, it was held that if a party suspects a fraud, and does not ask as to it, lest he should know it, he has sufficient notice. But one who takes a negotiable security *bonâ fide*, that is giving value for it, and having no notice at the time that the party from whom he takes it has no title, is entitled to recover upon it, even although he may at the time have had the means of knowledge of that fact, of which means he neglected to avail himself, and such negligence will not of itself amount to notice, though it may be evidence of it, *Raphael* v. *The Bank of England*, 17 C. B. 161; again, it has been decided that the question whether or not an indorsee was guilty of gross negligence is improper, and that gross negligence may be evidence of *mala fides*, but is not equivalent to it, *Goodman* v. *Harvey*, 4 A. & E. 870; see also *Swan* v. *The North British Company*, 2 H. & C. 184, where Mr Justice Byles said, " The object of the law merchant as to bills and notes made or become payable to bearer, is to secure their circulation as money ; therefore honest acquisition conveys title. To this despotic but necessary principle the ordinary rules of the common law are made to bend. The misapplication of a genuine signature written across a slip of stamped paper (which transaction being a forgery would in ordinary cases convey no title) may give a good title to any sum fraudulently inscribed within the limits of the stamp, and in America, where there are no stamp laws, to any sum whatsoever. Negligence in the maker of an instrument payable to bearer makes no difference in his liability to an honest holder for value, the instrument may be lost by the maker or stolen from him, still he must pay. The negligence of the holder, on the other hand, makes no difference in his title. However gross the holder's negligence, if it stop short of fraud, he has a title." Again, it is not enough if the party charged had incautiously neglected to make inquiries, but he must have designedly abstained from so doing, per Wigram, V.C, in *Jones* v. *Smith*, 1 Hare, 55, see also the observations of Lord Cranworth, L. C., in *Ware* v. *Lord Egmont*, 4 De G. M. & G. 473. But such indorsee must not "wilfully shut" his eyes to the means of knowledge of which he might avail himself; per Willes, J., in *May* v. *Chapman*, 16 M. & W. 361; see also the observations of Parke, B., in *The Bank of Ireland* v. *The Trustees of Evans' Charities*, 5 H. L. Cas. 411; *Stevens* v. *Foster*, 1 C. M. & R. 849; see further sect. 90 of this Act and the notes thereto.

(*v*) "No contract," says Patteson, J., in *Campbell* v. *Fleming*, 1 A. and E., p. 42, "can arise out of a fraud; and an action brought upon a supposed contract, which is shown to have arisen from fraud, may be resisted." But a contract obtained by fraud is only voidable, and not void, and hence can be ratified; or if not, it must be disaffirmed; *White* v. *Garden*, 10 C. B. 919; *Hawes* v. *Harness*, L. R. 10 C. P. 166; *Hogan* v. *Healy*, 11 Ir. R. C. L. 119. "Fraud," said Wilde, B., in *Rogers* v. *Hadley*, 2 H. & C 257, "does not vitiate a contract necessarily, but at the election of the party defrauded."

"Fraud generally consists either in the misrepresentation or in the concealment of a material fact. What does or does not amount to fraud, depends very much on the facts of each particular case, on the relative situation of the parties, and on their means of information. Where therefore one person misrepresents or conceals a material fact, that is, a fact which is substantially the consideration for the contract, and which is peculiarly within his own knowledge, or uses a device which is calculated to induce the other party to forego inquiry into a material fact, upon which the former has information, although such information be not exclusively within his reach, and such concealment or other deception is practised with respect to the particular transaction will be voidable on the ground of fraud." Chitty on Contracts (10th Edition), pp. 630 & 631. A misrepresentation as to the legal effect of an agreement does not avoid it, *Lewis* v. *Jones*, 4 B. & C. 509. But a fraudulent intention to break the contract, expressed at the time it was entered into, will not, if not carried out, affect it, *Hemingway* v. *Hamilton*, 4 M. & W. 115. If therefore a negotiable instrument be obtained by fraud it is void not only as between the immediate parties, but also between other parties, except *bonâ fide* holders for value without notice, *Mills* v. *Oddy*, 2 C. M. & R. 103; *Whistler* v. *Forster*, 14 C. B. N. S. 248; see further sub-sects. (2) and (3) of this section. It has been held that if a cheque is given on a verbal condition which the drawer finds to be broken or eluded, he has a right to stop the payment of the cheque, *Wienholt* v. *Spitta*, 3 Camp. 376; fraud in obtaining a cheque gives an option to the party defrauded to disaffirm the contract, *Dawes* v. *Harness*, L. R. 10 C. P. 166. If a horse be sold under a warranty and paid for by a cheque, and the horse afterwards turns out to be unsound, the breach of warranty is an answer to the action on the cheque, if the vendor knew of this unsoundness, and if the purchaser has tendered back the horse,

Lewis v. *Cosgrave*, 2 Taunt. 2; see also 1 Parsons on Bills, 205; *Fleming* v. *Simpson*, 1 Camp. 40. Mere inadequacy of consideration does not constitute fraud, unless there be evidence of other circumstances, *Solomon* v. *Turner*, 1 Stark. 51. A bill given by an insolvent debtor in fraud of his creditors is bad, *Cockshott* v. *Bennett*, 2 T. R. 763; *Knight* v. *Hunt*, 5 Bing. 432; Parsons on Bills, vol. 1, 216. If, however, a party to a contract has been deceived by the other party, but has received the benefit of it, he cannot afterwards get it set aside. Or, to use the words of Lord Chief Baron Pollock in *Rogers* v. *Hadley*, 32 L. J. Ex. 248, "the rule that applies to a case simply of fraud, where there has been a contract imposed upon a man by fraud, and which he may adopt or not as he pleases, is a very simple rule, and if he adopt it, he cannot afterwards repudiate it. It is at his option to say, I will not give my sanction to the contract, I repudiate it; but he cannot in the common phrase play fast and loose; he cannot at one time say, 'I will adopt it,' and then when he has done so, say, 'I will hark back and repudiate it.'" And in *Clarke* v. *Dixon*, E. B. & E. 148, it was held that a person induced by fraud to enter into a contract under which he pays money, may, at his option, rescind the contract and recover back the price, as money had and received, if he can return what he has received under it. But when he can no longer place the parties *in statu quo*, as if he has become unable to return what he has received in the same plight as that in which he received it, the right to rescind no longer exists; and his remedy must be by an action for deceit, and not for money had and received. Thus on a treaty of marriage a promissory note was given in consideration of the marriage, which was afterwards solemnised, and an action was subsequently brought by the indorsee against the makers of the note, it was held that as the marriage, the consideration for the note, could not be undone, it was not competent to the makers to avoid the note upon the ground of fraud practised during the marriage treaty, *Hogan* v. *Healy*, 11 Ir. R. C. L 119. It would seem that it is no defence to an action on a bill by an indorsee against the acceptor for value that the bill was indorsed upon an illegal consideration; the acceptor must shew that it was indorsed in fraud of himself; *Flower* v. *Sadler*, 10 Q. B. D. 572.

(*t*) "Duress may consist either in actual violence or in a threat thereof; any unlawful imprisonment or detention of a person in consequence of which he is obliged to enter into a contract, or in other words to give a bill or note, is duress; but not if the custody be lawful, e g., under the regular process of a court of competent jurisdiction, and to constitute duress by threat or *per minas* there must be a threat of some serious personal injury, e.g, threat to murder, wound, or imprison." Chitty on Contracts (10th Edit.), 186 and 187. A threat of trespass to lands or goods is not sufficient, *Skeate* v. *Beale*, 11 A. & E. 983. The duress must be suffered by the party who enters into the contract, and the consent of his agent or counsel at the time will not bind him, *Cumming* v. *Ince*, 11 Q. B. 112.

(*s*) These are synonymous with duress. See note (*t*) hereto.

(*r*) Other unlawful means, i e , ejusdem generis, as fraud, duress, or force and fear, the rule as to the construction of statutes being that where several words preceding a general word point to a confined meaning, the general word shall not have such a meaning as to extend its effect beyond subjects *ejusdem generis*, per Lord Denman, L. C. J., in *Reg.* v. *Nevill*, 8 Q B. 463; see also *Sandiman* v. *Breach*, 7 B. & C. 96.

(*q*) Considerations are illegal either at Common Law or by Statute; Story on Bills, s. 186. Considerations which are illegal at Common Law are those which are against morality (A.), or are against public policy (B.). As an instance of class (A.) a contract to hire a carriage to a prostitute for the purposes of prostitution; *Pearce* v. *Brooks*, L R. 1 Ex. 212. So also a contract to supply dresses to a prostitute for her calling, *Bowry* v. *Bennett*, 1 Camp. 348. So also an agreement made in consideration of future illicit cohabitation between the parties is void, *Walker* v. *Perkins*, 3 Burr. 1568; 1 W. Bl. 517; *Rex* v. *Inhabitants of Northwingfield*, 1 B. & Ad. 912. So also an agreement in consideration of past cohabitation unless it be under seal, *Binnington* v. *Wallis*, 4 B & Ald. 650; *Nye* v. *Moseley*, 6 B. & C. 133, so that a bill or note given in consideration of past cohabitation is void, as indeed was held in *Robinson* v. *Cox*, 9 Mad. 263. So also a bill or note given for the amount of the rent of rooms let to a prostitute for the purpose of receiving visitors there, *Girardy* v. *Richardson*, 1 Esp. 13; *Jennings* v. *Throgmorton*, Ry. & M. 251; but not if the woman merely lodges there and receives her visitors elsewhere, *Appleton* v. *Campbell*, 2 C. & P. 347. Other instances of class (A.) are contracts for the sale of obscene immoral or libellous pictures, see *Forbes* v. *Johnes*, 4 Esp. 97; *Poplett* v. *Stockdale*, Ry. & M. 337. Instances of class (B.) are contracts in restraint of trade, as to which see *Hilton* v. *Eckersley*, 6 E. & B. 47; *Ward* v. *Byrne*, 5 M. & W. 548. But an agreement in partial restraint of trade is not void, see *Davis* v. *Mason*, 5 T. R. 118; *Homer* v. *Ashford*, 3 Bing. 322, *Wickens* v. *Evans*, 3 Y. & J. 318; *Pilkington* v. *Scott*, 15 M. & W. 657; see also *Mitchel* v. *Reynolds*, 1 Smith's Leading Cases (8th edition), p. 417, and the cases cited therein. Another instance of class B. is a contract in restraint of marriage, as to which see *Lowe* v. *Peers*, 4 Burr. 2225; *Baker* v. *White*, 2 Vern. 215; *Woodhouse* v. *Shepley*, 2 Atk. 540; *Cock* v. *Richards*, 10 Ves. 429. Another instance is an agreement for compounding a prosecution for felony, or misdemeanor of a public nature, such as perjury, embezzlement, &c., as to which see *Collins* v. *Blantern*, 1 Smith's Leading Cases (8th Edition), p. 387; 2 Wils. 341, see also *Kirwan* v. *Goodman*, 9 Dowl. 330; *Ward* v. *Lloyd*, 6 M. & G. 785, *Keir* v. *Leeman*, 6 Q. B. 308; *Gibbs* v. *Hume*, 31 L. J. Ch. 37; and *Brown* v. *Brine*,

1 Ex. D. 5; even though the prosecution be withdrawn, *Ex parte
Critchley*, 3 D. & L. 527. But it seems that if no criminal proceedings have actually been commenced, or if there be no reasonable or probable cause for believing a criminal act to have been committed, the agreement, or bill, or note given for such a consideration is not invalid, *Bourke* v. *Mealy*, 14 Cox. C. C. 329. But a bill given on threat of prosecution is valid; *Flower* v. *Sadler*, 10 Q. B. D 572. A promissory note given for the amount of the penalty directed by a magistrate e.g., for a breach of the excise laws, is valid, *Sugars* v. *Brinkworth*, 4 Camp. 46; *Pilkington* v. *Green*, 2 B. & P. 151. And a promissory note given by a forger in lieu of a forged one is also valid unless there is an agreement to stifle a prosecution for forgery, *Wallace* v. *Hardacre*, 1 Camp 45. Agreements of maintenance and champerty, *Bradlaugh* v. *Newdigate*, 11 Q. B. D. 1. There are also many other contracts which are illegal at Common Law, as to which see Chitty on Contracts (10th Edition), pp. 611-639; Addison on Contracts (7th edition), pp. 190-234. As to contracts illegal by statute the rule is that every contract made for or in respect of something the doing of which is punished by a penalty by any statute, or impliedly prohibited by the nature and objects of the statute, is void, as to which see Story on Bills, s. 186; and Byles on Bills (13th Edition) pp 140-147; Chitty on Contracts (10th Edition), 639-655, Addison on Contracts (7th Edition), 209-224. But where a statute imposes a penalty merely for the purpose of revenue, as for instance a statute requiring a dealer in tobacco to have his name painted on his premises, the price of tobacco sold, by one who has not complied with the provisions of such a statute can be recovered, *Smith* v. *Mawhood*, 14 M & W. 452; or again the price of spirits of nitre distilled and sold by one without a licence, which is prohibited by statute, *Bailey* v. *Harris*, 12 Q. B. 905. Therefore a bill or note given for any illegal consideration is void except in the hands of a *bonâ fide* holder for value without notice. "There is," says Mr. Justice Story in his work on Bills, s. 187, "one peculiarity in cases of illegality of consideration, in which it is distinguishable from the want or failure of consideration. In the latter, if there be a partial want or failure of consideration, it avoids the bill only pro tanto; but where the consideration is illegal in part, it avoids the bill in toto."

(*p*) Thus in *Wienholt* v. *Spitta*, 3 Camp. 376, it was held that if a cheque is given on a verbal condition which the drawer finds is to be broken or eluded, he has a right to stop the payment of it; see also *Lloyd* v. *Howard*, 15 Q. B. 995.

(*o*) See note (*v*) to this section.

(*n*) "An innocent party may transfer a title in the bill to a person who is no party to the original fraud, though he have knowledge of it," per Pollock, L. C. B., in *May* v. *Chapman*, 16 M. & W. 355; a plea that the note was obtained from the defendant by D (not the plaintiff or his indorser) by fraud, and that there was no consideration for the indorsement to the plaintiff, was held bad, *Masters* v. *Ibberson*, 8 C. B 100; "A *bonâ fide* holder," said Lord Campbell, C J., in *Lloyd* v. *Howard*, supra, "who takes before the bill is due, for value and without notice, may recover without further proof of a prior endorsement than by proving the handwriting."

30.—(1). Every party whose signature appears on a bill is, *primâ facie,* deemed to have become a party thereto for value (*a*).

(2). Every holder of a bill is, *primâ facie,* deemed to be a holder in due course (*b*), but if in an action on a bill it is admitted or proved (*c*) that the acceptance, issue, or subsequent negotiation of the bill is affected with fraud (*d*), duress (*e*), or force and fear (*f*), or illegality, the burden of proof is shifted, unless and until the holder proves that, subsequent to the alleged fraud or illegality, value has in good faith been given for the bill (*g*).

Presumption of value and good faith
Ind Act, s.118, sub-s (*a*)
Ind. Act, s 118, sub-s. (*g*)

(*a*) This follows from the consideration of a bill or note being presumed, see the judgment of Parke, B , in *Foster* v. *Dawber*, 6 Ex. 853.

(*b*) So held before this Act, *Mills* v. *Barber*, 1 M. & W. 424; *Lloyd* v. *Howard*, 15 Q. B. 995, *Fitch* v. *Jones*, 5 E & B. 238.

(*c*) Thus it has been long established that as soon as the bill appears by evidence to be affected by fraud or illegality the *onus* is shifted and the plaintiff is put to the proof of the consideration, as was stated by Lord Blackburn in *Jones* v. *Gordon*, 2 Ap. Cas. 627: "When it is shewn that a bill of exchange was a fraudulent one, or an illegal one, or a stolen one, in any of those cases it being known that the person who holds it was a party to that fraud, to that illegality, or to that theft; and therefore could not sue upon it himself, the presumption is so strong that he would part with it to somebody who could sue for him that that shifts the burden;" see also *Bailey* v. *Bidwell*, 13 M & W. 73; *Hall* v. *Featherstone*, 3 H & N. 284; *Smith* v *Braine*, 16 Q. B. 246; *Mather* v. *Lord Maidstone*, 1 C. B. N. S. 273; *Fitch* v. *Jones*, 5 E. & B. 238. It will be noticed that this section provides four cases only, in which the burden of proof is shifted, viz, fraud, duress, force or fear, and illegality. It is therefore submitted that in none of the other cases or events mentioned in sub-sect (2) of the last preceding (the 29th) section, will the *onus* be shifted on the plaintiff as in this section is provided. So that it is submitted in such cases the defendant must first prove the absence of consideration not only for his acceptance but also for the indorsement of it to the plaintiff, that is to say, not

SS 30, 31.
———
Presumption
of value and
good faith.

only that his acceptance was obtained in breach of faith but also that the plaintiff had notice of such breach of faith when the bill was indorsed to him, and then only the plaintiff will be called upon to give any evidence.

(*d*) As to fraud see note (*v*) to the 29th section of this Act. As to cases in which the burden of proof has been shifted on the plaintiff on proof of the bill being affected with fraud, see *Hall* v. *Featherstone*, 3 H. & N. 284; *Smith* v. *Braine*, 16 Q. B. 244, *Mather* v. *Lord Maidstone*, 1 C. B. N. S. 273.

(*e*) As to duress, see note (*t*) to the 29th section of this Act.

(*f*) As to force or fear see note (*s*) to the 29th section of this Act.

(*g*) As to illegality see note (*q*) to the 29th section of this Act and as to cases in which the burden of proof has been shifted on the plaintiff on proof of the bill being affected with illegality, see *Hall* v. *Featherstone*, 3 H. & N. 284; *Smith* v. *Braine*, 16 Q. B. 244; *Bailey* v. *Bidwell*, 13 M. & W. 73, *Fitch* v. *Jones*, 5 E. & B. 238. In *Jones* v. *Gordon*, L. R. 2 Ap. Cas. at p. 628, Lord Blackburn thought it doubtful whether the onus lies on the plaintiff to shew that he gave value *bonâ fide*, this, however, is now settled by this sub-section But a plea by the defendant that he accepted without consideration will not cast the onus on the plaintiff; *Batley* v. *Catterall*, 1 Moo. and Rob. 379.

NEGOTIATION OF BILLS.

Negotiation
of bills.
Ind Act, s. 46.

31.—(1). A bill is negotiated when it is transferred from one person to another in such a manner as to constitute the transferee the holder of the bill (*a*).

Ind Act, s 47.

(2). A bill payable to bearer is negotiated by delivery (*b*).

Ind. Act, s. 48.

(3). A bill payable to order is negotiated by the indorsement of the holder completed by delivery (*c*).

(4). Where the holder of a bill payable to his order transfers it for value without indorsing it, the transfer gives the transferee such title as the transferor had in the bill (*d*), and the transferee in addition acquires the right to have the indorsement of the transferor (*e*).

Ind Act, s 29.

(5). Where any person is under obligation to indorse a bill in a representative capacity, he may indorse the bill in such terms as to negative personal liability (*f*).

(*a*) That is, transferred by delivery or indorsement; as to the modes of indorsement see sub-sects. (2) and (3) of this section.

(*b*) See notes (*h*) and (*k*) to sect. 2 and note (*m*) to sect. 3 of this Act. If indorsed, the indorser is liable on his indorsement; *Keene* v. *Beard*, 8 C. B. N. S. 372.

(*c*) See notes (*h*) and (*k*) to sect. 2, and note (*m*) to sect. 3 of this Act. Every indorser of a bill is a new drawer; and it is part of the inherent property of the original instrument that an indorsement operates as against the indorser in the nature of a new drawing of the bill by him; per Parke, B., in *Penny* v. *Innes*, 1 C. M. & R. 441. If a person indorse a bill which is not negotiable, he is liable on his indorsement as a new drawer; *Gwinnell* v. *Herbert*, 5 A. & E. 436; *Burmester* v. *Hogarth*, 11 M. & W. 97.

(*d*) In *Whistler* v. *Forster*, 14 C. B. N. S. 248, it was held that one who receives a bill of exchange unindorsed (though for value), acquires no better title under it than the person from whom he receives it himself has. In a recent case in America, it has been decided that a cheque payable to order may be transferred by the payee by delivery without indorsement, and that the transferee of such cheque only acquires the right which the payee had in it at the time of the transfer, *Freund* v. *The Importers' National Bank*, 76 N. Y. Rep. 352.

(*e*) A note being handed over for valuable consideration, the indorsement is a form which the party is entitled to call for; per Sir Thomas Plumer, M. R., in *Watkins* v. *Maule*, 2 Jac. & Walker, 237; following *Smith* v. *Pickering*, Peake's N. P. R. 69; Story on Bills, s. 201. Even after bankruptcy; *Ex parte Mowbray*, 1 Jac. & W. 428.

(*f*) A person who signs a bill in a representative capacity, or as agent for his principal, is personally liable, even though he be known to be an agent; *Leadbitter* v. *Farrow*, 5 M. & S. 345; or his representative character be described in the instrument; *Liverpool Bank* v. *Walker*, 4 De G. & J. 24, so also if he sign in an official character, *e.g.*, as director; see *Gray* v. *Raper*, L. R. 1 C. P. 694; *Courtauld* v. *Saunders*, 16 L. T. N. S. 562; *Dutton* v. *Marsh*, L. R. 6 Q. B. 361. But see *Alexander* v. *Sizer*, L. R. 4 Ex. 102, where the note was signed by the maker as secretary of a railway company, and the Lord Chief Baron distinguished it on that ground from the above cases, and held that those words excluded personal liability. This section would seem to be a sequel to that decision. Therefore a trustee, executor, overseer, &c., who is compelled to sign a bill in his fiduciary or official capacity, should under this sub-section so sign it as to negative personal liability.

32.—An indorsement in order to operate as a negotiation must comply with the following conditions, namely :—

(1.) It must be written on the bill itself and be signed by the indorser (*a*). The simple signature (*b*) of

S. 32

Requisites of a
valid indorse-
ment
Ind. Act, s 15.

the indorser on the bill without additional words is sufficient.

An indorsement written on an allonge (*c*), or on a "copy" of a bill issued or negotiated in a country where "copies" (*d*) are recognised, is deemed to be written on the bill itself.

Ind. Act, s 56.

(2.) It must be an indorsement of the entire bill. A partial indorsement, that is to say, an indorsement which purports to transfer to the indorsee a part only of the amount payable (*e*), or which purports to transfer the bill to two or more indorsees severally, does not operate as a negotiation of the bill.

(3.) Where a bill is payable to the order of two or more payees or indorsees who are not partners, all must indorse, unless the one indorsing has authority to indorse for the others (*f*).

(4.) Where, in a bill payable to order, the payee or indorsee is wrongly designated, or his name is mis-spelt, he may indorse the bill as therein described, adding, if he think fit, his proper signature (*g*).

Ind Act, s 118,
sub-s. (*c*)

(5.) Where there are two or more indorsements on a bill, each indorsement is deemed to have been made in the order in which it appears on the bill, until the contrary is proved.

Ind. Act, s. 15.

(6.) An indorsement may be made in blank (*h*) or special (*j*). It may also contain terms making it restrictive (*k*)

(*a*) No particular form or language or expression is necessary for an indorsement; Story on Bills, s. 204; a blank indorsement has generally been made by the signature of the indorser generally on the back of the bill, see *Gibson* v. *Minet*, 1 H. Bl. 569; *Lecann* v. *Kirkman*, 6 Jur N. S. 17; although it has not been necessary to make the indorsement on the back of the bill, for indorsements on the face of it have been allowed, see *Ex parte Yates*, 27 L. J. Bankr. 9. The effect of such an indorsement is to make the instrument thereafter payable to bearer, sect. 34, subs. 1; *Peacock* v. *Rhodes*, 2 Doug. 633. The allegation of the indorsement of a bill in an action by the indorsee against the acceptor does not necessarily mean such an indorsement as will give a right of action against the indorser, but only such an indorsement as gives the plaintiff a title to the bill; *Smith* v. *Johnson*, 3 H. & N. 222.

(*b*) So held hitherto, *Pinkney* v. *Hall*, 1 Ld Raym. 175. The indorsement may be made by a mark, *George* v. *Surrey*, 1 M. & M. 516.

(*c*) An allonge is a paper annexed to the bill, which is necessary, when there are a series of indorsements; see Story on Bills, s. 204; Byles on Bills (13th Edition), 152.

(*d*) Copies of bills are not much used in this country, Byles on Bills, 13th ed., 395; nor in America; 1 Parsons on Bills, 60.

(*e*) By sect 56 of the Indian Act, where a bill has been partly paid, a note to that effect may be indorsed on it, and it may be negotiated for the balance. If the indorsee pay only a part of the amount of the bill, he is still entitled to recover the whole amount of the bill, *Johnson* v. *Kennion*, 2 Wils. 262; *Reid* v. *Furnival*, 5 C. & P. 499, 1 Cr. & M. 538. If the holder receives payment in whole or in part from the drawer and recovers from the acceptor, he must pay over to the drawer the amount which he received from him; *Solomon* v. *Davis*, 1 Cab. & El. N. P. C. 85. But if the indorsee has been a party to a fraud, he can recover only the amount actually paid by him, *Jones* v. *Gordon*, L. R. 2 Ap. Cas. 627; *In re Gomersall*, L. R. 1 Ch D. 137.

(*f*) As to partners, see sec. 24, note (*b*).

(*g*) Thus where a bill was by the defendant indorsed thus: "Pay Messrs. Terney and Farley or order," and they indorsed it in blank by writing thereon, "Thomas Terney and Farelly," the indorsement was held to be good and the defendant liable, *Leonard* v. *Wilson*, 2 Cr. & M. 589.

(*h*) As to blank and special indorsements, see Byles on Bills (13th Edition), 151, note (*a*) hereto; and sect. 34 (1) of this Act and the notes thereto which defines a special indorsement. A blank indorsement may be converted into a special indorsement, *Clerk* v. *Pigot*, 1 Salk. 126, 12 Mod. 193; *Hirschfield* v. *Smith*, L. R. 1 C. P. 340; but when an instrument is once indorsed in blank, a special indorsement made afterwards will not restrain its negotiability, *Smith* v. *Clarke*, 1 Esp. 180; *Walker* v. *M'Donald*, 2 Ex. 527; *Sigourney* v. *Lloyd*, 8 B. & C. 622; Story on Bills, s. 207.

(*j*) As to a special indorsement, see Sect. 34 (2) of this Act and the notes thereto. Even before this Act (sect. 8, sub-s 4) an indorsement need not have had the words "or order." "It is well settled, that if a note be made payable to J. S. or order, and he indorse the note to S., without adding "or order," S. may convey a good title to any other person by indorsement, *Gay* v. *Lander*, 6 C. B. 362. See also the last preceding note (*h*) hereto as to the conversion of a blank into a special indorsement.

(*k*) "The payee or indorsee, having the property in the bill, can limit the payment to whom he pleases"; Story on Bills, s. 210. For

SS. 32, 33, 34.
———
Requisites of valid indorsement.

examples of such indorsements, see sect. 35. But the words "pay the contents of the bill to A. B , being part of the consideration in a certain deed of assignment, executed by the said A. B. to the indorser and others," have been held not to be a restrictive indorsement, *Potts* v. *Reed*, 6 Esp 57; nor the words "being the portion of a value as under deposited in security for the payment thereof," *Haussouillier* v. *Hartsinck*, 7 T. R. 733 , nor "pay J. S. or order value in account with H. C. D," *Buckley* v. *Jackson*, L. R. 3 Ex. 185. The omission of the words "*or order*" in the indorsement will not restrain the negotiability of the instrument, see note (*j*) to this section.

Conditional indorsement.
Ind. Act, ss. 50 and 52.

33.—Where a bill purports to be indorsed conditionally, the condition may be disregarded by the payer, and payment to the indorsee is valid whether the condition has been fulfilled or not (*a*).

(*a*) If the indorsement is made conditional before acceptance, the acceptor is bound by the acceptance, *Robertson* v. *Kensington*, 4 Taunt. 30; see also *Soares* v. *Glyn*, 8 Q. B. 24; 14 L J. Q. B. 313. By the present section it seems that no matter what condition is imposed by the indorsement, it may be totally disregarded by the payer.

Indorsement in blank and special indorsement
Ind. Act, s. 16.

Ind Act, s. 16.

Ind Act, s. 49.

34.—(1) An indorsement in blank specifies no indorsee, and a bill so indorsed becomes payable to bearer (*a*).

(2.) A special indorsement specifies the person to whom or to whose order the bill is to be payable (*b*).

(3) The provisions of this Act relating to a payee (*c*) apply with the necessary modifications to an indorsee under a special indorsement.

(4.) When a bill has been indorsed in blank, any holder may convert the blank indorsement into a special indorsement by writing above the indorser's signature a direction to pay the bill to or to the order of himself or some other person (*d*).

(*a*) See note (*h*) to sect. 32 of this Act.

(*b*) See note (*j*) to sect. 32 of this Act.

(*c*) See sub-sects. (1), (2) and (3) of sect. 7 of this Act and the notes thereto.

(*d*) So held in *Clerk* v. *Pigott*, 12 Mod. 193; 1 Salk. 126; *Hirschfield* v. *Smith*, L. R. 1 C. P. 340. But in *Vincent* v. *Horlock*, 1 Camp. 441, it was held that if A, the payee of a bill, indorses it in blank, and delivers it to B., and B. writes above A.'s indorsement "pay the contents to C.," B. is not liable to C. as an indorser of the bill. This

case seems almost self-evident, for no one can be liable on a bill unless
his name is on it, see sect. 23. See also note (*h*) to the 32nd section
of this Act.

SS. 34, 35.
—
Indorsement in
blank and
special in-
dorsement.
Restrictive
indorsement
Ind. Act, s 50

35.—(1) An indorsement is restrictive (*a*) which pro-
hibits the further negotiation of the bill or which expresses
that it is a mere authority to deal with the bill as thereby
directed, and not a transfer of the ownership thereof (*b*);
as for example, if a bill be indorsed "pay D. only" (*c*), or
'pay D. for the account of X." (*d*), or "pay D. or order
or collection" (*e*).

(2) A restrictive indorsement gives the indorsee the
right to receive payment of the bill, and to sue any
party thereto that his indorser could have sued,
but gives him no power to transfer his rights as
indorsee unless it expressly authorise him to do
so (*f*).

(3.) Where a restrictive indorsement authorises further
transfer, all subsequent indorsees take the bill with
the same rights and subject to the same liabilities
as the first indorsee under the restrictive indorsement (*g*).

(*a*) See note (*k*) to sect. 32 of this Act.

(*b*) "To be sure, he may give a mere naked authority to any person
to receive it for him ; he may write upon it, 'Pray pay the money to
my servant, for my use,' or use such expressions as necessarily import
that he does not mean to indorse it over, but is only authorising a
particular person to receive it for him and for his *own use.* In such
case it would be clear that no valuable consideration had been paid
him. But, at least, that intention must *appear upon the face of the
'indorsement,'*" per Wilmot, J., in *Edie* v. *The East India Company,*
2 Burr. 1227. In *Ancher* v. *The Bank of England,* 2 Doug. 637, the
following indorsement was held to restrain the negotiability of the bill,
viz., "The within must be credited to Captain Morten Larren Dahl,
value in account." But an indorsement, "Pay J. Spittal or order
value in account with H C. Drinkwater," has been held not to be a
restrictive indorsement, *Buckley* v. *Jackson,* L. R. 3 Ex. 135, following
Stuart v. *Murrow,* 8 Moo. P. C. 267 ; see also sect. 32, note (*k*).

(*c*) The word "only" is obviously necessary to make the indorsement restrictive, see sect. 8, sub-s. 4, and the notes thereto. There
has been no English decision giving an indorsement like this, except
Snee v. *Prescott,* 1 Atk. 219, where it was, "Pay the money to my
use." See also note (*d*).

SS. 35, 36.

Restrictive
indorsement.

(*d*) This is the same as the indorsement in *Treuttel* v. *Barandon*, 8 Taunt. 100.

(*e*) There are one or two American cases showing indorsements like this; they will be found in Chalmers' Digest of Bills, 2nd ed., 110, 111. But there seems to be no English case exactly like it, except three, the indorsements in which are somewhat similar. For instance, in *Snee* v. *Prescott, supra*; again, "Pay to A. or order for the use of B.," *Evans* v. *Cramlington*, 2 Show. 495; and "Pay B. or his order for my use," *Sigourney* v. *Lloyd*, 8 B. & C. 622.

(*f*) See notes (*b*) (*c*) (*d*) and (*e*).

(*g*) See the judgment of Lord Tenterden in *Sigourney* v. *Lloyd*, 8 B. & C 622; 5 Bing. 525.

Negotiation of overdue or dishonoured bill.

Ind Act, ss. 51, 60.

Ind. Act, s. 59.

36.—(1.) Where a bill is negotiable in its origin it continues to be negotiable until it has been (*a*) restrictively indorsed (*z*), or (*b*) discharged by payment (*y*) or otherwise.

(2.) Where an overdue bill is negotiated, it can only be negotiated subject to any defect of title affecting it at its maturity, and thenceforward no person who takes it can acquire or give a better title than that which the person from whom he took it had (*x*).

(3.) A bill payable on demand is deemed to be overdue within the meaning and for the purposes of this section, when it appears on the face of it to have been in circulation for an unreasonable length of time (*w*). What is an unreasonable length of time for this purpose is a question of fact (*v*).

Ind Act, s 118 (*d*)

(4.) Except where an indorsement bears date after the maturity of the bill, every negotiation is *primâ facie* deemed to have been effected before the bill was overdue (*t*).

Ind. Act, s 59

(5.) Where a bill which is not overdue has been dishonoured, any person who takes it with notice of the dishonour takes it subject to any defect of title attaching thereto at the time of dishonour, but nothing in this sub-section shall affect the rights of a holder in due course (*s*).

(*z*) See the judgment of Wilmot, J., in *Edie* v. *The East India Company*, 2 Burr. 1227, see also *Plimley* v. *Westley*, 2 Bing. N C.

249; also sect. 8, sub-s. 4 and the notes; also notes (*j*) and (*k*) to sect. 32, and notes (*b*) and (*c*) to sect. 35 of this Act.

(*y*) Payment here means payment at maturity, for it has been held that although a bill of exchange cannot be re-issued after it has arrived at maturity and been once paid, yet if it is paid and afterwards indorsed before it becomes due, it is a valid security in the hands of a *bonâ fide* indorsee, *Burbridge* v. *Manners*, 3 Camp. 194. As Lord Ellenborough said in his judgment in that case, " Payment means payment in due course and not by anticipation." It has also been decided that a promissory note payable on demand cannot be re-issued after it has been paid and has got into the hands of the maker, although the indorsee have no notice that the note has ever been paid or that payment has ever been demanded, *Bartrum* v. *Caddy* 9 A. & E. 275.

(*x*) The "defects of title" are set out in sect. 29, sub-sect. 2. They used to be called "equities attaching to the bill"; as to the former decisions showing what they were, see *Burrough* v. *Moss*, 10 B. & C. 558; *Holmes* v. *Kidd*, 3 H. & N. 891; *Oulds* v. *Harrison*, 10 Ex. 572; *Ex parte Swan*, L. R. 6 Eq. 344; Story on Bills, ss. 187, 220. That the bill was originally an accommodation bill, i.e. given without consideration, is not a defect of title; though this was not always considered so. Thus it was held in *Tinson* v. *Francis*, 1 Camp. 19, that although the *bonâ fide* holder of a promissory note, made without consideration, himself gave a full consideration for it; yet if he took it after it was due from an indorser who gave none, he cannot maintain an action upon it against the maker. In *Brown* v. *Davies*, 3 T. R. 80, it was held that where a promissory note had been indorsed to the plaintiff after it became due who sued the maker upon it, the latter might show by evidence that the note was paid as between him and the original payee, from whom the plaintiff received it. See further *Jones* v. *Broadhurst*, 9 C. B. 173; *Agra Bank* v. *Leighton*, L. R. 2 Ex. 56. But this was afterwards departed from in *Charles* v. *Marsden*, 1 Taunt. 224, in which it was held that it is not of itself a defence to an action by the indorsee of a bill of exchange to plead that it was accepted for the accommodation of the drawer without consideration, and was indorsed over to the plaintiff after it became due, unless it had been shewn also that it was agreed not to be indorsed after due. And this ruling was approved and followed in several cases, *Stein* v. *Yglesias*, 1 C. M. & R. 565; *Sturtevant* v. *Ford*, 4 M. & G. 101; *Carruthers* v. *West*, 11 Q. B. 143, and *Ex parte Swan*, *In re Overend, Gurney & Co.*, L. R. 6 Eq. 345, where the authorities are elaborately reviewed, and where it was held that the indorsee for value of a bill after dishonour has a right to recover against the acceptor, whether the bill was given for value or not, unless there be an equity attached to the bill itself amounting to a discharge of it. See also *Greenwell* v *Haydon*, 39 Am. Rep. 237. See also

S. 36.

———

Negotiation of
overdue or
dishonoured
bill.

sect. 10, note (*w*). But the rule of law as to bills and notes, that an indorsee taking them after maturity takes them upon the credit of and can stand in no better position than his indorser, does not apply to cheques, *The London & County Bank* v *Groome*, 8 Q. B. D. 288; 51 L. J. Q. B. D. 224, 46 L. T. N. S. 60; 30 W. R. 382. As to this see note to sect. 24, "overdue cheques." As to a prior defect of title, see sect. 29, sub-sect. 3. It has been decided that if the person who indorsed it to the plaintiff can himself sue upon it, any prior defect will not affect the plaintiff's rights; *Chalmers* v. *Lanion*, 1 Camp. 383. As regards the defect of title affecting a bill it must be such equities only as attach to the bill or note itself, or to use the language of Williams, J., "the equities must arise out of the original transaction;" *Holmes* v *Kidd*, 3 H. & N. 893, or to use the language of Malins, V.-C., "the equities of the bill, not the equities of the parties." Thus a set-off due from the payee to the maker is not such an equity, *Burrough* v. *Moss*, 10 B & C. 558; *Oulds* v. *Harrison*, 10 Ex. 572, 24 L J Ex 66 and *Ex parte Swan, In re Overend, Gurney & Co.*, L. R 6 Eq. 345. See further sect 38 (2) of this Act and note (*w*) thereto. A bill, given instead of one indorsed by an agent in breach of trust when overdue, cannot be recovered on, *Lee* v. *Zagury*, 8 Taunt. 114. The purchase of overdue bills with another person's money is an equity, *Ex parte Oriental Bank*, L. R. 5 Ch. 358, 39 L. J. Ch. 588

(*w*) This sub-section has been taken from the American law, *vide* Byles on Bills (5th American Edit.), p. 287. A promissory note payable on demand is sometimes considered as a continuing security, *vide* sect. 86 and the notes thereto.

(*v*) This subsection is not quite the same as what was laid down formerly by judicial decision, viz., that what is reasonable time is a mixed question of law and fact, for the determination of a jury with the assistance of a judge, where trial by jury exists, and for the determination of the Court, where they exercise the functions of a jury as well as those of judges, *Mullick* v. *Radakissen*, 9 Moo. P. C. C. 66, following *Mellish* v. *Rawdon*, 9 Bing. 423. As a question of fact it is one for the jury. What is a reasonable time will depend on the circumstances of each case. In *Mellish* v. *Rawdon*, *supra*, following *Muilman* v. *D'Eguino*, 2 H. Bl. 565, and *Fry* v. *Hill*, 7 Taunt. 397. It was held that in order to arrive at a proper determination of the question of reasonable time, the situation and interests not of the drawer only, or of the holder only, but the situation and interests of both must be taken into consideration. As to what has or has not been considered reasonable time, see the above cases and *Shute* v. *Robins*, 3 C. & P. 80; 1 M. & M. 133.

(*t*) On the principle that every negotiation is presumed to have been effected before the bill was due, so the onus lies on the defendant to show that the bill was overdue when indorsed, *Lewis* v. *Parker*,

4 A. & E. 838, *Parkin* v. *Moon*, 7 C. & P. 408; *Anderson* v. *Weston*, SS. 36, 37, 38.
6 Bing N. C. 296.

(s) The question in such cases always is whether the indorsee acted with good faith in taking the bill, see *Goodman* v *Harvey*, 4 A. & E. 870, 6 N. & M. 372, *Carlon* v. *Ireland*, 5 E. & B. 765 As to what is *bona* or *mala fides* see *Raphael* v. *Bank of England*, 17 C. B. 161.

Negotiation of overdue or dishonoured bill.

37.—Where a bill is negotiated back to the drawer (*a*), or to a prior indorser (*b*), or to the acceptor (*c*), such party may, subject to the provisions of this Act, re-issue and further negotiate the bill (*d*), but he is not entitled to enforce payment of the bill against any intervening party to whom he was previously liable (*e*).

Negotiation of bill to party already liable thereon

Ind Act, s 51

(a) As to bills negotiated back to the drawer, see *Roberts* v. *Eden*, 1 B. & P 398, *Callow* v. *Lawrence*, 3 M & S. 95, *Hubbard* v. *Jackson*, 3 C. & P. 134; 4 Bing. 390; *Wilders* v. *Stevens*, 15 M & W 208, *Morris* v. *Walker*, 15 Q. B. 589; *Woodward* v *Pell*, L. R. 4 Q. B 55, 38 L. J. Q. B. 30

(b) As to bills negotiated back to a prior indorser, see *Britten v. Webb*, 2 B. & C. 482, *Bishop* v. *Hayward*, 4 T R. 470, *Wilkinson* v. *Unwin*, 7 Q. B. D. 636, 50 L. J. Q B. D. 338. As to negotiation back by a surety, see sect. 85, note (*a*).

(c) As to bills negotiated back to the acceptor, see *Attenborough v Mackenzie*, 25 L. J Ex 244.

(d) In *Attenborough* v. *Mackenzie*, 25 L. J Ex 244, it was so decided.

(e) See *Beck* v. *Robley*, 1 H. Bl 89, n ; and the above cases.

38.—The rights and powers of the holder (*z*) of a bill are as follows :

Rights of the holder

(1.) He may sue on a bill in his own name (*y*) .

Ind Act, s 8.

(2.) Where he is a holder in due course, he holds the bill free from any defect of title of prior parties, (*x*) as well as from mere personal defences (*w*) available to prior parties among themselves, and may enforce payment against all parties liable on the bill (*v*) :

Ind Act, ss and 46

(3.) Where his title is defective (*a*) if he negotiates the bill to a holder in due course, that holder obtains a good and complete title to the bill (*t*), and (*b*) if he obtains payment of the bill the person who pays him in due course gets a valid discharge for the bill (*s*).

Ind Act, ss 9 and 46

Ind Act, ss 10 and 78

F

(z) As to the definition of a holder see sect. 2 of this Act and note (j) thereto, and as to the definition of a holder in due course see sect. 29 of this Act and the notes thereto.

(y) This is the same as hitherto, see Byles on Bills (13th edition), 410. Where the holder of a bill indorsed in blank, being unwilling to sue in his own name upon it, requested one K , who had guaranteed the payment of it, to get some one to sue for him upon it, and K. got the plaintiff, who however had neither any interest in the bill nor possession of it, it was held that he could not maintain the action, *Emmett* v *Tottenham*, 8 Ex. 884. But a person may ratify an action brought in his name, but without his knowledge or authority, by another professing to act as his agent and on his behalf, *Ancona* v. *Marks*, 7 H. & N. 686. It is competent to the holder to hand the bill over to a third person to sue upon it on his behalf, *Law* v. *Parnell*, 7 C. B. N. S. 282, and he may do so to a person to whom he is indebted and still sue, provided such person to whom the bill has been handed over be a trustee for him, *Stones* v. *Butt*, 2 Cr. & M. 416.

(x) See section 29 and notes (z) (y) (x) and (w) thereto, and also section 27 (2) and note (w) thereto. As to the defect of title of prior parties affecting a bill, see note (x) to section 36.

(w) As to the holder in due course of a bill being free from personal defences, as for example a set-off in respect of a debt due from the payee to the maker of a note, see *Burrough* v. *Moss*, 10 B. & C. 558; *Ex parte Swan*, *In re Overend, Gurney & Co.*, L. R. 6 Eq. 345.

(v) See note (y) hereto.

(t) A bill, accepted upon the terms of the sale and return of certain goods, a portion of which only had been sold, was indorsed by the drawer for a valuable consideration before it became due to B. & Co. After it became due, B. & Co. transferred it to the plaintiff by delivery; and at the time of the transfer the name of B. & Co. was erased from the back of the bill, it was held that the transfer by delivery from B. & Co passed their title in the bill to the plaintiff, and that the agreement between the drawer and the acceptor was no answer to an action on the bill, *Fairclough* v. *Pavia*, 9 Ex. 690; again in *Marston* v. *Allen*, 8 M. & W. 504, it was laid down (per Alderson, B.), that every person having possession of a bill has (notwithstanding any fraud on his part, either in acquiring or transferring it) full authority to transfer such bill, but with this limitation, that to make such transfer valid, there must be a delivery, either by him or some subsequent holder of the bill, to some one who receives such bill *bonâ fide* and for value, and who is either the holder of it or a person through whom the holder claims.

(s) As to such a discharge, see *Robarts* v. *Tucker*, 16 Q. B. 560; as to payment in due course, see n. (y) to section 36.

GENERAL DUTIES OF THE HOLDER.

39.—(1) Where a bill is payable after sight, present-ment for acceptance is necessary in order to fix the maturity of the instrument (*a*).

When present-ment for ac-ceptance is necessary

Ind Act, s 61

(2.) Where a bill expressly stipulates that it shall be presented for acceptance (*b*), or where a bill is drawn pay-able elsewhere than at the residence or place of business of the drawee, it must be presented for acceptance before it can be presented for payment (*c*).

Ind Act, s. 61 and s 76 sub-sect. (*a*).

(3.) In no other case is presentment for acceptance necessary in order to render liable any party to the bill (*d*).

(4.) Where the holder of a bill, drawn payable else-where than at the place of business or residence of the drawee, has not time, with the exercise of reasonable diligence, to present the bill for acceptance before presenting it for payment on the day that it falls due, the delay caused by presenting the bill for acceptance before presenting it for payment is excused, and does not discharge the drawer and indorsers (*e*).

(*a*) As to the necessity for presentment for acceptance see *Chitty on Bills* (9th Edit.), p. 237; *Byles on Bills* (13th Edit.), 182; *Story on Bills*, sect. 228; and *Chalmers' Digest of the Law of Bills of Exchange* (2nd edition), p. 130. The two cases mentioned in the first two sub-sections of this section are the only cases in which presentment for acceptance is necessary. By sub-sect (*a*) of sect. 10 (1) of this Act, re-enacting the provisions of 34 & 35 Vict. c. 74, a bill payable at sight or on presentation is payable on demand. Where a bill is pay-able at sight, acceptance and payment are simultaneous, therefore under the present section presentment for acceptance is not necessary but optional. To charge the drawer of an unaccepted bill, some actual evidence of a demand to accept on the drawee must be proved, *Cheek* v. *Roper*, 5 Esp. 174. In *Mullick* v. *Radakissen*, 9 Moore, P. C. C. 46, it was held that a foreign bill of exchange payable after sight must be presented for acceptance; and that within a reasonable time. By sect. 40 (1) a bill payable after sight must be presented within a reasonable time; as to the mode of determining the question of such reasonable time, see sub-sect. (3) of that section; also note (*v*) to section 36; also *Straker* v. *Graham*, 4 M. & W. 721. It is the regular and usual course of business in commercial transactions to deliver out a

When present-
ment for ac-
ceptance is
necessary.

bill, left for acceptance, to any person who mentions the amount, and describes any private mark or number upon it; and if the clerk of the party leaving it, by his conduct, enables a stranger to discover the mark or number, in consequence of which the bill is delivered out to him, the party leaving it cannot maintain trover for the bill against the party who so delivered it out, *Morrison* v. *Buchanan*, 6 C. & P. 18. But see now sect. 41 (1) of this Act, whereby a bill must be presented for acceptance by or on behalf of the holder.

(*b*) See Byles on Bills (13th Edition) 182; Chalmers' Digest of the Law of Bills of Exchange (2nd Edition), 131.

(*c*) This is new.

(*d*) *Vide* notes (*a*) and (*b*) hereto; see also *Crowe* v. *Clay*, 9 Ex. 604.

(*e*) As to such delay, see Brooke's Notary (3rd Edition), p. 73.

Time for pre-
senting bill
payable after
sight.
Ind. Act, ss. 61
and 62.

Ind. Act, ss 61
and 62

Ind. Act, s 105.

40.—(1.) Subject to the provisions of this Act, when a bill payable after sight is negotiated, the holder must either present it for acceptance (*a*), or negotiate it (*b*) within a reasonable time (*c*).

(2.) If he do not so, the drawer and all indorsers prior to that holder are discharged (*d*).

(3.) In determining what is a reasonable time (*e*) within the meaning of this section, regard shall be had to the nature of the bill (*f*), the usage of trade (*g*) with respect to similar bills, and the facts of the particular case (*h*).

(*a*) In *Fry* v. *Hill*, 7 Taunt. 397, it was held that the holder of an inland bill payable after sight, if he does not circulate it, should present it for acceptance within a reasonable time, and in *Mullick* v *Radakissen*, 9 Moo. P. C. C 46, it was held that a foreign bill must be presented for acceptance also within a reasonable time

(*b*) It was so laid down in *Goupy* v *Harden*, 7 Taunt 159, see also *Muilman* v. *D'Eguino*, 2 H. Bl 565.

(*c*) As to what is a reasonable time, see sub-section (3) hereof and note (*e*) thereto.

(*d*) See note (*a*) to sect. 39 (1); and note (*v*) to sect. 36.

(*e*) This is a question of fact, and depends on circumstances; see sub-sect (3) of sect. (36) and the notes thereto. As to the duties of an agent in presenting for acceptance and the time when he should do so, see *Bank of Van Diemen's Land* v. *Bank of Victoria*, L. R. 3 P. C. 526; 40 L. J. P. C. 28; 19 W. R. 857, where it was laid down that the duty of an agent is to obtain acceptance of the bill, if possible, but not to press unduly for acceptance in such a way as to lead to a refusal, provided that the proper steps are taken within that limit of time which will preserve the rights of his principal against the drawer.

(*f*) In order to determine what is a reasonable time the jury may take into consideration the situation and interests, not of the drawer only or of the holder only, but the situation and interests of both: per Tindal, C.J., in *Mellish* v. *Rawdon*, 9 Bing. 421; see also the judgment of Parke, B. in *Mullick* v. *Radakissen*, 9 Moore, P. C. C. 66.

(*g*) To determine what is a reasonable time one must look at the bill itself, and also take into consideration the ordinary practice relative to such bills, per Lord Tenterden, C J., in *Shute* v. *Robins*, 3 C. & P. 82.

(*h*) See the cases in the preceding notes to this section

41.—(1.) A bill is duly presented for acceptance which is presented in accordance with the following rules :

   (*a*) The presentment must be made by or on behalf of the holder (*z*) to the drawee (*y*), or to some person authorised to accept or refuse acceptance (*x*) on his behalf, at a reasonable hour (*w*) on a business day (*v*) and before the bill is overdue :

   (*b*) Where the bill is addressed to two or more drawees, who are not partners, presentment must be made to them all (*u*), unless one has authority to accept for all, then presentment may be made to him only (*t*).

   (*c*) Where the drawee is dead, presentment may be made to his personal representative (*s*) :

   (*d*) Where the drawee is bankrupt, presentment may be made to him or his trustee ·

   (*e*) Where authorised by agreement or usage, a presentment through the post-office is sufficient (*r*).

(2.) Presentment in accordance with these rules is excused, and a bill may be treated as dishonoured by non-acceptance—

   (*a*) Where the drawee is dead, or bankrupt, or is a fictitious person, or a person not having capacity to contract by bill (*q*) :

   (*b*) Where, after the exercise of reasonable diligence, such presentment cannot be effected (*p*)

   (*c*) Where, although the presentment has been irregular, acceptance has been refused on some other ground.

S. 41

Rules as to
presentment
for acceptance
and excuses
for non-pre-
sentment.

(3.) The fact that the holder has reason to believe that the bill on presentment will be dishonoured, does not excuse presentment (*o*).

(*z*) As to the necessity for presentment for acceptance, see sub-sect. 1 and note (*a*) thereto of sect. 39. A bill may be presented for acceptance by any person told or instructed to do so by or on behalf of the holder. As to the duties of an agent in presenting for acceptance, see *Bank of Van Diemen's Land* v. *Bank of Victoria*, cited in note (*e*) to sect 40 of this Act

(*y*) As to presentment for acceptance to the drawee, see Byles on Bills, 13th Ed., 185.

(*x*) It has been held that it is not sufficient to call at the residence of the drawee and to present the bill for acceptance to a person unknown to the person calling, *Cheek* v. *Roper*, 5 Esp. 175.

(*w*) "The usage on bills of exchange is established, they are payable any time on the last day of grace on demand, provided that demand be made within reasonable hours;" per Buller, J., in *Leftley* v. *Mills*, 4 T R. 174. The same rule applies to presentment for acceptance as is provided by this sub-section As to what is a reasonable hour on a business day, it is submitted that the words mean the usual hours of business Thus in *Parker* v. *Gordon*, 6 Esp 41, it was held that if a bill be made payable at a banker's, it must be presented within banking hours. So that a bill which has to be accepted by a banker must be presented within banking hours As to reasonable hour in any other business, see *Startup* v. *Macdonald*, 6 M. & G 593.

(*v*) By sect. 92 of this Act, "Non-business days for the purposes of this Act mean: (*a*) Sunday, Good Friday, Christmas Day, (*b*) A bank holiday under the Bank Holidays Act, 1871, or Acts amending it, (*c*) A day appointed by Royal Proclamation as a public fast or thanksgiving day." Any other day by that section is a business day Where the day on which a bill has to be presented for acceptance is a non-business day, other than a bank holiday, it must then be presented on the day preceding, unless the time within which the bill must be presented for acceptance is less than three days, in which case the non-business day must be excluded, and the day for presentment would be the day following, see sections 14 and 92 of this Act and the notes thereto

(*u*) See *Owen* v *Van Ulster*, 10 C. B. 318 As to acceptances by one partner, see note (*b*) to sect. 24 of this Act.

(*t*) See note (*b*) to sect. 24 of this Act.

(*s*) As to this see Byles on Bills (13th Edit. 186); *Smith* v. *Bank of New South Wales*, 8 Moore, P C. C (N. S), pp. 459-462; 41 L J. Ad. pp. 53-55. Where the executor has not proved the will, see same case.

(*r*) See *Kufh* v. *Weston*, 3 Esp. 54, where it was held that notice of the non-acceptance or non-payment of a bill is sufficiently given by proving that a letter was regularly put into the post informing the party of the fact.

(*q*) See note (*s*) hereto. As to the drawee being a fictitious person, see *Smith* v. *Bellamy*, 2 Stark. 223.

(*p*) As to what is reasonable diligence, see the judgment of Mellish, L.J., in *Smith* v. *Bank of New South Wales*, 8 Moore, P. C. C. (N. S.) pp. 459–462; 41 L. J. Ad. 54, 55; see also note (*v*) to sect. 36, and sect. 40, sub-s. 3, and the notes thereto.

(*o*) See *Hill* v. *Heap*, D. & R. N. P C. 57.

42.—(1.) When a bill is duly presented for acceptance, and is not accepted within the customary time, the person presenting it must treat it as dishonoured by non-acceptance. If he do not, the holder shall lose his right of recourse against the drawer and indorsers (*a*).

(*a*) Customary time here means, it is submitted, reasonable time, or to use the language of Lord Cairns in *Bank of Van Diemen's Land* v. *Victoria Bank*, L. R. 3 P. C. 542; 40 L. J P. C. 8, "that limit of time which will preserve the right of the holder against the drawer." As we have seen, the drawee is entitled to reasonable time, generally twenty-four hours, to deliberate whether or not to accept; and so it is provided by ss. 63 and 83 of the Indian Act. In one case it was held that where more than twenty-four hours are given, the holder should inform the antecedent parties, *Ingram* v. *Foster*, 2 Smith, 242.

43.—(1.) A bill is dishonoured (*z*) by non-acceptance (*y*).

> (*a*) When it is duly presented (*x*) for acceptance, and such an acceptance (*w*) as is prescribed by this Act is refused or cannot be obtained; or
>
> (*b*) When presentment for acceptance is excused (*v*) and the bill is not accepted.

(2.) Subject to the provisions of this Act, when a bill is dishonoured by non-acceptance, an immediate right of recourse against the drawer and indorsers accrues to the holder (*t*), and no presentment for payment is necessary.

(*z*) As to what an acceptance is see section 19 of this Act, and the sub-sections of the same and the notes thereto. As to when a bill may be accepted, see sect. 18 of this Act, and the sub-sections of the

---

Side notes:

SS. 41, 42, 43

Rules as to presentment for acceptance and excuses for non-presentment.

Non-acceptance.
Ind Act, s 61

Ind Act, s 63

Ind Act, s. 83

Dishonour by non-acceptance and its consequences
Ind Act, s. 61.

Dishonour by
non-acceptance
and its conse-
quences.

same and the notes thereto. As to the drawee being allowed a reasonable time for deliberating as to whether he will accept or not, see note to last section.

(*y*) As to when a bill may be accepted see sect. 18 of this Act and the sub-sections of the same and the notes thereto.

(*x*) As to what is a due presentment for acceptance see sect. 41 (1) of this Act and subdivisions (*a*) (*b*) (*c*) (*d*) and (*e*) thereof, and the notes thereto.

(*w*) That is to say, an unqualified acceptance, as to which see sect 44 (1) of this Act and the notes thereto.

(*v*) As to when presentment for acceptance is excused, see sub-sect. (2) of sect. 41 of this Act, and the subdivisions (*a*) (*b*) and (*c*) thereof and the notes thereto.

(*t*) See sub-sect. (1) of sect. 39 of this Act and the notes thereto

Duties as to
qualified
acceptance

Ind Act, s. 91.

Ind Act, s. 86.

44.—(1.) The holder of a bill may refuse (*a*) to take a qualified (*b*) acceptance, and if he does not obtain an unqualified acceptance, may treat the bill as dishonoured (*c*) by non-acceptance.

(2.) Where a qualified acceptance is taken, and the drawer or an indorser has not expressly or impliedly authorized the holder to take a qualified acceptance, or does not subsequently assent thereto, such drawer or indorser is discharged from his liability on the bill (*d*).

The provisions of this sub-section do not apply to a partial acceptance, whereof due notice has been given (*e*). Where a foreign bill has been accepted as to part, it must be protested as to the balance (*f*).

(3.) When the drawer or indorser of a bill receives notice of a qualified acceptance, and does not within a reasonable time express his dissent to the holder, he shall be deemed to have assented thereto

(*a*) "A man is not bound to receive a limited and qualified acceptance; he may refuse it and resort to the drawer, per Chambre, J., in *Gammon* v. *Schmoll*, 5 Taunt. 353, see also the judgment of Lord Ellenborough in *Boehm* v. *Garcias*, 1 Camp. 425, and of Bayley, J, in *Sebag* v. *Abitbol*, 4 M. & S. 462; Story on Bills, s. 240, Byles on Bills (13th Edit.), 195.

(*b*) As to qualified acceptances see sect. 19 (*z*) of this Act, and subdivisions (*a*) (*b*) (*c*) (*d*) and (*e*) thereof, and notes (*l*) (*m*) (*n*) (*o*) (*p*) and (*r*) thereto

(*c*) See note (*a*) hereto.

(*d*) "If the holder take a qualified acceptance, it may be a question whether he ought not to give notice to all the parties to the bill, and whether, by omitting to do so, he does not discharge them," per Bayley, J., in *Sebag* v. *Abitbol*, 4 M. & S. 462. See also note (*b*) hereto.

(*e*) As to partial acceptance contemplated by this sub-section see *Julian* v *Shobrooke*, 2 Wils 9; *Wegersloffe* v. *Keene*, 1 Stra. 214.

(*f*) There has been no decision exactly to this effect. See Story on Bills, s. 241.

45.—Subject to the provisions of this Act a bill must be duly presented for payment. If it be not so presented the drawer and indorsers shall be discharged (*z*) Rules as to presentment for payment

A bill is duly presented for payment which is presented in accordance with the following rules :— Ind. Act, s 64.

(1.) Where the bill is not payable on demand, presentment must be made on the day it falls due (*y*). Ind. Act, s. 66

(2.) Where the bill is payable on demand, then, subject to the provisions of this Act, presentment must be made within a reasonable time after its issue, in order to render the drawer liable; and within a reasonable time after its indorsement, in order to render the indorser liable (*x*). Ind Act, s. 74.

In determining what is a reasonable time, regard shall be had to the nature of the bill, the usage of the trade with regard to similar bills, and the facts of the particular case (*w*). Ind Act, s 105

(3.) Presentment must be made by the holder or by some person authorised to receive payment on his behalf at a reasonable hour (*u*) on a business day (*v*), at the proper place as hereinafter defined (*t*), either to the person designated by the bill as payer, or to some person authorised to pay or refuse payment on his behalf (*s*), if with the exercise of reasonable diligence such person can there be found. Ind Act, s 61.

Ind Act, s 75

(4.) A bill is presented at the proper place :— Ind Act, ss 68, 69

   (*a*) Where a place of payment is specified in the bill, and the bill is there presented (*r*).

   (*b*) Where no place of payment is specified, but the address of the drawee or acceptor is given in the bill, and the bill is there presented (*q*). Ind Act, ss 68 and 69.

S. 45.

Rules as to
presentment
for payment

Ind Act, s. 70.
Ind. Act, s. 71

Ind. Act, s. 76,
sub-s (a).

Ind. Act, s. 75

(c) Where no place of payment is specified and no address given, and the bill is presented at the drawee's or acceptor's place of business if known, and if not, at his ordinary residence if known (*p*).

(d) In any other case if presented to the drawee or acceptor wherever he can be found, or if presented at his last known place of business or residence (*o*).

(5.) Where a bill is presented at the proper place, and after the exercise of reasonable diligence no person authorised to pay or refuse payment can be found there, no further presentment to the drawee or acceptor is required (*n*).

(6.) Where a bill is drawn upon or accepted by two or more persons who are not partners, and no place of payment is specified, presentment must be made to them all.

(7.) Where the drawee or acceptor of a bill is dead, and no place of payment is specified, presentment must be made to a personal representative, if such there be, and with the exercise of reasonable diligence he can be found (*m*).

(8.) Where authorised by agreement or usage, a presentment through the post-office is sufficient (*l*).

(*z*) "Every bill is to be properly presented for payment, and in an action thereon against the drawer or indorser, a presentment according to the usage and custom of merchants must be averred and proved, per Bayley, J., in *Rowe* v *Young*, 2 Bligh, H L 468, and in *Peacock* v. *Purssell*, 32 L. J. C P 266, it was held that a bill taken as collateral security must be presented for payment when it becomes due, and the omission so to present discharges the debtor both on the bill and on the original consideration; see also *Crowe* v. *Clay*, 9 Ex. 206; 23 L. J. Ex 150. "In an action on a bill against the acceptor, presentment (generally speaking) need not be averred or proved, per Bayley, J., in *Rowe* v. *Young, supra*.

(*y*) By sect 14 of this Act and sub-sect. (1) thereof three days of grace are, in every case where the bill itself does not otherwise provide, added to the time of payment as fixed by the bill, and the bill is due and payable on the last day of grace See further sub-sects (2) (3) and (4), and subdivisions (*a*) and (*b*) of sub-sect. (1) of that section, and notes (*l*) (*m*) (*n*) (*o*) (*p*) (*q*) and (*r*) thereto. Payment is demandable when the bill is due, and not before; Story on Bills, s. 324,

Wiffen v. *Roberts*, 1 Esp. 261. The holder of a bill is entitled to know, on the day when it becomes due, whether it is honoured or dishonoured, *Cocks* v. *Masterman*, 9 M & W. 902 In the time for the presentment of a bill, the day of presentment is excluded, *Lester* v. *Garland*, 15 Ves 255.

(x) See Byles on Bills (13th Edition) 211; Chalmers' Digest of the Law of Bills of Exchange (2nd Edition) 140, Story on Bills, s. 325

(w) This is the same, in language, as sub-sect (3) of sect. 40 of this Act, which see, and also notes *(d)* *(e)* *(f)* and *(g)* thereto.

(u) See note *(m)* to section 41

(v) See note *(v)* to section 41. As we have seen already if a bill is payable at a banker's it must be presented during banking hours, *Parker* v. *Gordon*, 7 East, 385, but it has been held that if a bill is presented at a bank or other place of business at other than the usual banking or business hours, and no objection is made thereto, it is a good presentment, *Garnett* v. *Woodcock*, 6 M. & S. 44. It has been held that if a bill is payable at a banker's, and it is before its maturity indorsed to him, presentment is not necessary, *Bailey* v. *Porter*, 14 M. & W. 44

(t) As to the definition of a proper place, see sub-section 4 and the notes thereto.

(s) As to who is such an agent of the payer as is contemplated by this sub-section, see *Cromwell* v. *Hynson*, 2 Esp. 211, *Reynolds* v. *Chettle*, 2 Camp. 596, *Robson* v *Bennett*, 2 Taunt. 388; *Philips* v. *Astling*, 2 Taunt. 206

(r) It was formerly held that an acceptance payable at a particular place was a qualified acceptance, and that presentment at such place was absolutely necessary, *Rowe* v *Young*, 2 B. & B. 165, 2 Bligh, H. L 468. In consequence of this the statute 1 & 2 Geo. 4, c. 78, was passed, which provided that an acceptance payable at a particular place is a general acceptance unless it was stated to be payable there only and not elsewhere. Since this statute there have been decisions to the same effect, see *Turner* v *Hayden*, 4 B & C. 1, *Selby* v *Eden*, 3 Bing. 611, 11 Moo. 511, *Fayle* v. *Bird*, 6 B. & C 531, 2 C & P. 303. Where a bill was made payable in a particular town it was held that a presentment at the two banking-houses at that place was sufficient, *Hardy* v. *Woodroofe*, 2 Stark 319; and where a bill was made payable at one of two towns a presentment at either was sufficient, *Beeching* v. *Gower*, *Holt* N. P. C. 313. The present sub-division *(a)* of sub-sect. (4) of this section does not seem to have made any alteration in the law on this point

(q) Before this Act it was held that if the place of payment was mentioned in a memorandum in the margin, and not in the body of the bill or note, presentment at that place was not necessary, as such memorandum was only a direction, *Price* v. *Mitchell*, 4 Camp. 200; *Williams* v. *Waring*, 10 B. & C. 2, 5 M & R. 9. And it was in

SS. 45, 46.
—
Rules as to
presentment
for payment.

another case held that a memorandum is no part of the bill, *Masters* v. *Baretto*, 19 L. J. C. P. 50. But see *Trecothick* v. *Edwin*, 1 Stark. 468, where the contrary was held. The latter case, however, proceeded on the ground of the body of the note and the place of payment being printed. See further sect. 87 and the notes thereto

(*p*) And this, even though the acceptor has removed, provided the new address be not known to the holder, *vide Buxton* v. *Jones*, 1 M. & G. 86; *Brown* v. *M'Dermot*, 5 Esp. 265.

(*o*) Where a bill was made payable at a particular house, it was held that presentment at the door was sufficient if the house was shut up, *Hine* v. *Allely*, 4 B. & Ad. 624; 1 N. & M. 433. And where the house was not shut up, presentment to any inmate was considered sufficient, *Cromwell* v. *Hynson*, 2 Esp. 211; *Buxton* v. *Jones*, 1 M. & G. 83.

(*n*) *Vide* note (*o*) hereof.

(*m*) As to presentment to a personal representative, see *Caunt* v. *Thompson*, 7 C. B. 400.

(*l*) As to presentment through the post see note (*r*) to section 41.

Excuses for
delay or non-
presentment
for payment

46.—(1.) Delay in making presentment for payment is excused when the delay is caused by circumstances beyond the control of the holder, and not imputable to his default, misconduct, or negligence (*z*); when the cause of delay ceases to operate presentment must be made with reasonable diligence.

Ind. Act, s. 76,
sub-s (*a*).

(2.) Presentment for payment is dispensed with—

(*a*) Where, after the exercise of reasonable diligence, presentment as required by this Act cannot be effected (*y*).

The fact that the holder has reason to believe that the bill will, on presentment, be dishonoured, does not dispense with the necessity for presentment (*w*).

(*b*) Where the drawee is a fictitious person (*v*).

(*c*) As regards the drawer, where the drawee or acceptor is not bound, as between himself and the drawer, to accept or pay the bill, and the drawer has no reason to believe that the bill would be paid if presented (*t*).

(*d*) As regards an indorser, where the bill was accepted or made for the accommodation of that indorser, and he has no reason to expect that the bill would be paid if presented (*s*).

(*e*) By waiver of presentment, express or implied (*r*).

(z) This is the same as a part of Lord Denman's judgment in *Rothschild* v. *Currie*, 1 Q. B. 47, which is as follows: "It appears to us that the delay was attributable to circumstances over which the notary had no control, and therefore was satisfactorily accounted for." "If by an alteration of the local law pending the currency of the bill, the obligations of the acceptor are rendered more onerous, those of the indorser becomes so likewise. On the other hand, if the time of payment were postponed by a period of grace being allowed, or by an enactment that a bill falling due on a day appointed to be kept as a holiday, should be payable a day after, the period at which the liability of the indorser on nonpayment by the acceptor would arise, would be *pro tanto* delayed. If the right of the holder as against the acceptor and the antecedent parties can be thus modified in respect of the time of payment, there can be no injustice or hardship towards them in holding him exempted from the obligations of presenting the bill earlier than his right of payment accrues, or of giving notice of dishonour in order to preserve his right of recourse to them"; per Cockburn, L.C J., in *Rouquette* v. *Overmann*, L. R. 10 Q. B. 525. In this case the bill was accepted by French subjects at Paris, and was payable on the 5th October, 1870. In consequence of the Franco-German war the time for presenting and protesting current bills was from time to time enlarged till the 5th Sept. 1871. On that day the bill was presented to the acceptors and payment refused, thereupon it was duly protested and notice of dishonour given; it was held that the defendants (drawers) were liable. See also Byles on Bills (13th Edition), p. 219.

(y) An averment that the bill when due was presented and shewn to the acceptor for payment is supported by proof that the holder went to the acceptor's place of business to present it, but found the house shut up and no one there, *Hine* v. *Allely*, 4 B. & Ad. 624, 1 N. & M. 433. But an allegation that the plaintiffs were ready to present and would have presented, but that the defendant was not to be found, will not do, *Sands* v. *Clarke*, 19 L. J. C. P. 84; 8 C B. 751. If a bill is payable at a banker's and the defendant is not to be found, presentment at the banker's is sufficient, *Hardy* v. *Woodroofe*, 2 Stark, 319.

(w) See *Bowes* v. *Howe*, 5 Taunt. 30; *Ex parte Bignold*, 1 Deac. 712, 2 Mont. & Ayr. 633. Nor will the bankruptcy of the drawer or acceptor dispense with presentment or notice of dishonour, see *Esdaile* v. *Sowerby*, 11 East, 117; *Bowes* v. *Howe*, 5 Taunt. 30; *Ex parte Johnston*, 1 Mont. & Ayr. 622, 3 Deac. & Chitty, 443; Story on Bills, sect. 326. See also *Quinn* v. *Fitzgerald*, 1 Ir. C. L. R. 552. As to cheques, see sect 74 of this Act, note (a) thereto.

(v) So laid down by Lord Ellenborough in *Smith* v. *Bellamy*, 2 Stark. 223.

(t) For example, absence of effects of the drawer in the drawee's

SS. 46, 47, 48
———
Excuses for
delay or non-
presentment
for payment.

hands at the time of drawing the bill and of its maturity, *Dennis* v. *Morrice*, 3 Esp. 158; *Terry* v. *Parker*, 6 A. & E. 502. As to cheques see the cases cited under sect. 74, note (*a*).

(*s*) In *Turner* v. *Samson*, 2 Q. B. D. 23, it was held that if the intention of all parties to an accommodation bill is that it should be met by the last indorser, he need not have notice of dishonour.

(*r*) As where the indorser had paid part of the note: *Vaughan* v. *Fuller*, 2 Stra. 1246; or an application for further time to pay, with knowledge of the want of due presentation, *Hopely* v. *Dufresne*, 15 East, 275; *Lundie* v. *Robertson*, 7 East, 231; or if there be an agreement on the part of the bankrupt that the bill should not be presented, per Erskine, C.J., in *Ex parte Bignold*, 1 Deac. 737; *Gunson* v. *Metz*, 1 B. & C. 193; Story on Bills, sect. 373.

Dishonour by
non-payment.
Ind. Act, s. 92.

47.—(1.) A bill is dishonoured by non-payment (*a*) when it is duly presented for payment (*z*) and payment is refused or cannot be obtained, or (*b*) when presentment is excused (*y*) and the bill is overdue and unpaid.

Ind. Act, s. 92.

(2.) Subject to the provisions of this Act, when a bill is dishonoured by non-payment, an immediate right of recourse against the drawer and indorsers accrues to the holder (*x*).

(*z*) As to when a bill is duly presented for payment, see sub-sects. (1) (2) (3) (4) (5) (6) (7) and (8) of sect. 45 of this Act, and the notes thereto.

(*y*) As to when presentment is excused, see sub-sects. (1) and (2) of sect. 46 and the notes to the same.

(*x*) It was so laid down by Lord Lyndhurst in *Siggers* v. *Lewis*, 1 C. M. & R. 370, overruling *Walker* v. *Barnes*, 5 Taunt. 240, where it was held that a tender within a reasonable time after notice of dishonour prevented the plaintiff from recovering damages for the time between the notice of dishonour and the tender.

Notice of
dishonour and
effect of non-
notice.
Ind. Act, s. 93.

48.—Subject to the provisions of this Act, when a bill has been dishonoured by non-acceptance (*a*) or by non-payment (*b*), notice of dishonour (*c*) must be given to the drawer and each indorser (*d*), and any drawer or indorser to whom such notice is not given is discharged (*e*). Provided that—

(1) Where a bill is dishonoured by non-acceptance and notice of dishonour is not given, the rights of a holder in due course subsequent to the omission shall not be prejudiced by the omission (*f*).

(2.) Where a bill is dishonoured by non-acceptance, and due notice of dishonour is given, it shall not be necessary to give notice of a subsequent dishonour by non-payment unless the bill shall in the meantime have been accepted (*g*).

(*a*) As to dishonour by non-acceptance, see sub-sect. (1) of sect. 43 of this Act and the notes thereto.

(*b*) As to dishonour by non-payment, see sub-sect. (1) of sect. 47 of this Act and the notes thereto.

(*c*) Unless the want of such notice is excused by sect. 50 of this Act. It has been held before this Act that a creditor who holds a bill as collateral security must give notice of dishonour, *Peacock* v. *Purssell*, 14 C. B N. S. 728; 32 L. J. C. P. 266.

(*d*) The drawer and every indorser of a bill of exchange has always been entitled to notice of dishonour, see *Bridges* v. *Berry*, 3 Taunt. 130; unless there are any circumstances to excuse it, per Blackburn, J., in *Berridge* v. *Fitzgerald*, L. R. 4 Q. B 642. But the acceptor of a bill or the maker of a note is not entitled to notice of dishonour, *Treacher* v. *Hinton*, 4 B. & Ald. 413; the rule is that the party, other than the acceptor, is entitled to notice of dishonour within a reasonable time, per Jervis, C.J., in *Rowe* v. *Tipper*, 22 L. J. C. P. 137; nor is the maker of a note entitled to dishonour, *Pearse* v. *Pemberthy*, 3 Camp. 261.

(*e*) See notes (*c*) and (*d*) hereto.

(*f*) It was laid down in *Dunn* v. *O'Keefe*, 5 M. & S. 282. But such drawer or indorser is discharged as regards the holder at the time of dishonour and all subsequent holders with notice thereof, *Roscoe* v. *Hardy*, 12 East, 434.

(*g*) It was so held in *Whitehead* v. *Walker*, 9 M. & W. 506, see also *Hickling* v. *Hardey*, 7 Taunt. 312.

49.—Notice of dishonour in order to be valid and effectual must be given in accordance with the following rules:

(1.) The notice must be given by or on behalf of the holder (*z*), or by or on behalf of an indorser, who at the time of giving it is himself liable on the bill (*y*).

(2.) Notice of dishonour may be given by an agent either in his own name (*x*), or in the name of any party entitled to give notice whether that party be his principal or not (*w*).

(3.) Where the notice is given by or on behalf of the

S. 49.

Rules as to
notice of
dishonour.

Ind. Act, s. 93.

Ind Act, s. 94.

Ind. Act s. 94.

Ind. Act, s. 94.

Ind Act, s 94.

Ind Act, s 94.

Ind. Act, s. 94.

holder, it enures for the benefit of all subsequent holders and all prior indorsers who have a right of recourse against the party to whom it is given (*v*).

(4.) Where notice is given by or on behalf of an indorser entitled to give notice as hereinbefore provided, it enures for the benefit of the holder and all indorsers subsequent to the party to whom notice is given (*t*).

(5.) The notice may be given in writing or by personal communication (*s*), and may be given in any terms which sufficiently identify the bill, and intimate that the bill has been dishonoured by non-acceptance or non-payment (*r*).

(6.) The return of a dishonoured bill to the drawer or an indorser is, in point of form, deemed a sufficient notice of dishonour (*q*).

(7.) A written notice need not be signed (*p*), and an insufficient written notice may be supplemented and validated by verbal communication (*o*). A misdescription of the bill shall not vitiate the notice unless the party to whom the notice is given is in fact misled thereby (*n*).

(8). Where notice of dishonour is required to be given to any person, it may be given either to the party himself, or to his agent in that behalf (*m*).

(9.) Where the drawer or indorser is dead, and the party giving notice knows it, the notice must be given to a personal representative if such there be, and with the exercise of reasonable diligence he can be found (*l*).

(10.) Where the drawer or indorser is bankrupt. notice may be given either to the party himself or to the trustee (*k*).

(11.) Where there are two or more drawers or indorsers who are not partners, notice must be given to each of them, unless one of them has authority to receive such notice for the others (*j*).

(12.) The notice may be given as soon as the bill is dishonoured (*i*), and must be given within a reasonable time thereafter (*h*).

In the absence of special circumstances, notice is not

deemed to have been given within a reasonable time, unless—

(*a*) Where the person giving and the person to receive notice reside in the same place, the notice is given or sent off in time to reach the latter on the day after the dishonour of the bill (*g*).

(*b*) Where the person giving and the person to receive notice reside in different places, the notice is sent off on the day after the dishonour of the bill, if there be a post at a convenient hour on that day (*f*), and if there be no such post on that day, then by the next post thereafter (*e*).

(13.) Where a bill when dishonoured is in the hands of an agent, he may either himself give notice to the parties liable on the bill, or he may give notice to his principal. If he gives notice to his principal, he must do so within the same time as if he were the holder, and the principal upon receipt of such notice has himself the same time for giving notice as if the agent had been an independent holder (*d*).

(14.) Where a party to a bill receives due notice of dishonour, he has after the receipt of such notice the same period of time for giving notice to antecedent parties that the holder has after the dishonour (*c*).

(15.) Where a notice of dishonour is duly addressed and posted, the sender is deemed to have given due notice of dishonour, notwithstanding any miscarriage by the post-office (*b*).

S 49.

Rules as to notice of dishonour
Ind Act,s 106.

Ind Act,s 106.

Ind Act, s 96.

Ind Act, s 95

Ind. Act, s 94

(z) It was so held in *Stewart* v. *Kennett*, 2 Camp. 177, where Lord Ellenborough said that the notice must come from the person who can give the drawer or indorser his immediate remedy upon the bill, and not from a stranger; and notice of dishonour may be given by any party to the bill, *Jameson* v. *Swinton*, 2 Camp. 373; in *Chapman* v. *Keane*, 3 A. & E. 193, it was held that the holder of a bill is entitled to avail himself of notice of dishonour given by any party to the bill, and that therefore an indorsee, who has indorsed over, and is not the holder at the time of the maturity and dishonour, may give notice at such time to an earlier party, and upon afterwards taking up the bill and suing such party, may avail himself of such notice. It has also been held that the holder need not inform a party, to whom he gives

G

notice of dishonour, that he looks to him for payment, *Miers* v. *Brown*, 11 M. & W. 372. Notice of dishonour by an agent is sufficient, as, for example, by the defendant's clerk, *Newen* v. *Gill*, 8 C. & P. 367; or by an agent to indorse, *Firth* v. *Thrush*, 8 B. & C. 387; or by an agent to receive payment, *Rowe* v. *Tipper*, 13 C. B. 249, and a mistake by such an agent in the notice in the name of the holder is immaterial, *Harrison* v. *Ruscoe*, 15 M. & W. 231; Story on Bills, s. 303.

(*y*) See *Chapman* v. *Keane*, and *Miers* v. *Brown*, *supra*.

(*x*) A notice of dishonour given by an attorney in his own name, was held sufficient, *Woodthorpe* v. *Lawes*, 2 M. & W. 109.

(*w*) See *Harrison* v. *Ruscoe*, *supra*; *Woodthorpe* v. *Lawes*, *supra*; any agent in possession of the bill may give the notice, and it need not state at whose request it was given, or who was the owner of the bill (Kent's Commentaries, vol. iii. p. 108).

(*v*) So stated in Bayley on Bills (6th Edit.), p. 251; Byles on Bills (13th Edit.), p. 291.

(*t*) It was decided in *Lysaght* v. *Bryant*, 19 L. J. C. P. 160, that a notice of dishonour given by a party to the bill liable to be sued, or who may be entitled to sue, enures to the benefit of antecedent parties, but the present sub-section goes farther, and now such a notice enures to the benefit of subsequent holders as well as prior indorsers.

(*s*) No particular form or language has ever been necessary, nor has it been necessary to give it in writing. The notice of dishonour, it was once held, should inform the party either by express terms or by necessary implication, that the bill has been dishonoured, and that the holder looks to him for payment, *Solarte* v. *Palmer*, 1 Bing. N. C. 194; *East* v. *Smith*, 16 L. J. Q. B. 292; but it has been decided in other cases that the notice need not state that the holder looks to the party addressed for payment, but must state the dishonour either expressly, *Furze* v. *Sharwood*, 2 Q. B. 388; *Miers* v. *Brown*, 11 M. & W. 372; or by implication, *Bain* v. *Gregory*, 14 L. T. N. S. 601, *Stocken* v. *Collins*, 9 C. & P. 653. As to the various forms of such notices, see the cases already cited under this section, and *Messenger* v. *Southey*, 1 M. & G. 76; *Hedgar* v. *Steavenson*, 2 M. & W. 299; *Boulton* v. *Welsh*, 3 Bing. N. C. 688; *Houlditch* v. *Cauty*, 4 Bing. N. C. 411; *Robson* v. *Curlewis*, 2 Q. B. 421; *Everard* v. *Watson*, 22 L. J. Q. B. 222; *Paul* v. *Joel*, 28 L. J. Ex. 143. A notice of dishonour headed with the name of the bank (the holder's) is sufficient, though it has no signature at the foot, *Maxwell* v. *Brain*, 10 L. T. N. S. 301. In *Metcalfe* v. *Richardson*, 11 C. B. 1011, it was held that a verbal notice of dishonour is not to be construed with the same strictness as a written notice, provided there be enough to warrant the jury in assuming that the party to whom the notice is given is informed that the bill has been duly presented and dishonoured, and that he is looked to for payment. Even though a protest has in fact been made, the notice of dishonour need not mention the fact, *Ex parte Lowenthal, In re Lowenthal*, L. R. 9 Ch. 591.

(*r*) See the last preceding note.

(*q*) In *Housego* v. *Cowne*, 2 M. & W. 348, the bill was taken by a person sent by the holder to the drawer's house and the drawer being away, a verbal message was left for the drawer, this was held sufficient notice of dishonour.

(*p*) So held in *Maxwell* v. *Brain*, 10 L. T. N. S. 301.

(*o*) See *Houlditch* v. *Cauty*, 4 Bing. N. C. 411, where such evidence was admitted; see also *Metcalfe* v. *Richardson*, 11 C. B. 1011.

(*n*) A notice of dishonour described an instrument as a note instead of a bill; it was held a sufficient notice, *Stockman* v. *Parr*, 11 M. & W. 809; or *vice versâ*, *Messenger* v. *Southey*, 1 M. & G. 76; so where the notice of dishonour to the defendant described the bill as "your acceptance," whereas it was really drawn by the defendant, it was held sufficient, *Mellersh* v. *Rippen*, 7 Ex. 578; so also where the bill was in the notice referred to as "your draft" without any date, &c., it was held sufficient, *Shelton* v. *Braithwaite*, 7 M. & W. 436; so where the name of the acceptor was wrongly described in a notice of dishonour, such notice was held sufficient, *Harpham* v. *Child*, 1 F. & F 652. Again, where the notice stated that the bill was payable at the London and Westminster Bank, whereas it was made payable at the London Joint Stock Bank, it was held sufficient; *Bromage* v *Vaughan*, 9 Q. B. 608; 16 L. J. Q B. 10.

(*m*) *Crosse* v. *Smith*, 1 M. & S. 545; it was held in this case that it is the duty of a merchant to have his counting-house open during business hours and some one there, and a verbal notice sent there, though it be closed or no one there, is sufficient. The wife of the drawer of a bill of exchange is an agent for this purpose, *Wharton* v. *Wright*, 1 C. & K. 585; *Cromwell* v. *Hynson*, 2 Esp. 511; *Housego* v. *Cowne*, 2 M. & W. 348. So also notice to one who has authority to indorse for the drawer is a sufficient notice, per Lord Tenterden, C.J, in *Firth* v. *Thrush*, 8 B. & C. at p. 391; but a contrary decision has been come to in America; 1 Parsons on Bills, 500. The clerk of a merchant has been held to be an agent to receive notice of dishonour, provided such notice be given to, or left with, such clerk at the counting-house of his employer, *Crosse* v. *Smith*, *supra*, at p. 554, citing *Goldsmith* v. *Bland*. But a tradesman's foreman or servant is *not* to be presumed to have authority to give a notice of dishonour for his master, *East* v. *Smith*, 16 L. J. Q B. 292. Nor is the solicitor of the person to whom notice of dishonour should be given such an agent, 1 Parsons on Bills, 499.

(*l*) There has been no English decision to this effect, so far as we know, but the point has been so decided in America; see 1 Parsons on Bills, 500, Story on Bills, sec. 305; see also s. 94 of the Indian Act.

G 2

S. 49

Rules as to notice of dishonour.

(*k*) It has been held that notice of a dishonoured bill to a bankrupt, as drawer, before the choice of assignees is good, *Ex parte Moline*, 19 Ves. 216; and if he abscond, the notice must be sent to his house, *Rhodes* v. *Proctor*, 4 B. & C. 517; *Ex parte Johnston, In re Cohen*, 1 Mont. & Ayr. 622; again in *Ex parte Chappel*, 3 Mont. & Ayr. 490, it was held that notice of dishonour must be given to the bankrupt before the choice of assignees, and to them afterwards; but this was not followed in *Ex parte Baker*, 4 Ch. D. 795; 46 L. J. Bankr. 60; 36 L. T. N. S. 339; 25 W. R. 454, where it was decided that such notice may be given either to the bankrupt or to the trustee, by which decision the present sub-section seems to be suggested.

(*j*) So held in America; see the cases cited in Parsons on Bills, vol. i. p. 502; Story on Bills, s. 299. But there has not, so far as we know, been any English decision to this effect.

(*i*) So held in *Burbridge* v. *Manners*, 3 Camp. 193, where the bill was dishonoured in the forenoon of the day it became due, and notice of dishonour was immediately sent to the defendant, an indorser. Story on Bills, s. 382.

(*h*) As to reasonable time see sub-sect. (3) of sect. 40 of this Act, and notes (*e*) (*f*) (*g*) and (*h*) thereto, and sub-sect. (2) of sect. 45 of this Act and notes (*x*) and (*w*) thereto. Before this Act it was held that in the consideration of the question of what is a reasonable time, non-business days should be excluded, *Lindo* v. *Unsworth*, 2 Camp. 602. And now by sect. 92 of this Act (which also defines non-business days) such non-business days are excluded, where by this Act the time limited for doing any act or thing is less than three days.

(*g*) So held before this Act; see *Smith* v. *Mullett*, 2 Camp. 208; allowing only one day to each party where all the parties reside in the same town is the established rule, per Lawrence, J., in *Jameson* v. *Swinton*, 2 Camp. 374; the true rule is that a party in order to avoid laches must give notice by the same day's post and not by the next possible post, *Williams* v. *Smith*, 2 B. & Ald. 496; see also *Rowe* v. *Tipper*, 13 C. B., at p. 256; *Gladwell* v. *Turner*, L. R. 5 Ex. 59.

(*f*) This is the same as before this Act; *Hawkes* v. *Salter*, 4 Bing. 715; *Williams* v. *Smith*, 2 B. & Ald. 496.

(*e*) So laid down in *Geill* v. *Jeremy*, 1 M. & M. 61, where Lord Tenterden said: "The general rule is that the party need not write on the very day that he receives the notice; if there be no post on the following day it makes no difference; the next post after the day on which he receives the notice is soon enough. See also *Hawkes* v. *Salter*, 4 Bing. 715.

(*d*) So held hitherto, see *Clode* v. *Bayley*, 12 M. & W. 51; see also *In re Leeds Banking Company*, L. R. 1 Eq. 1; 35 L. J. Ch. 311, the decision in which seems to be overruled by the present sub-section.

(*c*) See *Geill* v. *Jeremy*, 1 M. & M. 61.

(*b*) In *Mackay* v. *Judkins*, 1 F. & F. 208, following *Saunderson* v.

Judge, 2 H. Bl. 509; and *Scott* v. *Lifford,* 9 East, 347, it was held that it is not necessary that the notice should be shewn to have come to the defendant's hands, nor is it any answer that it has not. It is enough that the plaintiff has duly posted it; see also *Castrique* v. *Bernabo,* 14 L. J. Q. B. 3; again in *Woodcock* v. *Houldsworth,* 16 M. & W. 124, it was held that if a notice of dishonour be posted in due time, the holder is not prejudiced, if through mistake or delay of the post-office, it is not delivered in due time. It has been held that a letter directed "Mr. Haynes, Bristol," containing notice of the dishonour of a bill is too general a direction to raise a presumption that the letter reached the particular individual intended, *Walter* v. *Haynes,* R. & M. 149, but the fact that the holder had previously sent a letter to the drawer, addressed as he had dated the bill, is evidence on which a jury is warranted in finding that due diligence has been used to give notice of dishonour, though no inquiry had been made of the acceptor who knew the drawer's address, *Burmester* v. *Barron,* 17 Q B. 828; following *Mann* v. *Moore,* R. & M. 249; *Clarke* v. *Sharpe,* 3 M. & W. 166. But where notice of dishonour reaches the drawer too late, having first by mistake been sent to a wrong person, and such mistake arose from the indistinctness of the drawer's writing on the bill, he is not discharged, *Hewitt* v. *Thompson,* 1 Moo. & Rob. 543.

50.—(1.) Delay in giving notice of dishonour is excused where the delay is caused by circumstances beyond the control of the party giving notice, and not imputable to his default, misconduct, or negligence (*z*). When the cause of delay ceases to operate, the notice must be given with reasonable diligence (*y*).

(2.) Notice of dishonour is dispensed with—

(*a*) When, after the exercise of reasonable diligence, notice as required by this Act cannot be given or does not reach the drawer or indorser sought to be charged (*x*) :

(*b*) By waiver express or implied. Notice of dishonour may be waived before the time of giving notice has arrived, or after the omission to give due notice (*w*) :

(*c*) As regards the drawer in the following cases, namely, (1) where drawer and drawee are the same person (*v*); (2) where the drawee is a fictitious person or a person not having capacity to contract (*t*) ; (3)

where the drawer is the person to whom the bill is presented for payment (*s*) ; (4) where the drawee or acceptor is as between himself and the drawer under no obligation to accept or pay the bill (*r*) ; (5) where the drawer has countermanded payment (*q*) :

(*d*) As regards the indorser in the following cases, namely, (1) where the drawee is a fictitious person or a person not having capacity to contract, and the indorser was aware of the fact at the time he indorsed the bill (*p*) ; (2) where the indorser is the person to whom the bill is presented for payment (*o*) ; (3) where the bill was accepted or made for his accommodation (*n*).

(*z*) It has been held that where the holder does not know the indorser's address he is excused for not giving regular notice of dishonour if he use reasonable diligence to discover where the indorser may be found, *Bateman* v. *Joseph*, 2 Camp. 461 ; see also *Baldwin* v. *Richardson*, 1 B. & C. 245 ; and *Gladwell* v *Turner*, L. R. 5 Ex. 59. As to the delay in giving the notice of dishonour being caused by circumstances beyond one's control, see *Berridge* v. *Fitzgerald*, L. R. 4 Q. B. 639. But it is not enough to make such inquiries at the place where the bill is payable, *Beveridge* v. *Burgis*, 3 Camp 262. Again the delay is excused if the notice of dishonour is sent by mistake to a wrong person, through the indistinctness of the drawer's writing on the bill, *Hewitt* v. *Thompson*, 1 Moo. & Rob. 543.

(*y*) See *Dixon* v. *Johnson*, 1 Jur. N. S. 70, where the holder on the maturity of the bill not knowing the defendant's address, wrote for it to another indorsee, and on the day he received an answer sent notice of dishonour to the defendant, and it was held sufficient.

(*x*) As to reasonable diligence see section 36, sub-s. (3), and note (*v*) thereto ; section 39, sub-sec. (4), and note (*e*) thereto.

(*w*) There can be no difficulty as to an express waiver. But as to the circumstances from which a waiver will be implied, see *Brett* v. *Levett*, 13 East, 214 ; *Bishop* v. *Rowe*, 3 M. & S. 362 ; *Campbell* v. *Webster*, 15 L. J. C. P. 4 ; *Mills* v. *Gibson*, 16 L. J. C. P. 249, *Jackson* v. *Collins*, 17 L. J. Q. B. 142 ; *Brownell* v. *Bonney*, 1 Q. B. 39 ; *Raybey* v. *Gilbert*, 30 L. J. Ex. 170 ; *Woods* v. *Dean*, 3 B. & S. 101 ; 32 L. J. Q. B. 1 ; *North Stafford Company* v. *Wythies*, 2 F. & F. 563 From these cases it would seem that if, on the maturity of a bill, the party entitled to notice of dishonour, acknowledges the debt, or promises to pay it, or asks for time, that is a waiver of the want of notice of dishonour: although mere acknowledgment without a promise to pay has not been considered sufficient to amount to waiver, see *Baker* v. *Birch*, 3 Camp. 107; *Pickin* v. *Graham*, 1 Cr. & M. 725; *Hicks* v. *Beaufort*, 4 Bing. N. C. 229; *Lecaan* v. *Kirkman*, 6 Jur. N. S. 17; Story on Bills, s. 320.

S. 50.

———

Excuses for non-notice and delay.

(*v*) Because the instrument is then a promissory note, the drawer being the maker, and so not entitled to notice of dishonour; see sect. 5 (2) and the notes thereto.

(*t*) So held in *Smith* v. *Bellamy*, 2 Stark. 223

(*s*) "If, for example, A. draws on himself, payable to himself, and then accepts, and then indorses, a holder need not first demand of him as drawee, and then notify him of non-payment as drawer, and then notify him again as indorser," 1 Parsons on Bills, 521. See *Caunt* v. *Thompson*, 7 C. B. 400; 18 L. J. C. P. 125.

(*r*) This is the case of an acceptor who has accepted for the accommodation of the drawer whom the drawer has not put in funds for the purpose of meeting the bill, see *Bickerdike* v. *Bollman*, 2 Sm. L. C. (8th Edition), p. 51; 1 T. R. 405; and *Goodall* v. *Dolley*, 1 T. R. 712, *Rogers* v. *Stephens*, 2 T. R. 713; *Legge* v. *Thorpe*, 12 East, 171; *Claridge* v. *Dalton*, 2 M. & S. 226; *Carter* v. *Flower*, 16 M. & W. 743; *Everard* v. *Watson*, 1 E & B. 804, and the other cases discussed in the notes to the same. But it has been held that the drawer is entitled to notice if he had reasonable ground to expect that the bill would be honoured on the strength of the consignment, *Rucker* v. *Hiller*, 3 Camp. 217. And that, too, although the funds may not have actually arrived, *Robins* v. *Gibson*, 3 Camp. 334. But the drawer is not entitled to notice if the funds either in the hands of or on their way to the acceptor are not sufficient for meeting the bill, *Carew* v. *Duckworth*, L. R. 4 Ex. 317. But it is submitted that the drawee or acceptor is, to use the words of this sub-section, under no obligation to pay unless he is actually put in funds for that purpose by the drawer at or before the maturity of the bill, and that therefore, unless such is the case, the drawer is not entitled to notice of dishonour. Knowledge that the bill will probably be dishonoured does not operate as a notice of dishonour, *Caunt* v. *Thompson*, 7 C. B. 400.

(*q*) It was so held in *Hill* v. *Heap*, D. & R. N. P. C. 57. See 1 Parsons on Bills, 584.

(*p*) In *Leach* v. *Hewitt*, 4 Taunt. 731, it was held that one who, without consideration but without fraud, indorses a bill in which both the holder and acceptor are fictitious persons, is entitled to notice of the dishonour of the bill.

(*o*) See *Caunt* v. *Thompson*, 7 C. B. 400, 18 L. J. C. P. 125, where the bill was taken to the defendant when it became due, and he said that the acceptor was dead, and that he was his executor, at the same time he asked for time saying that he would see the bill paid. See note (*s*) above.

SS. 50, 51.

Excuses for non-notice and delay.

Noting or protest of bill.

Ind. Act, s. 99.

Ind Act, ss. 100 & 104

Ind Act, s 99

Ind. Act, s. 100.

Ind Act, s 100.

Ind. Act, s. 103.

(*n*) Because he would have no remedy over against any other party to the bill, per Brett, L.J., in *Turner* v. *Samson*, 2 Q. B. D. 23, where the authorities are reviewed.

51.—(1.) Where an inland bill has been dishonoured, it may, if the holder think fit, be noted (*z*) for non-acceptance or non-payment as the case may be; but it shall not be necessary to note or protest any such bill in order to preserve the recourse against the drawer or indorser.

(2.) Where a foreign bill, appearing on the face of it to be such, has been dishonoured by non-acceptance, it must be duly protested for non-acceptance, and where such a bill, which has not been previously dishonoured by non-acceptance, is dishonoured by non-payment, it must be duly protested (*y*) for non-payment. If it be not so protested the drawer and indorsers are discharged (*x*). Where a bill does not appear on the face of it to be a foreign bill, protest thereof in case of dishonour is unnecessary (*w*).

(3.) A bill which has been protested for non-acceptance may be subsequently protested for non-payment (*v*).

(4.) Subject to the provisions of this Act, when a bill is noted or protested, it must be noted on the day of its dishonour (*t*). When a bill has been duly noted the protest may be subsequently extended as of the date of the noting (*s*).

(5.) Where the acceptor of a bill becomes bankrupt or insolvent or suspends payment before it matures, the holder may cause the bill to be protested for better security against the drawer and indorsers (*r*).

(6.) A bill must be protested at the place where it is dishonoured (*q*): Provided that,

(*a*) When a bill is presented through the post-office, and returned by post dishonoured, it may be protested at the place to which it is returned, and on the day of its return if received during business hours, and if not received during business hours, then not later than the next business day (*p*):

(*b*) When a bill drawn payable at the place of business

or residence of some person other than the drawee,
has been dishonoured by non-acceptance, it must
be protested for non-payment at the place where
it is expressed to be payable (*o*), and no further
presentment for payment to, or demand on, the
drawee is necessary.

(7.) A protest must contain a copy of the bill, and must   Ind Act, s. 101,
be signed by the notary making it, and must   sub-s. (*a*) & (*o*).
specify (*n*):

(*a*) The person at whose request the bill is pro-   Ind Act, s 101,
tested (*m*):   sub-s. (*b*).

(*b*) The place and date of protest, the cause or reason   Ind. Act, s 101,
for protesting the bill, the demand made, and the   sub-s. (*c*) & (*d*)
answer given, if any, or the fact that the drawee
or acceptor could not be found (*l*).

(8.) Where a bill is lost or destroyed, or is wrongly
detained from the person entitled to hold it, protest may be made on a copy or written particulars
thereof (*k*).

(9.) Protest is dispensed with by any circumstance
which would dispense with notice of dishonour (*j*).
Delay in noting or protesting is excused when the
delay is caused by circumstances beyond the control
of the holder (*h*), and not imputable to his default,
misconduct, or negligence. When the cause of
delay ceases to operate, the bill must be noted or
protested with reasonable diligence (*g*).

(*z*) "Noting is a minute made on the bill by the officer at the time
of refusal of acceptance or payment. It consists of his initials, the
month, the day, the year, and his charges for minuting; and is considered as the preparatory step to protest." Byles on Bills (13th
Edition), pp. 263; see also Brookes' Notary, 3rd Edit., p. 73. As to
the expense of noting, see sub-division (*c*) of sub-sect. (1) of sect. 57
of this Act, and note (*q*) thereto.

(*y*) "When a foreign bill is refused acceptance or payment, it was   Ind. Act,
and still is necessary, by the custom of merchants, in order to charge   ss. 100, & 101.
the drawer, that the dishonour should be attested by a protest. For,
by the law of most foreign nations, a protest is or was essential in case
of dishonour of any bill; and, though by the law of England it is
unnecessary in case of an inland bill, yet, for the sake of uniformity, in

international transactions a foreign bill must be protested," Byles on Bills (13th Edition), 261. See also Story on Bills, sect. 277; *Hoare* v. *Cazenove*, 16 East, at p. 398; *Brough* v. *Parkings*, 2 Ld. Raym. 993. The protest should be made by a notary public, and when made by such person, it must be signed by him; see sub-sect. 7 of his section, but if there be no notary at the place where the bill is dishonoured, it may be made by a householder or substantial resident of the place in the presence of two witnesses; see sect. 94 of this Act and the notes thereto. "A protest is an instrument in writing signed by the notary, and passed under his official seal, it must state correctly the date of the dishonour and give a concise account of the refusal to accept or pay, or other circumstances incident thereto; and it generally (though this is not necessary) states at whose request the bill is protested; but it is commonly stated in the protest to be done at the request of the 'holders' or 'the bearer', a protest in this country does not require any attesting witness." Brooke's Notary (3rd Edition), 75. "A notary is a public officer of the civil and canon law, appointed by the Archbishop of Canterbury, who, in the instrument of appointment decrees 'that full faith be given, as well in as out of judgment, to the instrument by him to be made.'" Byles on Bills (13th Edition), p. 262; 1 Parsons on Bills, 634. As to forms of protests to be made when the services of a notary cannot be obtained, see the first schedule to this Act. It may be added here that a foreign promissory note need not be protested, sect. 89, sub-sect. 4.

(*x*) It was held in *Rogers* v. *Stephens*, 2 T. R. 713; *Orr* v. *Maginnis*, 7 East, at p. 360; *Gale* v. *Walsh*, 5 T. R. 239.

(*w*) See note (*y*) to this section.

(*v*) A second protest is gratuitous, *De la Torre* v. *Barclay*, 1 Stark at p. 8. It is not necessary to do so, because the holder by the non-acceptance acquires the most complete right of action against the drawer which the nature of the case admits, and no subsequent act or omission of the drawee can give him a more extensive right against the drawer than he has already acquired; see the judgment of Parke, B., in *Whitehead* v. *Walker*, 9 M. & W. 506.

(*t*) This is new; for though the noting of a bill has generally hitherto been done on the day of the dishonour, it has not been compulsory to do so, see Brooke's Notary (3rd Edition), 73.

(*s*) See sect. 93 of this Act and the notes thereto, which section follows the decision in *Chaters* v. *Bell*, 4 Esp. 48; and in *Geralopulo* v. *Wieler*, 10 C. B. 690, it was held, in the case of a foreign bill paid, *supra* protest for the honour of the indorser, that the formal protest may be drawn up or extended even after the commencement of an action by the person so paying; see 1 Parsons on Bills, 644.

(*r*) See Brooke's Notary (3rd Edition), p. 80; and Byles on Bills (13th Edition), 263.

(*q*) That is to say, at the place where the drawee resides, as was

the opinion of the Court of King's Bench in *Mitchell* v. *Baring*, 4   SS 51, 52.
C. & P. 35.   See 1 Parsons on Bills, 640.

*Noting or
protest of bill.*

(*p*) See note (*s*) hereto.

(*o*) This is almost the same as the provisions of 2 & 3 Will. 4
c. 98, which has been by this Act repealed ; but there is this distinction
between the two statutes, that the older one used the words " shall or
may be protested."

(*n*) See Brooke's Notary (3rd Edition), p. 75 ; 1 Parsons on Bills,
645 ; see also note (*y*) hereto.

(*m*) This has been generally stated in a protest, see Brooke's
Notary (3rd Edition), p. 75 , see also note (*y*) hereto.

(*l*) See Brooke's Notary (3rd Edition), pp. 75, 76 ; see also note (*y*)
hereto.

(*k*) This was decided in the old case of *Debers* v. *Harriot*, 1 Shower,
p. 159 , Story on Bills, sect. 279, note.

(*j*) As to the circumstances under which notice of dishonour may be
dispensed with, see sub-sect. (2) of sect. 50 of this Act, and subdivisions (*a*), (*b*), (*c*) and (*d*) thereof, and notes (*x*), (*w*), (*v*), (*t*), (*s*),
(*r*), (*q*), (*p*) and (*o*).   This sub-section adopts the decision of the Court
in *Legge* v. *Thorpe*, 12 East, 171.

(*h*) As to the circumstances under which delay in giving notice
of dishonour is excused, see sub-sect. (1) of sect. 50, and notes (*z*), (*y*)
and (*x*) thereto.

(*g*) As to reasonable diligence see sect. 36, sub-sect (3), and note
(*v*) thereto ; sect. 39, sub-sect. (4), and note (*e*) thereto.

52.—(1.) When a bill is accepted generally present-   *Duties of
holder as re-
gards drawee
or acceptor.*
ment for payment is not necessary in order to render the
acceptor liable (*a*).

(2.) When by the terms of a qualified acceptance   Ind Act, s 93
presentment for payment is required, the acceptor, in the
absence of an express stipulation to that effect, is not
discharged by the omission to present the bill for payment
on the day that it matures (*b*).

(3.) In order to render the acceptor of a bill liable it   Ind. Act, s. 93
is not necessary to protest it, or that notice of dishonour
should be given to him (*c*).

(4.) Where the holder of a bill presents it for payment,   Ind Act, s 81
he shall exhibit the bill to the person from whom he
demands payment (*d*), and when a bill is paid the holder
shall forthwith deliver it up to the party paying it (*e*).

(*a*) " Every bill is to be properly presented for payment ; and in an
action thereon against the drawer or indorser, a presentment according

SS. 52, 53.

Duties of holder as regards drawee or acceptor.

to the custom and usage of merchants must be averred and proved; in an action thereon against the acceptor presentment (generally speaking) need not be averred or proved. This is clear, settled, undisputed law," per Bayley, J., in *Rowe* v. *Young*, 2 Bligh, H. L. at p. 468; again in *Fayle* v. *Bird*, 6 B. & C. 531, it was decided that presentment to the acceptor is not necessary, where the bill is accepted generally.

(*b*) So held in *Smith* v. *Vertue*, 9 C. B. N. S. 214; and so held in *Rhodes* v. *Gent*, 5 B. & Ald 244, but the Court seemed to think with this qualification, that the acceptor has not sustained any actual loss through the delay in presenting the bill. It must be remembered that the acceptance in *Rhodes* v. *Gent* would now be a general acceptance; see sect. 19, sub.-s. 2 (C.) of this Act, and the notes thereto.

(*c*) It was so held in *Treacher* v. *Hinton*, 4 B. & Ald. 413. "The rule is, that the party, other than the acceptor, sought to be charged, is entitled to notice of dishonour," per Maule, J , in *Rowe* v. *Tipper*, 22 L J. C. P. 185 , nor is the maker of a promissory note entitled to notice of dishonour, *Pearse* v. *Pemberthy*, 3 Camp. 261.

(*d*) Presentment for payment means presentment according to mercantile usage; the document itself must be present though not the holder , per Blackburn, J., in *Griffin* v. *Weatherley*, L. R. 3 Q. B. 753 "The custom of merchants," says Lord Tenterden in *Hansard* v. *Robinson*, 9 D. & R. 860 , 7 B & C. 90; "is that the holder shall present the bill, at its maturity, demand payment of its amount, and upon receipt of the money deliver up the bill."

(*e*) See Brooke's Notary (3rd Edit.), p 59. See also the judgment of Lord Tenterden, C.J., in *Hansard* v. *Robinson*, *supra*; also *Alexander* v. *Strong*, 9 M. & W. 733, and *Crowe* v. *Clay*, 9 Ex. 604; 23 L. J. Ex. 150. But it has been held that where a bill or note is not negotiable, the acceptor or maker cannot refuse to pay it on the ground that the payee has not got it in his possession or power, and cannot produce it for the purpose of delivering it up to the acceptor or maker on payment, *Wain* v. *Bailey*, 10 A. & E. 616; 2 P. & D. 507. But a banker receiving bills from his correspondents to whom they had been indorsed, to present for payment, is not guilty of negligence in giving up such bills to the acceptor upon receiving a cheque upon a banker for the amount, although it turn out that such cheque is dishonoured, *Russell* v. *Hankey*, 6 Term, 12. See also *Vernon* v. *Bouverie*, 2 Show. 303.

LIABILITIES OF PARTIES.

Funds in hands of drawee

Ind Act, ss. 7 & 33.

53.—(1.) A bill, of itself, does not operate as an assignment of funds in the hands of the drawee available for the payment thereof (*a*), and the drawee of a bill who does not accept as required by this Act is not liable on the instrument (*b*). This sub-section shall not extend to Scotland.

(2.) In Scotland, where the drawee of a bill has in his hands funds available for the payment thereof, the bill operates as an assignment of the sum for which it is drawn in favour of the holder, from the time when the bill is presented to the drawee (*c*).

(*a*) In *Hopkinson* v. *Forster*, L. R. 19 Eq. 74, it was held that a cheque is not an equitable assignment of the drawer's balance at his bankers. In this case the observations of Mr. Justice Byles in *Keene* v. *Beard*, 8 C B. N. S. 381, that a cheque is an appropriation of so much money of the drawer's in the hands of the banker upon whom it is drawn for the purpose of discharging a debt or liability of the drawer to a third person were commented on, the late Master of the Rolls adding, "I am quite sure that learned Judge never meant to lay down that a banker who dishonours a cheque is liable to a suit in equity by the holder" The decision in *Hopkinson* v. *Forster* is in a great measure supported by that in *Hill* v. *Royds*, L. R. 8 Eq. 290. In that case the acceptor of a bill of exchange paid the amount to his bankers in order to meet the bill; on the day it arrived at maturity the acceptor died, and the bankers dishonoured the bill, which was returned to the drawers and subsequently paid by them. Upon bill filed by the drawers against the bankers to make good the amount, it was held that there was no privity between the plaintiffs and the defendants. Further, *Hopkinson* v *Forster*, has been approved and followed in *Schroeder* v *The Central Bank of London, Lim.*, 34 L. T. N. S. 735. But though a cheque is not an assignment of funds belonging to the drawer in the hands of a banker, the banker, if he dishonour such cheque when he has such funds, is liable in damages to the drawer, per Jessel, M.R., in *Hopkinson* v. *Forster, supra*. A bill of exchange is still less than a cheque an assignment of funds in the hands of a drawee, for the latter is not bound to accept, and until acceptance he is not liable on the bill, as is provided in the latter part of this sub-section, see notes (*b*) hereto and also section 2 of this Act and note (*a*) thereto, and sects. 17 and 54 of this Act and the notes thereto. See also note [(*b*) (4)] to sect. 73 of this Act. In America the law seems to be the same, see Parsons on Bills; as to bills, vol. i. pp. 331–336, and the cases cited therein; as to cheques, vol. ii. pp 59–62, and the cases cited therein.

(*b*) But though not liable on the bill, he may be liable on an agreement to accept, *Laing* v. *Barclay*, 1 B. & C. 398, see also the judgment of Cockburn, L.C J, in *Godwin* v. *Robarts*, L. R. 10 Ex. at p 351.

SS. 53, 54.
———
Funds in hands
of drawee.

(c) In a recent case in Scotland it was held that a cheque granted for value, and presented for payment, operates as an intimated assignation of any funds of the drawer in the hands of the bank up to the amount of the cheque, *British Linen Co. Bank* v. *Carruthers,* Court of Sess. Cas. 4th series, vol. x 923. Referring to the present and 73rd sections of this Act, Lord Shand in his judgment says. "The result of these sections is that a cheque to a third party has the force of a bill, and 2nd, that the statute enacts the common law of Scotland, that a cheque or a bill of exchange, when intimated, is effectual as an intimated assignation. . . . That being so, the only question remaining is whether, because the bank was in debt to the grantor to a less amount than that contained in the cheque, the assignation is useless? If this had been an ordinary assignation of a fund and not a cheque, that circumstance would not have prevented the intimated assignation from carrying the amount in the debtor's hands, and the circumstance that this is in form a cheque can make no difference."

Liability of
acceptor.
Ind Act, s. 32.

54.—The acceptor of a bill, by accepting it—

(1.) Engages that he will pay it according to the tenor of his acceptance (*z*) :

(2.) Is precluded from denying to a holder in due course :

Ind Act, s. 120.

 (*a*) The existence of the drawer, the genuineness of his signature, and his capacity and authority to draw the bill (*y*) ;

Ind. Act, s. 121.

 (*b*) In the case of a bill payable to drawer's order, the then capacity of the drawer to indorse (*x*), but not the genuineness or validity of his indorsement (*w*) ;

Ind Act, s. 121.

 (*c*) In the case of a bill payable to the order of a third person, the existence of the payee and his then capacity to indorse (*v*), but not the genuineness or validity of his indorsement (*t*).

(*z*) The acceptance of a bill, like the making a note, has always been considered to be an absolute undertaking, on the part of the acceptor or maker, to pay the payee, or order or bearer, in the manner directed by the instrument; see *Walton* v. *Mascall,* 13 M. & W. at pp. 457, 458; see also the judgment of Byles, J., in *Smith* v. *Vertue,* 9 C. B. N. S. 214; 30 L. J. C. P. 56. Story on Bills, s. 113.

(*y*) So held hitherto; as to the signature of the drawer, per Lord Ellenborough, C J , in *Bass* v. *Clive,* 4 M & S. 13; per Lord Tenterden, C.J., in *Cooper* v. *Meyer,* 10 B. & C. 468; see also *Sanderson* v.

Collman, 4 M. & G. 209; and *Phillips* v. *Im Thurn,* L. R. 1 C. P. 463; 35 L. J. C. P. 220; 18 C. B. N. S. 694; as to the capacity and authority of the drawer, see *Porthouse* v. *Parker,* 1 Camp. 82; *Prince* v. *Brunatte,* 1 Bing. N. C. 435; and *Braithwaite* v. *Gardiner,* 8 Q. B. 473.

(*x*) See Story on Bills, s. 113. The defendant by making a note payable to C. or order, intimates to all persons that he considers C. capable of making an order sufficient to transfer the property in the note; per Bayley, J., in *Drayton* v. *Dale,* 2 B. & C. 293, at p. 299; as the maker of a note stands in the same position as the acceptor of a bill, the acceptor of a bill payable to C. or order would also be taken to admit C.'s power to make an order as above, as is provided by this sub-section; see also *Smith* v. *Marsack,* 6 C. B 486; 18 L. J. C. P. 65, *Pitt* v. *Chappelow,* 8 M. & W. 616, *Hallifax* v. *Lyle,* 3 Ex 446.

(*w*) The mere acceptance proves the drawing, but never the indorsement; per Parke, J., in *Robinson* v. *Yarrow,* 7 Taunt. 455, see also the judgment of Lord Tenterden, C J., in *Cooper* v. *Meyer,* 10 B & C. 468; the judgment of Parke, B., in *Beeman* v. *Duck,* 11 M. & W 251; an acceptor, though he admits the authority of the person drawing the bill to draw it, does not admit the authority of the same person to indorse it; per Blackburn, J., in *Garland* v. *Jacomb,* L R. 8 Ex. 216.

(*v*) See *Drayton* v. *Dale, supra.*

(*t*) So held in *Smith* v. *Chester,* 1 T. R. 654; see also the judgment of Parke, B., in *Robarts* v. *Tucker,* 16 Q. B. 560. And this is so, notwithstanding that the indorsement was on the bill at the time it was accepted; *Smith* v. *Chester, supra.* Story on Bills, s. 412.

55.—(1.) The drawer of a bill by drawing it—

(*a*) Engages that on due presentment it shall be accepted and paid according to its tenor, and that if it be dishonoured he will compensate the holder or any indorser who is compelled to pay it (*z*), provided that the requisite proceedings on dishonour be duly taken (*y*),

(*b*) Is precluded from denying to a holder in due course the existence of the payee and his then capacity to indorse (*x*).

(2.) The indorser of a bill by indorsing it—

(*a*) Engages that on due presentment it shall be accepted and paid according to its tenor, and that if it be dishonoured he will compensate the holder

Liability of drawer or indorser
Ind Act, s 30

Ind. Act, ss 120 & 121.

Ind Act, s. 35

or a subsequent indorser who is compelled to pay it (*w*), provided that the requisite proceedings on dishonour be duly taken (*v*) ;

(*b*) Is precluded from denying to a holder in due course the genuineness and regularity in all respects of the drawer's signature and all previous indorsements (*t*) ;

(*c*) Is precluded from denying to his immediate or a subsequent indorsee that the bill was at the time of his indorsement a valid and subsisting bill, and that he had then a good title thereto (*s*).

(*z*) As to the legal effect of drawing a bill, see Byles on Bills (13th Edit.), 3, and Chalmers' Digest of the Law of Bills of Exchange (2nd Edit.), 185. The drawer comes under an obligation to the holder to pay him, if the person on whom the bill is drawn does not accept and pay it, and the drawer has notice of dishonour, *Steele* v. *McKinlay*, 5 Ap. Cas. 769. The contract of the drawer is an undertaking that the acceptor shall pay the bill, per Lord Lyndhurst, C.B., in *Siggers* v. *Lewis*, 1 C. M. & R. 371 ; the acceptor is primarily liable, the drawer is liable only upon the contingencies of the acceptor's or drawee's making default, and of the holder's performing certain conditions precedent, such as presenting the bill, giving due notice of dishonour, &c. ; per Cresswell, J., in *Jones* v. *Broadhurst*, 9 C B. 181 ; see also the judgment of Parke, B., in *Whitehead* v. *Walker*, 9 M. & W. 516

(*y*) As to the requisites on dishonour see sects. 48, 49, 50, 51, and 52, the sub-sections thereof, and the notes to the same.

(*x*) In *Phillips* v. *Im Thurn*, 18 C B N. S. 694, it was held that the acceptor *supra* protest of a bill of exchange, for the honour of the drawer, is, like the drawer himself, estopped from denying that the bill is a valid bill ; and consequently it is not competent to him to set up as a defence to an action against him by an indorsee that the payee is a fictitious person, and that he was ignorant of that fact at the time he accepted the bill. The drawer is not precluded from denying the genuineness and regularity of the payee's indorsement, even though he has seen the bill with such indorsement, and does not object to it ; *Duncan* v. *Scott*, 1 Camp. 101.

(*w*) "The contract of an indorser is an engagement by him that if the drawee shall not at maturity pay the bill, he, the indorser, will on due notice pay the holder the sum which the drawee ought to have paid, together with such damages as the law prescribes, or allows as an indemnity," per Byles, J., in *Suse* v. *Pompe*, 8 C. B. N. S. 538, at p. 563 ; 30 L. J. C. P. 75, at p 78, see also the judgment of Lord Selborne in *Duncan Fox & Co.* v. *N. & S. Wales Bank*, 6 Ap. Cas. at

p. 13; the judgment of Brett, L.J., in *Horne* v. *Rouquette*, 3 Q. B. D. 519; and per Lord Blackburn in *Steele* v. *McKinlay*, 5 Ap. Cas. at p 769; see further Byles on Bills (13th Edit.), 154; and Story on Bills, s. 107. In a recent case it was held that the liabilities *inter se* of successive indorsers of a bill or note must in the absence of evidence to the contrary be determined according to the ordinary principles whereby a prior indorser must indemnify a subsequent one; but the whole circumstances may be looked at for the purpose of ascertaining the true relation of the parties to each other, *Macdonald* v. *Whitfield*, 8 Ap. Cas. 733.

(*v*) See note (*y*) to this section.

(*t*) See the judgment of Lord Campbell in *M'Gregor* v. *Rhodes*, 25 L. J. Q. B. 318; 6 E. & B. 266. This sub-section overrules the opinion expressed in *The East India Co* v. *Tritton*, 3 B & C. 280, that an indorser does not impliedly warrant the validity of prior indorsements. In America it has been held also that the indorsement is an implied warranty that the previous signatures are genuine, *Turnbull* v. *Bowyer*, 40 N Y. Rep. 456.

(*s*) See the last preceding note hereto; Story on Bills, s. 110; see also sect. 74 of this Act and the notes thereto, title " forged cheques," and " altered cheques."

56.—Where a person signs a bill otherwise than as drawer or acceptor, he thereby incurs the liabilities of an indorser to a holder in due course (*a*).

(*a*) It was so laid down by Lord Blackburn in *Steele* v. *M'Kinlay*, 5 Ap. Cas. at p. 772 where all the authorities are discussed. See also *Macdonald* v. *Union Bank of Scotland*, Court Sess. Cas., 3rd Series, vol. ii. 963; and *Matthews* v. *Bloxome*, 33 L. J. Q. B. 209 (where the defendant put his name on the back of a stamped paper, which was afterwards filled in as a bill for £50; held, that he was liable as an indorser); but see this case commented on in *Steele* v. *McKinlay*, 5 Ap. Cas. at p 773; if a man write his name across the back of a blank bill-stamp, and the paper is afterwards improperly filled up, he is liable as indorser; per Byles, J., in *Foster* v. *Mackinnon*, L. R 4 C. P. at p. 712.

57.—Where a bill is dishonoured. the measure of damages, which shall be deemed to be liquidated damages, shall be as follows:

Measure of damages against parties to dishonoured bill.

Ind. Act. s 117.

Ind. Act, s. 117, sub-ss. (c) & (d).

(1.) The holder (*z*) may recover from any party liable on the bill, and the drawer (*y*) who has been compelled to pay the bill may recover from the acceptor (*x*), and an indorser (*w*) who has been compelled to pay the bill

S. 57.

Measure of
damages
against parties
to dishonoured
bill.

Ind. Act, s 117,
sub-s. (a)

Indian Civil
Procedure
Code, s. 532

Ind. Act, s 117,
sub.-s (a).

Ind. Act, s 117,
sub-s. (b)

Ind Act, s 79.

may recover from the acceptor or from the drawer, or from a prior indorser—

(a) The amount of the bill (v):

(b) Interest thereon from the time of presentment for payment if the bill is payable on demand (t), and from the maturity of the bill in any other case (s):

(c) The expenses of noting (r), or, when protest is necessary, and the protest has been extended, the expenses of protest (q).

(2.) In the case of a bill which has been dishonoured abroad, in lieu of the above damages, the holder may recover from the drawer or an indorser, and the drawer or an indorser who has been compelled to pay the bill may recover from any party liable to him, the amount of the re-exchange with interest thereon until the time of payment (p).

(3.) Where by this Act interest may be recovered as damages, such interest may, if justice require it, be withheld wholly or in part (o), and where a bill is expressed to be payable with interest at a given rate, interest as damages may or may not be given at the same rate as interest proper (n).

(z) As to the rights of a holder see sect. 38 of this Act, and the notes thereto.

(y) See note (v) to sub-sect. (1) of sect. 3 of this Act, and sub-sect. (1) of sect. 55 of this Act, and sub-sect. (a) thereof, and the notes thereto.

(x) See note (a) to sect. 2 of this Act, and sect. 17 and the notes thereto, and also sub-sect. (1) of sect. 54 of this Act and the notes thereto.

(w) See sub-sect. (2) of sect 55 of this Act and the notes thereto.

(v) This is a matter of course; see *Deverill* v. *Burnell*, L. R. 8 C. P. 475; 42 L. J. C. P. 214; 28 L. T. N. S. 874. And this, too, though the amount given for a bill or note be less than the actual amount of such instrument, provided such amount be given for the purchase of it; see note (e) to sect. 32 of this Act. But where the amount given is advanced upon the security of the bill, the amount so advanced can only be recovered; see *Re Gomersall*, 1 Ch. D. 137. But if, in the case of the purchase of a bill, the amount

S. 57.
Measure of
damages
against parties
to dishonoured
bill.

given for it is considerably less than the actual amount of the
bill, it will be an important element in considering whether the
person who gave the undervalue was acting *bonâ fide*, or was assisting
in committing a fraud, though the under value *per se* will not be
sufficient to affect the title of the holder, *Jones* v. *Gordon*, 2 Ap. Cas.
632 (per Lord Blackburn).

(*t*) See *Hudson* v. *Fawcett*, 7 M. & G. 348; *Lowndes* v. *Collins*, 17
Ves. 27. Where there has been no other demand than the writ,
interest runs from the service of such writ, *Pierce* v. *Fothergill*, 2 Bing.
N. C. 167.

(*s*) See *Parker* v. *Hutchinson*, 3 Ves. 134; *Cameron* v. *Smith*, 2 B.
& Ald. 305; *In re Burgess*, 2 Moore, 745, *Laing* v. *Stone*, 2 M. & R.
561; *Keene* v. *Keene*, 3 C. B. N. S. 144; 27 L. J. C. P. 88; *Ackerman*
v. *Ehrensperger*, 16 M. & W. 103 (where it was held that a party who
guarantees the payment of a bill is liable for interest in the same way
as the principal would be); and *Maxwell* v. *Tuohill*, 1 L. R. Ir. 250.
Where a bill is expressed to be payable with interest, until the
maturity of the bill the interest is a debt; after its maturity, the
interest is given as damages at the discretion of the jury, who may
adopt, if they please, the rate of interest which the parties themselves
had fixed; *Keene* v. *Keene*, *supra*, and so it is now provided by sub-
sect. 3 of this section.

(*r*) Formerly the expenses of noting, except in actions under the 18
& 19 Vict. c. 67, have not been recoverable unless claimed as special
damage; see *Kendrick* v. *Lomax*, 2 C. & J. 405.

(*q*) See *Suse* v. *Pompe*, 8 C. B. N. S. 538; *Prehn* v. *Royal Bank of
Liverpool*, L. R. 5 Ex. 92; 39 L. J. Ex. 41; 21 L. T. N. S. 830;
18 W. R. 463, *Re General South American Co. Limited*, 7 Ch. D. 637;
47 L. J. Ch. 67; 37 L. T. N. S. 599; 26 W. R. 232; in these last two
cases the telegraphic expenses were also allowed.

(*p*) "Re-exchange is the difference in the value of a bill occasioned
by its being dishonoured in a foreign country in which it was payable.
The existence and amount of it depend on the rate of exchange between
the two countries. The theory of the transaction is this: A merchant
in London indorses a bill for a certain number of Austrian florins
payable at a future date in Vienna. The holder is entitled to receive
in Vienna, on the day of the maturity of the bill, a certain number of
Austrian florins. Suppose the bill to be dishonoured. The holder is
now, by the custom of merchants, entitled to immediate and specific
redress, by his own act, in this way. He is entitled, being in Vienna,
then and there to raise the exact number of Austrian florins, by drawing
and negotiating a cross bill, payable at sight, on his indorser in London,
for as much English money as will purchase in Vienna the exact
number of Austrian florins, at the rate of exchange on the day of
dishonour; and to include in the amount of that bill the interest and
necessary expenses of the transaction. According to English practice,

SS. 57, 58.

Measure of
damages
against parties
to dishonoured
bill.

the *retraite* or re-exchange bill is now seldom drawn, but the right of the holder to draw it is settled by the law-merchant of all nations, and it is only by a reference to this supposed bill that this re-exchange—in other words, the true damages in an action on the original bill—can be scientifically understood and computed;" Byles on Bills (13th Edit.), 418. This passage along with that in Story on Bills, section 399, is cited in full in *Suse* v *Pompe*, 8 C. B. N. S. 538; 30 L. J. C. P. 75, where all the authorities are reviewed and discussed. In *Willans* v. *Ayers*, 3 Ap. Cas. 133; 47 L. J. P. C. 1, it was held that the right to "re-exchange," in the absence of express agreement, arises when the holder of a bill who has contracted for the transfer of funds from one country to another has sustained damages by its dishonour through having to obtain funds in the country where the bill was payable, and "re-exchange" is the measure of those damages. In a recent case it was held that when a bill of exchange is dishonoured at maturity, the drawer of the bill is entitled to recover, as against the acceptor, not only the amount of the bill, and interest and notarial and telegraphic charges, but also the re-exchange, *Re The General South American Company, Limited*, 7 Ch. D. 637; 47 L. J. Ch. 67. This case treated *Woolsey* v *Crawford* (2 Camp. 445) and *Napier* v. *Schneider* (12 East, 420) as overruled.

(*o*) The holder must have done something to disentitle him to interest; *Laing* v. *Stone*, 2 M. & R 561, there must be a default in the holder to deprive him of his right to interest, *Cameron* v. *Smith*, 2 B. & Ald. 305.

(*n*) See *Keene* v. *Keene*, 3 C. B. N. S. 144, cited in note (*s*) to this section.

58.—(1.) Where the holder of a bill payable to bearer negotiates it by delivery without endorsing it, he is called a "transferor by delivery" (*a*).

(2.) A transferor by delivery is not liable on the instrument (*b*).

(3.) A transferor by delivery who negotiates a bill thereby warrants to his immediate transferee being a holder for value that the bill is what it purports to be, that he has a right to transfer it, and that at the time of transfer he is not aware of any fact which renders it valueless (*c*).

(*a*) See notes (*h*) and (*k*) to sect. 2 of this Act and note (*m*) to sect. 3 of this Act.

(*b*) See Story on Bills, s. 109 Thus in *Ex parte Roberts*, 2 Cox, Equity Cases, 171, it was held that a mere discount of a bill without the indorsement of the party who receives the money does not give the holder of the bill any claim against him; see also *Fenn* v. *Harrison*, 3 T. R. at p. 761, where Buller, J, said: "The acceptor, the drawer, and the indorsers of a bill are all liable in their turns, but they are only liable because they have written their names on the bill. But this is an attempt to make some other persons liable, whose names do not appear on the bill;" see further the judgment of Park, J, in *Evans* v. *Whyle*, 5 Bing. at p 488, and also notes (*h*) and (*k*) to sect. 2 of this Act.

(c) So held: *Jones* v. *Ryle*, 5 Taunt. 488; *Gurney* v. *Womersley*, 24 L. J. Q. B. 46; *Fenn* v. *Harrison*, 3 T. R. at p 761; *Camidge* v. *Allenby*, 6 B. & C. 373, at p. 385; *Gompertz* v. *Bartlett*, 2 E. & B. 849; Story on Bills, s. 111.

DISCHARGE OF BILL.

59.—(1.) A bill is discharged by payment in due course by or on behalf of the drawee or acceptor (*z*).

"Payment in due course" means payment made at or after the maturity of the bill (*y*) to the holder thereof (*x*) in good faith and without notice (*w*) that his title to the bill is defective.

(2.) Subject to the provisions heinafter contained, when a bill is paid by the drawer or an indorser it is not discharged (*v*); but

    (a)   Where a bill payable to, or to the order of, a third party is paid by the drawer, the drawer may enforce payment thereof against the acceptor, but may not reissue the bill (*t*).

    (b)   Where a bill is paid by an indorser, or where a bill payable to drawer's order is paid by the drawer, the party paying it is remitted to his former rights as regards the acceptor or antecedent parties, and he may, if he thinks fit, strike out his own and subsequent indorsements, and again negotiate the bill (*s*).

(3.) Where an accommodation bill is paid in due course by the party accommodated the bill is discharged (*r*).

(*z*) Story on Bills, sect. 269; *Fentum* v. *Pocock*, 5 Taunt. 192. "I am of opinion," said Parke, B, "that nothing will discharge the acceptor or the drawer, except *payment according to the law-merchant*, that is, payment of the bill at maturity, if a party pays it

before, he purchases it, and is in the same situation as if he had
discounted it.   The rule is laid down correctly by Lord Ellenborough
in *Burbridge* v. *Manners* (3 Camp. 194) that a payment before a bill
becomes due, does not extinguish it any more than if it were merely
discounted ; and that payment means payment in due course, and not
by anticipation," *Morley* v. *Culverwell*, 7 M. & W. at p. 182.   The
cases on the subject of discharge by payment are reviewed in *Jones* v.
Broadhurst, 9 C. B. 173, and so only a few are given below ; see also
Beck v. *Robley*, 1 H. Bl. 89, n. ; *Purssord* v *Peek*, 9 M. & W. 196 ;
Callow v. *Lawrence*, 3 M. & S 97 ; *Lyon* v *Maxwell*, 18 L. T. N. S
28 ; if payment is made in the name and on behalf of another without
authority, in may be ratified by the debtor, *Walter* v. *James*, L. R. 6 Ex.
124   Payment by a stranger of the amount of a bill of exchange to the
bankers at whose house the bill is, by the acceptance, made payable,
under an arrangement with such bankers, whereby the party paying
obtains possession of the bill for a collateral purpose of his own, is not
a payment of the bill by the acceptor.   Nor can such payment, if made
before the bill becomes due, be considered as payment for the honour
of an indorser, *Deacon* v. *Stodhart*, 2 M. & G. 317.   See also *Jones*
v. *Broadhurst*, 9 C. B. 173 ; *Agra Bank* v. *Leighton*, L. R. 2 Ex. 56 ;
Thornton v *Maynard*, L. R 10 C. P. 695.   These cases were reviewed
in a recent case where it was held that the rule that payment by the
drawer of a bill to the holder does not discharge the holder's claim
against the acceptor does not apply where the bill has been accepted
for the accommodation of the drawer, *Solomon* v. *Davis*, 1 Cababe
and Ellis, N. P. Rep. 83 (per Stephen, J.).   It has been held that part
payment of a bill in due course is a discharge *pro tanto*, *Cook* v.
Lister, 13 C. B. N. S. 543 ; 32 L. J. C. P. 121, where all the
authorities are discussed.   See also *Bacon* v. *Searles*, 1 H. Bl. 88 ;
Solomon v. *Davis, supra.*

(*y*) Story on Bills, s 217, *Harmer* v *Steele*, 4 Ex. at p 13 ; *Attenborough* v. *Mackenzie*, 25 L. J. Ex. 244.   As to payment of a note
payable on demand, see *Bartrum* v. *Caddy*, 9 A. & E. 275.

(*x*) It has been for a long time established that payment should be
made to the holder of the bill or note ; see sect. 45, sub-sect. 3 ; the
acceptor paying the bill has a right to the possession of the instrument, *Hansard* v. *Robinson*, 7 B. & C. at p. 94 ; *Robarts* v. *Tucker*,
16 Q. B. 579.

w) See sect. 90, and the notes thereto, also Story on Bills, sect.
416

(*v*) That is to say, the drawer retains his remedy against the
acceptor, or the indorser against all parties prior to himself ; *Jones*
v *Broadhurst*, 9 C. B. 173 ; *Williams* v. *James*, 15 Q. B 498 ; 19 L.
J Q B. 445 ; see also the judgment of Stephen, J., in *Solomon* v. *Davis,
supra*

(*t*) If the bill is drawn payable to the drawer, then the drawer, having paid it, can re-issue it, provided it does not prejudice any of the indorsers; *Callow* v. *Lawrence*, 3 M. & S. 95; sub-sect. (b) hereto. SS, 59, 60, 61, 62.

(s) See note (t) hereto.

Payment in due course

(r) The party accommodated being in the same situation as the acceptor of a bill for value; *Lazarus* v. *Cowie*, 3 Q. B. 459, at p. 465; see also *Solomon* v. *Davis, supra.*

60.—When a bill, payable to order on demand, is drawn on a banker, and the banker on whom it is drawn pays the bill in good faith and in the ordinary course of business, it is not incumbent on the banker to shew that the indorsement of the payee or any subsequent indorsement was made by or under the authority of the person whose indorsement it purports to be, and the banker is deemed to have paid the bill in due course, although such indorsement has been forged or made without authority (a). Banker paying demand draft whereon indorsement is forged

(a) This section is nearly the same as 16 & 17 Vict. c. 59, s. 19, see also *Ogden* v. *Benas*, L. R 9 C. P. 513, *Halifax Union* v. *Wheelwright*, L. R 10 Ex. 183, *Arnold* v. *Cheque Bank*, 1 C. P. D. 586; but the customer must not by any act of his contribute to the fraud, forgery, &c. See further the notes to sect. 74 of this Act, title "forged and altered cheques," where the cases are discussed. As to bankers paying cheques which bear marks of having been cancelled, see *Ingham* v *Primrose*, 7 C. B. N. S. 82.

61.—When the acceptor of a bill is or becomes the holder of it at or after its maturity, in his own right, the bill is discharged (a). Acceptor the holder at maturity.
Ind. Act, s 90

(a) "It appears to us on the authority of the case of *Freakley* v. *Fox* (9 B. & C. 130), and on principle, that the fact of the defendant, one of the acceptors being, at the time the bill became due, the holder, and entitled to receive as well as liable to pay the amount of the bill, operated, in respect of all the defendants, as a performance of the contract to pay the bill at maturity, and put an end to the contract of acceptance," per Wilde, C.J., in *Harmer* v. *Steele*, 4 Ex. 1

62.—(1.) When the holder of a bill at or after (a) its maturity absolutely (b) and unconditionally renounces his rights against the acceptor, the bill is discharged. Express waivers
Ind Act, s. 82, sub-s (b)

The renunciation must be in writing (c), unless the bill is delivered up to the acceptor.

(2.) The liabilities of any party to the bill may in like manner be renounced by the holder before, at, or after its maturity (d); but nothing in this section shall affect the rights of a holder in due course without notice of the renunciation.

(a) It has been decided that a bill of exchange may be discharged by an express waiver by the holder of his claim, per Parke, B., in *Foster* v. *Dawber*, 6 Ex. 851, his lordship saying the rule has often been so laid down and acted upon, although there is no case precisely on the point between immediate parties ; see also *Dingwall* v. *Dunster*, 1 Doug. 247 , *Harmer* v. *Steele*, *supra*.

(b) The renunciation must be express ; *vide* note (a) hereto.

(c) This is new, for prior to this Act the renunciation need not have been in writing; *vide* Byles on Bills (13th Edition), 200 Not only must such renunciation be in writing, but also any parol agreement contemporaneous with a promissory note to the effect that the note, though on the face of it payable on demand, should not be enforced for three years, is inoperative to contradict the terms of the note, *Stott* v. *Fairlamb*, 52 L. J. Q. B. D. 420; 47 L. T. N. S. 574, following *Woodbridge* v. *Spooner*, 3 B. & Ald. 233, and *Abrey* v. *Crux*, L. R. 5 C. P. 37 , 39 L. J. C. P. 9.

(d) See *Smith* v. *Knox*, 3 Esp. 46 ; *Carstairs* v. *Rolleston*, 5 Taunt. 551; *English* v. *Darley*, 2 B. & P. 62 ; *Dingwall* v. *Dunster*, 1 Dougl. at p. 249; see also *Martin* v. *Cole*, 14 Otto. Sup. Ct. U. S. 30.

63.—(1.) Where a bill is intentionally (a) cancelled by the holder or his agent, and the cancellation is apparent thereon, the bill is discharged.

(2.) In like manner any party liable on a bill may be discharged by the intentional cancellation of his signature by the holder or his agent. In such case any indorser who would have had a right of recourse against the party whose signature is cancelled, is also discharged (b).

(3.) A cancellation made unintentionally, or under a mistake, or without the authority of the holder, is inoperative; but where a bill or any signature thereon appears to have been cancelled the burden of proof lies on the party who alleges that the cancellation was made unintentionally, or under a mistake, or without authority (c).

(a) As has been shewn before an acceptor may cancel his acceptance before delivery of the bill (which completes the contract), see note (*a*) to section 2; note (*z*) to section 17; and note (*z*) to section 21; see also *Ingham* v. *Primrose*, 7 C. B. N. S. 82.

(*b*) The cancellation of the name of an indorsee to whom a bill had been specially indorsed, and who after erasing his name transferred the bill by delivery, is immaterial; *Fairclough* v. *Pavia*, 9 Ex. 693, where all the authorities are discussed; see further section 64 and the notes thereto.

(*c*) The mere fact of cancelling the signature of the makers of a dishonoured promissory note and writing "paid" on the note, corrected before the note is sent back to the plaintiffs by a memorandum thereon "cancelled in error," cannot be effectual to charge a bank with the receipt of the money, *Prince* v. *Oriental Bank*, 3 Ap. Cas. 325, following *Warwick* v. *Rogers*, 5 M. & G. 340, in which was approved *Novelli* v. *Rossi*, 5 B. & Ad. 757.

64.—(1.) Where a bill or acceptance is materially altered (*a*) without the assent (*b*) of all parties liable on the bill, the bill is avoided except as against a party who has himself made, authorised, or assented (*c*) to the alteration, and subsequent indorsers.

Provided that,

Where a bill has been materially altered, but the alteration is not apparent, and the bill is in the hands of a holder in due course, such holder may avail himself of the bill as if it had not been altered, and may enforce payment of it according to its original tenor (*d*).

(2.) In particular the following alterations are material (*e*), namely, any alteration of the date (*f*), the sum payable (*g*), the time of payment (*h*), the place of payment (*j*), and, where a bill has been accepted generally, the addition of a place of payment (*k*) without the acceptor's assent (*l*).

(*a*) Every written contract is avoided by an alteration in a material part; see *Master* v. *Miller*, 2 H. Bl. 141, 1 Smith, L. C. (8th Edition), 857; see also the cases in the notes to the same; the alteration discharges not only the liability on the bill but on the consideration also, *Alderson* v. *Langdale*, 3 B. & Ad. 660. But it has been held that a bill may at any time be altered in pursuance of the original intention of the parties, or for the purpose of correcting a mistake, *Webber* v. *Maddocks*, 3 Camp. 1; *Kershaw* v. *Cox*, 3 Esp. 246; *Byrom* v. *Thompson*, 11 A. & E. 31; *Hamelin* v. *Bruck*, 9 Q. B. 306; *Bradley* v. *Bardsley*, 14 M. & W. 873. See also the cases in notes (*b*), (*e*) and (*g*) hereto, and in note (*c*) to the last preceding section.

(*b*) As to material alterations made without the assent of the parties, see *Kuill* v. *Williams*, 10 East, 431; *Perring* v. *Hone*, 4 Bing. 28; *Cowie* v. *Halsall*, 4 B. & Ald. 197; *Langton* v. *Lazarus*, 5 M. & W. 629; but in *Sutton* v. *Toomer*, 7 B. & C. 416, the alteration of the rate of interest, though made with the consent of the parties, was held to vitiate the instrument.

(*c*) As to alterations made with the consent of the parties, see *Bathe* v. *Taylor*, 15 East, 412; *Sherrington* v. *Jermyn*, 3 C. & P. 374, *Stevens* v. *Lloyd*, M. & M. 292; *Cariss* v. *Tattersall*, 2 M. & G. 890; approval will do as well as assent, *Jacobs* v. *Hart*, 6 M. & S. 142; so also request, *Walter* v. *Cubley*, 2 C. & M. 151. If altered before it is issued, a new stamp is not requisite; *Downes* v. *Richardson*, 5 B. & Ald 674; *Wright* v. *Inshaw*, 6 Jur. 857; *Sherrington* v. *Jermyn*, *suprà*.

(*d*) In *Burchfield* v. *Moore*, 23 L. J. Q. B. 261; 3 E. & B 683, it was held that an unauthorised alteration of a bill discharges the acceptor, even as against a *bonâ fide* holder, subsequently taking it for value, and without notice of the alteration. But according to the present sub-section that case will not apply if the alteration is not apparent. The word " apparent " does not mean that the holder only should not have had the means of detecting the alteration; but that if the party sought to be bound can at once discern by some incongruity on the face of the note, and point out to the holder that it is not what it was, that is to say, that it has been materially and fraudulently altered, the alteration is an "apparent" one, even though not obvious to all mankind, per Denman, J., in *Leeds Bank* v. *Walker*, 11 Q. B. D. 90.

(*e*) Any alteration of an instrument is material which alters the business effect of the instrument; it need not be such an alteration as affects the contract, *Suffel* v. *Bank of England*, 9 Q. B. D. 555. In addition to those mentioned in the preceding and following notes hereto, the following have been held material alterations, viz.: the addition of the name of a maker, *Gardner* v. *Walsh*, 5 E. & B. 83; 24 L. J. Q. B. 285; and cutting off the name of a maker, *Mason* v. *Bradley*, 11 M. & W. 590; the addition of a party as surety, *Clerk* v. *Blackstock*, Holt's N. P. C. 474. In a recent case it has been held that the alteration of the number of a Bank of England note is material, *Suffell* v. *The Bank of England*, 51 L. J. Q. B. D. 401; 9 Q. B. D. 555, where all the authorities are reviewed and discussed. As regards immaterial alterations, see *Marson* v. *Petit*, 1 Camp. 82 n.; *Trapp* v. *Spearman*, 3 Esp. 57; *Kershaw* v. *Cox*, 2 Esp. 246; *Farquhar* v. *Southey*, M. & M. 14; *Attwood* v. *Griffin*, 2 C. & P. 368; *Calvert* v *Baker*, 4 M. & W. 417; *Simmons* v. *Taylor*, 4 C. B. N. S. 463; 27 L J. C. P. 248; *Walter* v. *Cubley*, 2 Cr & M. 151, *Aldous* v. *Cornwall*, L R. 3 Q. B. 573; 37 L J. Q B. 201; *London and Provincial Bank* v. *Roberts*, 22 W. R. 402.

(*f*) See *Master* v. *Miller*, 2 H. Bl 141; 1 Smith's L C. (8th

Edition) 857; *Bowman* v. *Nicholl*, 5 T. R. 537, 1 Esp. 81; *Sloman* v. *Cox*, 1 C. M. & R. 471, *Outhwaite* v. *Luntly*, 4 Camp. 179; *Walton* v. *Hastings*, 4 Camp. 223; *Leykariff* v. *Ashford*, 12 Moore, 281; *Cardwell* v. *Martin*, 9 East, 190, *Hirschman* v. *Budd*, L. R. 8 Ex. 171; also the alteration of the date of a cheque, *Vance* v. *Lowther*, 1 Ex. D. 176.

(*g*) See *Hamelin* v. *Bruck*, 9 Q. B. 306. So also the addition of interest, *Warrington* v. *Early*, 2 E & B. 763; 23 L. J Q. B. 47. Again, the addition of a particular rate of exchange has been held to be material, *Hirschfield* v. *Smith*, L. R. 1 C. P. 340; 35 L. J. C. P. 177. The cases are collected in the notes to *Master* v. *Miller*, 1 Sm. L. C (8th Ed.) 899 It has been held that a person who accepts a bill which has figures for the amount in the margin, but a blank in the body of it for such amount, holds out the person to whom it is entrusted as having authority to fill in the bill as he pleases within the limits of the stamp, and that no alteration of such marginal figures (which are only an index of the contents), however fraudulent, vitiates the bill as a bill for the full amount inserted in the body when in the hands of a *bonâ fide* holder for value without notice, *Garrard* v. *Lewis*, 10 Q. B. D. 30; 47 L. T. N. S. 408, 31 W. R. 475.

(*h*) See *Paton* v. *Winter*, 1 Taunt. 420; *Alderson* v. *Langdale*, 3 B. & Ad. 660; *Brutt* v. *Picard*, R. & M. 37; *Bathe* v. *Taylor*, 15 East, 412; *Tarleton* v. *Shingler*, 7 C. B. 812.

(*j*) See *Jacobs* v. *Hart*, 6 M. & S. 142; *Stevens* v. *Lloyd*, M. & M. 292; *Cowie* v. *Halsall*, 4 B. & Ald. 197; *Tidmarsh* v. *Grover*, 1 M. & S. 735; *Rex* v. *Treble*, 2 Taunt. 328.

(*k*) And this is so; even though after the addition of the place of payment, the acceptance is still a general acceptance, *Macintosh* v. *Haydon*, Ry. & M. 362; *Desbrowe* v. *Wetherby*, 1 Moo. & Rob. 438; *Taylor* v. *Moseley*, 1 Moo. & Rob. 439, n, *Cowie* v. *Halsall*, 4 B. & Ald 197; *Calvert* v. *Baker*, 4 M. & W. 417, *Crotty* v. *Hodges*, 4 M. & G. 561; *Burchfield* v. *Moore*, 23 L. J. Q. B. 261; 3 E. & B 683, *Hanbury* v. *Lovett*, 18 L. T. N. S. 366, 16 W. R. 795.

(*l*) See *Walter* v. *Cubley*, 2 Cr. & M. 151.

ACCEPTANCE AND PAYMENT FOR HONOUR.

65.—(1.) Where a bill of exchange has been protested for dishonour by non-acceptance (*z*), or protested for better security (*y*), and is not overdue, any person not being a party already liable thereon, may, with the consent of the holder, intervene and accept the bill *suprà protest*, for the honour of any party liable thereon (*x*), or for the honour of the person for whose account the bill is drawn (*w*)

S. 65.

Acceptance
for honour
suprà protest

Ind. Act, ss. 108
& 109.

Ind. Act, s 110

Ind. Act,
ss. 108 & 109

(2.) A bill may be accepted for honour for part only of the sum for which it is drawn (*v*).

(3.) An acceptance for honour *suprà protest* in order to be valid must—

(*a*) be written on the bill, and indicate that it is an acceptance for honour (*t*):

(*b*) be signed by the acceptor for honour (*t*):

(4.) Where an acceptance for honour does not expressly state for whose honour it is made, it is deemed to be an acceptance for the honour of the drawer (*s*).

(5.) Where a bill payable after sight is accepted for honour, its maturity is calculated from the date of the noting for non-acceptance, and not from the date of the acceptance for honour (*r*).

(*z*) See *Mitford* v. *Walcot*, 12 Mod. 410, where the Court said that "if A. draws a bill upon B. and B. refuses to accept it, and C. offers to accept it for the honour of A., the drawee (or holder) need not acquiesce, but may protest, but if he do acquiesce, this acceptance will bind C."

(*y*) As to when and against whom a bill may be protested for better security, see sub-sect. (5) of sect. 51 of this Act and the notes thereto; see also *Ex parte Wackerbath*, 5 Ves. 574, where there was an acceptance by the original drawee, and then an acceptance for the honour of the drawers after protest for better security. An acceptance for honour cannot properly be made until the bill has been protested for non-acceptance; 1 Parsons on Bills, 314; *Hoare* v *Cazenove*, 16 East, 395.

(*x*) Save in the case of acceptances for honour or per procuration, no one can become a party to a bill *quâ acceptor* who is not an addressee, per Lord Watson in *Steele* v. *McKinlay*, 5 Ap. Cas. at p. 779. The difference between an acceptor and an acceptor for honour is that the former is absolutely liable, but the latter only if there has been a presentment of the bill to the drawees for payment, and a protest for non-payment, and that he receives notice of these facts; see sub-sect. (1) of sect. 66 of this Act and the notes thereto, see also *Hoare* v. *Cazenove*, 16 East, 391, 1 Parsons on Bills, 315; Story on Bills, s. 123.

(*w*) There may be successive acceptances for honour by as many persons as there are parties to the bill, each for the honour of one party; but there can be only one such acceptance for one person, 1 Parsons on Bills, s. 315; Story on Bills, s. 122.

(*v*) As an acceptance may be partial (sect. 19, sub-s. 2 (*b*)), so may an acceptance for honour.

(*t*) The method of accepting, *supra protest*, is as follows, viz.: the acceptor, *supra protest*, must personally appear before a notary public, with witnesses, and declare that he accepts such bill for honour, and designate for whose honour he so accepts, and then he must subscribe the bill thus: "Accepted, *supra protest*, in honour of A. B.," &c.; or, as it is more usual. "Accepted, S P;" 1 Parsons on Bills, 318.

(*s*) *Vide* Byles on Bills (13th Edit.), 268; 1 Parsons on Bills, 313.

(*r*) This is new; for hitherto the time has been computed from the date of the acceptance *supra protest*, Byles on Bills (13th Edit.), 270; *Williams* v. *Germaine*, 7 B. & C. 468; 1 Parsons on Bills, 318.

SS. 65, 66, 67.

Acceptance for honour *supra protest.*

Ind. Act, ss. 108 & 109.

66.—(1.) The acceptor for honour of a bill by accepting it engages that he will, on due presentment, pay the bill, according to the tenor of his acceptance, if it is not paid by the drawee, provided it has been duly presented for payment, and protested for non-payment, and that he receives notice of these facts (*a*).

(2.) The acceptor for honour is liable to the holder and to all parties to the bill subsequent to the party for whose honour he has accepted (*b*).

Liability of acceptor for honour.

Ind Act, ss. 111 & 112.

Ind Act, s. 111

(*a*) The undertaking of the acceptor, *supra protest*, is an undertaking to pay, if the original drawee, upon a presentment to him for payment, should persist in dishonouring the bill, and such dishonour be notified, by protest, to the person who has accepted for the honour of the indorser, per Lord Ellenborough in *Hoare* v. *Cazenove*, 16 East, 391; *Williams* v. *Germaine*, 7 B. & C 468, Story on Bills, s 261. The acceptor, *supra protest*, is estopped from denying the genuineness of the signature of the drawer, if he has induced the plaintiffs to part with the money upon the faith of his authentication of the bill, *Phillips* v. *Im Thurn*, L. R. 1 C. P. 464. See Story on Bills, s 262. As to where the protest must be made see sect. 51, sub-s. 6, and the notes thereto.

(*b*) Subject of course to the conditions required by the last preceding sub-section, which see, as also the notes to the same. See Story on Bills, s. 123; and he has his recourse over against the person for whose honour he accepted, and any parties liable to that person, see sect. 68, sub-s. 5, and the notes thereto; Story on Bills, s. 124.

67.—(1.) Where a dishonoured bill has been accepted for honour *supra protest*, or contains a reference in case of need, it must be protested for non-payment before it is presented for payment to the acceptor for honour, or referee in case of need (*a*).

Presentment to acceptor for honour

Ind Act, s 112.

Presentment to
acceptor for
honour.
Ind. Act, s. 111.

(2.) Where the address of the acceptor for honour is in the same place where the bill is protested for non-payment, the bill must be presented to him not later than the day following its maturity (*b*); and where the address of the acceptor for honour is in some place other than the place where it was protested for non-payment, the bill must be forwarded not later than the day following its maturity for presentment to him (*c*).

(3.) Delay in presentment or non-presentment is excused by any circumstance which would excuse delay in presentment for payment or non-presentment for payment (*d*).

(4.) When a bill of exchange is dishonoured by the acceptor for honour, it must be protested for non-payment by him (*e*).

(*a*) See note (*a*) to the last section; also *Hoare* v. *Cazenove*, 16 East, 391; *Williams* v. *Germaine*, 7 B. & C. 468, seems to have decided that protest for non-payment by the drawee was unnecessary. At any rate this sub-section makes such a protest necessary; see also Story on Bills, ss. 123, 396.

(*b*) *Vide* subdivision (*a*) of sub-sect. (12) of sect. 49 of this Act and the notes thereto. The language of this sub-section is similar to that of 6 & 7 Will. 4, c. 58, s. 1, which has been repealed by this Act.

(*c*) See the last preceding note (*b*) hereto.

(*d*) As to the circumstances which would excuse delay in presentment for payment, or non-presentment for payment, see sub-sects. (1) and (2) of sect. 50 of this Act and the subdivisions thereof and notes thereto.

(*e*) See note (*a*) to this section. Mr. Justice Story, in his work on Bills, s. 326, so lays it down. Any of these protests may be waived, *Patterson* v. *Becher*, 6 Moore, 319; *Campbell* v. *Webster*, 2 C. B. 258. See also *Cox* v. *Earle*, 3 B. & Ald. 430.

Payment for
honour *suprà*
protest.
Ind. Act, s 113.

68.—(1.) Where a bill has been protested for non-payment, any person may intervene and pay it *suprà protest* for the honour of any party liable thereon, or for the honour of the person on whose account the bill is drawn (*a*).

(2.) Where two or more persons offer to pay a bill for the honour of different parties, the person whose payment will discharge most parties to the bill shall have the preference (*b*).

S. 68.

Payment for honour *suprà protest.*

(3.) Payment for honour *suprà protest*, in order to operate as such, and not as a mere voluntary payment, must be attested by a notarial act of honour, which may be appended to the protest or form an extension of it (*c*).

Ind. Act, s. 113.

(4.) The notarial act of honour must be founded on a declaration made by the payer for honour, or his agent in that behalf, declaring his intention to pay the bill for honour, and for whose honour he pays (*d*).

Ind Act, s 113

(5.) Where a bill has been paid for honour, all parties subsequent to the party for whose honour it is paid are discharged, but the payer for honour is subrogated for, and succeeds to both the rights and duties of the holder as regards the party for whose honour he pays, and all parties liable to that party (*e*).

Ind Act, s 114

(6) The payer for honour, on paying to the holder the amount of the bill and the notarial expenses incidental to its dishonour, is entitled to receive both the bill itself and the protest (*f*). If the holder do not on demand deliver them up he shall be liable to the payer for honour in damages.

Ind. Act, s. 114.

(7.) Where the holder of a bill refuses to receive payment, *suprà protest*, he shall lose his right of recourse against any party who would have been discharged by such payment.

(*a*) Byles on Bills (13th Ed.), p. 272. Chitty on Bills (11th Ed.), p. 350.

(*b*) There is no section in the Indian Act to correspond with this.

(*c*) "No person could, by paying money simply to the holder of a bill, by a subsequent declaration cause a payment so made to assume the character of a payment for honour," *Geralopulo* v. *Wieler*, 10 C. B. at p. 709. In that case it was pointed out that in *Vandewall* v. *Tyrrell*, M. & M. 87, the payment was made without any declaration before a notary.

(*d*) *Vide* note (c) hereto. This sub-section adopts almost the words of the Court in *Geralopulo* v. *Wieler*, *supra*, at p. 709.

(*e*) So held before this Act, *Ex parte Swan*, *In re Overend, Gurney, & Co*, L. R 6 Eq 344 "The person who takes up a bill *suprà*

SS. 68, 69, 70.

Payment for
honour *suprà*
protest.

protest for the honour of a particular party to the bill, succeeds to the title of the person from whom he receives it, and discharges the parties to the bill subsequent to the one for whose honour he took it up, and he cannot indorse it over," per Malins, V.-C., in *Ex parte Swan, supra*, at p. 367.

(*f*) The holder of the bill, upon payment of it, is bound to deliver it up, per Lord Tenterden, C.J., in *Hansard* v. *Robinson*, 7 B. & C. 90.

LOST INSTRUMENTS.

Holder's right
to duplicate of
lost bill.

69.—Where a bill has been lost before it is overdue, the person who was the holder of it may apply to the drawer to give him another bill of the same tenor, giving security to the drawer, if required, to indemnify him against all persons whatever in case the bill alleged to have been lost shall be found again (*a*). If the drawer on request as aforesaid refuses to give such duplicate bill, he may be compelled to do so (*b*).

(*a*) This is the same as sect. 3 of 9 & 10 Will. 3, c. 17, the provisions of which were afterwards extended to promissory notes by the 3 & 4 Anne, c. 9, which also see. Both these statutes, however, have been repealed by this Act. See the 2nd schedule. If the holder wish to preserve his remedies upon the lost bill, he must give the usual notice of dishonour, *Thackray* v. *Blackett*, 3 Camp. 164.

(*b*) There was a similar provision in section 3 of 9 & 10 Will. 3, c. 17. And this power will, it is submitted, be exercised by the Courts of Equity or the Chancery Division of the High Court of Justice, unless the claim for a duplicate Bill be not a substantial part of the claim in an action, see sub-sect. (3) of sect. 34 of the Judicature Act of 1873. In *Rhodes* v. *Morse*, 14 Jur. 800, this power was exercised.

Action on lost
bill.

70. In any action or proceeding upon a bill, the Court or a Judge may order that the loss of the instrument shall not be set up, provided an indemnity be given to the satisfaction of the Court or Judge against the claims of any other person upon the instrument in question (*a*).

(*a*) This is the same as sect. 87 of the 17 & 18 Vict. c. 125, and 19 & 20 Vict. c. 102, s. 90, within which bank-notes have been held to come, *M'Donnell* v. *Murray*, 9 Ir. Com. Law Rep. 495; see also *Noble* v. *Bank of England*, 2 H. & C. 355; 33 L. J. Ex. 81; 9 Jur. N. S. 778; 8 L. T. N. S. 733. Half-notes have also been held to be within the 87th section of that Act. *Redmayne* v. *Burton*, 2 L. T. N. S. 324; see also *Smith* v. *Mundy*, 3 E. & E. 22; 6 Jur. N. S. 977; 29 L. J. Q. B. 172; 2 L. T. N. S. 373. See note (*h*) to sect. 83, "Bank Notes." Where a plaintiff brought an action on a lost bill of exchange against the acceptor without first offering to give him an indemnity against the claims of other persons on the bill, the Court, in the exercise of its discretion under sect. 87 of the Common Law Procedure Act, 1854, ordered that the loss of the bill should not be set up as a defence to the action, only on the terms that the plaintiff should pay the defendant his costs of the action up to that time as well as give a proper indemnity against such claims, *King* v. *Zimmerman*, 40 L. J. C. P. 278, L. R. 6 C. P. 466. Sect. 87 of the 17 & 18 Vict. only applied to the Superior Courts. A plaintiff who sued on a lost bill or note in the County Court, could not avail himself of the privilege given by that Act, *vide Noble* v. *The Bank of England* (*supra*). It is submitted that as the language of the present section is the same as that of sect. 87 of the former statute, and that as the words, the Court or a judge, are used (which always relate to actions in the High Court of Justice, and especially to applications in them which have to be made in the first instance before a Master), a plaintiff who may happen to bring an action on a lost bill in a County Court, cannot now either avail himself of such privilege.

BILL IN A SET.

71.—(1.) Where a bill is drawn in a set, each part of the set being numbered, and containing a reference to the other parts, the whole of the parts constitute one bill (*a*).

(2.) Where the holder of a set indorses two or more parts to different persons, he is liable on every such part, and every indorser subsequent to him is liable on the part he has himself indorsed as if the said parts were separate bills (*b*).

(3.) Where two or more parts of a set are negotiated to different holders in due course, the holder whose title first accrues is as between such holders deemed the true owner of the bill (*c*); but nothing in this sub-section shall affect the rights of a person who in due course accepts or pays the part first presented to him (*d*).

(4.) The acceptance may be written on any part (*e*), and

Rules as to sets.

Ind. Act, s 132

Ind. Act, s. 132 Exception.

Ind. Act, s 133

Ind Act, s. 132. Exception

S. 71.

Rules as to
sets.

it must be written on one part only (*f*). If the drawee accepts more than one part, and such accepted parts get into the hands of different holders in due course, he is liable on every such part as if it were a separate bill (*g*).

(5.) When the acceptor of a bill drawn in a set pays it without requiring the part bearing his acceptance to be delivered up to him, and that part at maturity is outstanding in the hands of a holder in due course, he is liable to the holder thereof (*h*).

Ind. Act,s 132.

(6.) Subject to the preceding rules, where any one part of a bill drawn in a set is discharged by payment or otherwise, the whole bill is discharged (*j*).

(*a*) It is common, says Mr. Justice Story, in his work on Bills, to deliver to the payee several parts, commonly called a set, of the same bill of exchange, any one of which being paid, the others are to be void, s 66. See also *Société Générale* v. *The Metropolitan Bank, Lim.,* 27 L. T. N. S. 849. Where a bill drawn in different parts was negotiated by (among other persons) the defendants, and it was ultimately indorsed to the plaintiff, and neither the plaintiff nor the defendants had ever had possession of any part other than the first, nor were the defendants able to obtain possession of the other parts, and the plaintiff, having lost the part which was indorsed to him, brought an action against the defendants for not delivering over the other parts, it was held that no action would lie against them as there was no obligation upon them to hand the other parts to the plaintiff, *Pinard* v. *Klockman,* 3 B. & S 388; 32 L. J. Q. B. 82. It has been held that if two bills are given for the same debt, and for the whole amount of it, *bonâ fide* holders for value can enforce each bill; *Davison* v. *Robertson,* 3 Dow, 218. It is only necessary to stamp one part (33 & 34 Vict. c. 97, s. 55), but it is not negligence to stamp more than one, *Société Générale* v. *Metropolitan Bank, supra.*

(*b*) Per Lord Tenterden, C.J., and Parke, J., in *Holdsworth* v. *Hunter,* 10 B. & C. 449.

(*c*) Per Lord Tenterden, C.J., in *Holdsworth* v. *Hunter, supra,* at p. 454.

(*d*) See *Kearney* v. *The West Granada Gold and Silver Mining Company,* 1 H. & N. 412; Story on Bills, s. 226.

(*e*) This is the same as the provision in sect. 6 of 19 & 20 Vict. c. 97, which has been repealed by this Act.

(*f*) See *Holdsworth* v. *Hunter,* 10 B. & C. 449.

(*g*) Following the opinion of Lord Tenterden, C.J., and Parke, J., in *Holdsworth* v. *Hunter,* 10 B. & C. 449, *supra.*

(*h*) See per Watson, B., in *Kearney* v. *West Granada Gold and Silver Mining Company,* 1 H. & N. 412; Story on Bills, sect. 226.

(*j*) See Story on Bills, sect. 226; Byles on Bills (13th Edition), 394.

SS. 71, 72.

Rules as to sets.

CONFLICT OF LAWS.

72.—Where a bill drawn in one country is negotiated, accepted, or payable in another, the rights, duties, and liabilities of the parties thereto are determined as follows (*a*):

Rules where laws conflict.

> (1.) The validity of a bill as regards requisites in form is determined by the law of the place of issue, and the validity as regards requisites in form of the supervening contracts, such as acceptance, or indorsement, or acceptance *suprà protest,* is determined by the law of the place where such contract was made (*b*).

Ind. Act, s. 134

Provided that—

(*a*) Where a bill is issued out of the United Kingdom, it is not invalid by reason only that it is not stamped in accordance with the law of the place of issue (*c*):

(*b*) Where a bill, issued out of the United Kingdom, conforms, as regards requisites in form, to the law of the United Kingdom, it may, for the purpose of enforcing payment thereof, be treated as valid as between all persons who negotiate, hold, or become parties to it in the United Kingdom.

> (2.) Subject to the provisions of this Act, the interpretation of the drawing (*d*), indorsement (*e*), acceptance (*f*), or acceptance *suprà protest* (*g*), of a bill, is determined by the law of the place where such contract is made.

Ind Act, s 134

Provided that where an inland bill is indorsed in a foreign country, the indorsement shall as regards the payer be interpreted according to the law of the United Kingdom (*h*).

> (3.) The duties of the holder with respect to presentment for acceptance or payment and the necessity for or

Ind Act, ss. 134 & 135.

S. 72.

Rules where
laws conflict.

sufficiency of a protest or notice of dishonour, or otherwise, are determined by the law of the place where the act is done (*j*) or the bill is dishonoured (*k*).

(4.) Where a bill is drawn out of but payable in the United Kingdom, and the sum payable is not expressed in the currency of the United Kingdom, the amount shall, in the absence of some express stipulation, be calculated according to the rate of exchange for sight drafts at the place of payment on the day the bill is payable (*l*).

Ind. Act, s. 135.

(5) Where a bill is drawn in one country and is payable in another, the due date thereof is determined according to the law of the place where it is payable (*m*).

(*a*) See Story's Conflict of Laws (8th Edit.), Chapter VIII.; also Byles on Bills (13th Edit.), pp. 400, 401.

(*b*) The general rule established *ex comitate et jure gentium* is that the place where the contract is made, and not where the action is brought, is to be considered in expounding and enforcing the contract, unless the parties have a view to a different kingdom, that is to say, unless the contract is to be performed in another place, then it is to be governed by the law of the place where it is to be performed, *Robinson* v. *Bland*, 1 W. Blackstone, 258 (per Lord Mansfield, C.J.); *Gibbs* v. *Fremont*, 9 Ex. 25; *Scott* v. *Pilkington*, 2 B. & S. 11; 31 L. J. Q. B. 81; or unless it is forbidden in or contrary to the public policy of the country where it is made, *Forbes* v. *Cochrane*, 2 B. & C. 471, *Hope* v. *Hope*, 8 De G. M. & G. 731, 26 L. J. Ch. 417. So also as to bills or notes, their validity as regards requisites in form is, as provided in this section, determined by the law of the place of issue. All the various provisions of this section are founded upon the abovementioned principles.

(*c*) "No country," said Lord Mansfield, C.J., "takes notice of the revenue laws of another," *Holman* v. *Johnson*, Cowp at p. 343. See also Story on Bills, p. 150, note; *Bristow* v. *Sequeville*, 5 Ex. 279 (where it was held that if a bill be *void* without a stamp in the foreign country, it cannot be enforced here), following *Clegg* v. *Levy*, 3 Camp. 166.

(*d*) See note (*b*) hereto; also *Allen* v. *Kemble*, 6 Moo. P. C. C. 314; remarked on in *Rouquette* v. *Overmann*, L. R 10 Q. B. at p. 540.

(*e*) See note (*b*) hereto. See also *Trimby* v. *Vignier*, 1 Bing N. C. 151; 6 C. & P. 25, *Bradlaugh* v. *De Rin*, L. R. 3 C. P. 538; 5 C. P. 473, and the remarks about this last case in Story's Conflict of Laws, 8th Ed., p. 440, n. But see the exception in the latter part of this sub-section and note (*h*).

(*f*) See note (*b*) hereto. The acceptor cannot be made liable under any law but his own, *Rouquette* v. *Overmann*, L. R. 10 Q. B. at p. 536. See also *Burrows* v. *Jemino*, 2 Stra. 733; *Sprowle* v. *Legge*, 1 B. & C. 16; *Kearney* v. *King*, 2 B. & Ald. 301. But if a bill is made payable at a particular place the contract of acceptance is governed by the law of acceptance at that place; see the cases on the question of the *lex loci solutionis* in the note (*b*) hereto.

(*g*) See note (*f*) hereto.

(*h*) So decided in *Lebel* v. *Tucker*, L. R. 3 Q. B. 77; *Bradlaugh* v. *De Rin*, L R. 5 C. P. 473; 39 L. J. C. P. 254. See the observations upon these two cases in Story's Conflict of Laws, 8th Ed., p. 440, n., where he says that *Lebel* v. *Tucker* is clearly correct.

(*j*) See *Burrows* v. *Jemino*, 2 Stra. 733; *Wilkinson* v. *Simson*, 2 Moo P. C. C. 275; *Potter* v. *Brown*, 5 East, 124; *Allen* v. *Kemble*, 6 Moo. P. C. C. 314; *Ralli* v. *Dennistoun*, 6 Ex. 483; *Symons* v. *May*, 6 Ex. 707; see also *Bartley* v. *Hodges*, 30 L. J. Q. B. 352, *Ellis* v. *M'Henry*, L. R. 6 C. P. at p. 234; *Rouquette* v. *Overmann*, L. R. 10 Q. B. at p. 535.

(*k*) See *Rothschild* v. *Currie*, 1 Q. B 43; *Hirschfield* v. *Smith*, 35 L. J. C. P. 177; L. R. 1 C. P. 340. "The liability of each of the contracting parties to the other is to be determined by the law of the country in which the contract was made," per Brett, L.J., in *Horne* v. *Rouquette*, 3 Q. B. D. at p. 520.

(*l*) See Story's Conflict of Laws, 2nd Ed., p. 426; *Hirschfield* v. *Smith*, 35 L. J. C. P. 177; L. R. 1 C. P. 340.

(*m*) See *Rouquette* v. *Overmann*, L. R. 10 Q. B. at p. 535.

S. 72.

Rules where laws conflict.

PART III.

——

CHEQUES ON A BANKER.

73.—A cheque is a bill of exchange drawn on a banker payable on demand (*a*).

Except as otherwise provided in this Part, the provisions of this Act applicable to a bill of exchange payable on demand apply to a cheque (*b*).

(*a*) By sect. 3, sub-sect. 1, a bill of exchange payable on demand is defined to be "an unconditional order in writing, addressed by one person to another, signed by the person giving it, requiring the person to whom it is addressed to pay on demand a sum certain in money to or to the order of a specified person or to bearer." Substituting the word "banker" in this definition where necessary, we have the following definition of a cheque:—"A cheque is an unconditional order in writing, addressed by a person to a banker, signed by the person giving it, requiring the banker to whom it is addressed to pay on demand a sum certain in money to or to the order of a specified person or to bearer." As to the different terms in this definition, see sect 3, and the notes thereto. As to the relation between banker and customer see note to sect. 2.

A cheque may be ante-dated or post-dated, or it may be dated on a Sunday; sect. 13, sub-sect. 2, of this Act. There is now no minimum limit for which a cheque may be drawn. As to the old law on the subject, see Byles on Bills, 13th Edit., 17. It may happen that the sum written in words is different from the sum expressed in figures. In that case the law is the same now (sect. 9, sub-sect. 2) as it was before this Act, namely, that the sum denoted by the words is the amount payable, *Saunderson* v. *Piper*, 5 Bing. N. C. 425; 7 Scott, 408. In America the rule is that the figures in the margin are merely a memorandum for convenience of reference, and form no part of the bill or cheque, and an alteration in them making them conform to the body of the instrument, does not vitiate the instrument; see Parsons on Notes, vol. 1, p. 28, note (*w*). In the recent case of *Garrard* v. *Lewis*,

10 Q. B. D. 30; 47 L. T. N. S. 408; 31 W. R. 475, it was held that where a bill was signed in blank with marginal figures only, the bill was not a perfect bill, till the amount in the body was filled in, and hence that an alteration, however fraudulent, of the marginal figures does not vitiate the bill for the full amount inserted in the body, when in the hands of a holder in due course, who has no notice of the improper alteration. If the words are written in the body of the cheque so obscurely that their meaning is doubtful, the figures in the margin and the stamp may be referred to as shewing the intention of the parties, *Hutley* v *Marshall*, 46 L. T. N. S. 186, so held also in America in *Riley* v. *Dickens*, 19 Ill. 29. Where both the sum mentioned in the body and the sum mentioned in the margin or at the foot are expressed in figures, and there is a discrepancy between the two, there is a patent ambiguity on the face of the cheque, and evidence cannot be produced to explain what sum was intended to be payable (*Saunderson* v. *Piper*, *supra*), and the question arises for which sum is the cheque to be taken as drawn. It is submitted that in such a case the amount expressed in the body of the cheque, though in figures, would, on the authority of *Garrard* v. *Lewis* (*supra*), be the amount for which the cheque would be payable. An omission in the body may be aided by figures in the margin, where they are not contradictory, as for instance, where the sum was in the body expressed to be "twenty-five, seventeen shillings, and three pence," the figures in the margin being "25 „ 17 „ 3," the Court held the sum to be twenty-five pounds, seventeen shillings and three pence, *Phipps* v. *Tanner*, 5 C. & P 488, Tindal, C.J., saying, it must mean pounds, it cannot mean anything else, again, where "fifty" was put in the body, the word "pounds" being omitted, while £50 was in the margin, *Elliot's Case*, 1 Leach, 175. A mere slip, which renders the statement of the sum payable merely inaccurate, will not invalidate a cheque. For instance, an instrument which stated "pay A. B. seventeen, or bearer pounds," was held good for £17 payable to A. B. or bearer; *R.* v. *Boreham*, 2 Cox, C. C. 189; see also *Burnham* v. *Allen*, 67 Mass. Rep. 496, where the note was expressed to be for "three hundred dollars," and the figures in the margin were "$300," it was held that the note was good for three hundred dollars. A cheque must be signed by the party drawing it; see sect. 3, note (*w*), and sect. 23. The drawer's initials will be sufficient, *Merchant's Bank* v. *Spicer*, 6 Wend. 443, which was a decision in America that an indorsement by initials was sufficient to charge the indorser; though, of course, the banker on whom the cheque is drawn would not be liable, if he refused to pay such a cheque, unless he knew whose the initials were, or had usually paid the drawer's cheques so signed. A cheque of any sort may now be post-dated; see sect. 13, sub-sect. 2. As to the old law upon this point, see *Fisher on the Stamp Act*, 1870. If a person takes a cheque, whether payable to order or to bearer, that is post-dated, with know-

ledge of its having been post-dated, such cheque only having a penny stamp upon it, it was held that he could sue upon it, and that it was admissible in evidence, the question being, is the stamp sufficient upon the face of the instrument? *Bull* v. *O'Sullivan*, L. R. 6 Q. B. 209; 40 L. J. Q. B. 141; *Gatty* v. *Fry*, 2 Ex. D. 265, 36 L. T. N. S. 152.

(*b*) In the decisions prior to this act cheques were always considered as analogous to bills of exchange; " a cheque is a bill of exchange payable at a bankers," per Jessel, M.R., in *Hopkinson* v. *Forster*, L. R. 19 Eq. at p. 76; *Cruger* v. *Armstrong*, 3 John. Cas. 5; see also *Keene* v. *Beard*, 8 C. B. N. S. 372; 29 L. J. C. P. 287; *Deener* v. *Brown*, 28 Amer. Rep. 602, note, *British Linen Co. Bank* v. *Carruthers*, Court of Sess. Cas., 4th Ser., vol. 10, at p. 926. The following are some of the differences between cheques and bills of exchange:

(1) A banker does not generally accept a cheque, per Erle, C.J., in *Keene* v. *Beard*, *supra*; the reason being that the banker is the debtor of his customer to the extent of the funds that he holds on his customer's account, with the obligation imposed upon him arising out of the custom of bankers of honouring his customer's drafts, so that he has no option but to pay his customer's cheques to the extent of his customer's funds, *Foley* v. *Hill*, 2 H. L. C. 28. The bank only acts as the agent for the depositor, and so under ordinary circumstances owes no duty to the holder of a cheque, and is liable to no action by him for refusing to pay it, although it has sufficient funds for the purpose, as there is no privity between them, *Schroeder* v. *Central Bank of London*, 34 L. T. N. S. 735; 24 W. R. 710; unless the bank has, so to speak, accepted it by marking it, and communicated such marking to the holder, *Warwick* v. *Rogers*, 5 M. & G. 340, see also observations of Parke, B, in *Bellamy* v. *Marjoribanks*, 7 Ex. at p. 404; see also the American cases (which are contradictory, though on the whole they agree with the English cases), collected in *Parsons on Notes and Bills*, vol. 2, p. 61, note (*j*). It is said in *Parsons*, vol 2, at p. 61, that "while, therefore, we admit that a bank may be liable in a proper action to a holder of a cheque for a wanton or fraudulent refusal to pay the cheque, whereby the holder lost the funds, we should say that only in such cases could any action be maintained against the bank for the refusal." In *Risley* v. *Phœnix Bank*, 83 N. Y Rep. 318, it was held that a verbal promise to pay a cheque created no cause of action   See also *Security Bank* v. *National Bank*, 23 Amer. Rep 129, 67 N. Y. Rep. 458, where it is said that a bank, by certifying a cheque, undertakes that the signature of the drawer is genuine, and that there are sufficient funds to meet it, and engages that they will not be withdrawn to the prejudice of the holder, but does not warrant the genuineness of the body of the cheque. Such " marking" occurs frequently between bankers in the case of cheques paid in after clearing time, as to which see sect. 74 note (*a*), but not as between bankers and private persons.

(2.) The drawer of a cheque is only discharged by the holder making delay in presenting it for payment, when he has thereby suffered damage, and then to the extent of such damage, see next section, and the notes thereto.

(3.) Notice of the death of the drawer of a cheque is a determination of the authority of the banker to pay it. This is dealt with in sect. 75, sub-sect. 2, and note thereto. As to a banker paying a cheque in ignorance of the drawer's death, see note to sect. 75, sub-sect. 2.

(4.) A cheque is supposed to be drawn against funds. It was at one time thought that a cheque was an appropriation of so much money of the drawer's in the hands of the banker upon whom it was drawn for the purpose of discharging a debt or liability of the drawer to the payee. The case of *Hopkinson* v. *Forster*, L. R. 19 Eq. 74; 23 W. R. 301, however, decided that a cheque was not an equitable assignment of money in the hands of a banker. This was followed and approved in *Schroeder* v. *Central Bank*, 34 L. T. N. S. 735, 24 W. R. 710. And sect. 53, sub-sect. 1, of this Act now provides that a cheque is not an appropriation of a particular sum of money, except in Scotland, where, if the drawee has in hand funds available for the payment thereof, the bill operates as an assignment of the sum for which it is drawn in favour of the holder, from the time when the bill is presented to the drawee; sect. 53, sub-sect. 2, and the notes thereto. The law is the same in America; *Lunt* v. *Bank of North America*, 49 Barb. 221.

74.—Subject to the provisions of this Act—

(1.) Where a cheque is not presented (*a*) for payment within a reasonable time of its issue (*b*), and the drawer or the person on whose account it is drawn had the right at the time of such presentment, as between him and the banker, to have the cheque paid, and suffers actual damage through the delay, he is discharged to the extent of such damage, that is to say, to the extent to which such drawer or person is a creditor of such banker to a larger amount than he would have been had such cheque been paid (*c*).

(2) In determining what is a reasonable time regard shall be had to the nature of the instrument, the usage of trade and of bankers, and the facts of the particular case (*d*).

(3) The holder of such cheque as to which such drawer or person is discharged shall be a creditor, in

S 74.

Presentment of cheque for payment.

lieu of such drawer or person, of such banker to the extent of such discharge, and entitled to recover the amount from him.

(a) Banking hours in London are from 9 a.m. to 4 p m., and on Saturdays from 9 a.m. to 3 p.m , during which hours cheques must be presented. Open, *i e.* uncrossed, cheques are paid over the counter in large numbers, but crossed cheques are paid into the holder's bank, and presented by it. Instead of sending round to each bank upon which a cheque is drawn and presenting it there, the London bankers have established the Clearing House, where all cheques are sent, presentment there being a good presentment, *Reynolds* v. *Chettle,* 2 Camp. 596; *Harris* v. *Packer,* 3 Tyr. 370, n. The following account of the Clearing House has been furnished by the courtesy of a gentleman of high position in one of the leading London Banks. The Clearing House was established by private bankers, and the joint-stock banks were afterwards admitted. The banks belonging to it are twenty-eight in number, no banks west of Temple Bar being admitted. Country bankers clear through their London correspondents. The Clearing House is a large room in which each bank using it has a certain number of seats, where its clearing clerks sit. All cheques received by one bank drawn upon other banks are entered at the receiving bank on a sheet against the name of the bank on which they are drawn; and between the hours of 10.30 and 11 a m., and 2.30 and 3.55 p m. (in the case of country cheques between 12 and 12.30 p.m) these cheques are sent on to the Clearing House, and given to the clearing clerks of the banks on which they are drawn. Each clearing clerk enters the cheques drawn on his bank, and sends them on to his bank, when they are cancelled and retained, or returned the same day if there are no funds to meet them. At the close of the day the sheets of the different banks are compared and balances struck. An account is kept at the Bank of England called the Clearing Bankers' account, and if the balance is against any particular bank, that bank gives a cheque for such balance upon its private account at the Bank of England to the Clearing Bankers' account, by which means accounts are adjusted. When cheques are paid into a bank too late for clearing, it is the practice to send such cheques on to the banks on which they are drawn, where as a matter of courtesy between bankers they are "marked" if intended to be paid. If so marked, the bank marking them is bound to pay them the next day when passed through the Clearing House, and in fact they are entered as paid when they are marked. This custom of marking cheques has, for some time, received judicial sanction; for instance in *Robson* v. *Bennett,* 2 Taunt., 388, where such marking was considered equivalent to an acceptance; again, in *Goodwin* v. *Robarts,* L. R. 10 Ex. at p. 351, the Court said that a

custom had grown up among bankers of "marking" cheques as good
for the purpose of clearance by which they became bound to one
another (per Cockburn, C.J.). The name of the London agent on a
country cheque is put on for clearing purposes; and though it has
been held that presentment to the London agent is not sufficient
(*Bailey* v. *Bodenham*, 16 C. B. N. S. 288; 33 L. J. C. P. at p.
255), still if presented to him through the Clearing House in the
customary manner, as is invariably the case, such presentment might
now be held sufficient. A presentment must be made by some person
authorised to receive the money for the cheque; see sect. 45, sub-
sect. 3. A presentment by post, however, may be made where
authorised by agreement or usage; see sect. 45, sub-sect. 8, and the
notes thereto. It would seem that presentment for payment is dispensed with in the case of the notorious stoppage of the bank on
which the cheque is drawn, Byles on Bills, 13th Edit., 207; but under
such circumstances the holder is only bound to give notice within a
reasonable time after he has acquired the knowledge of the stoppage of
the bank, and not, necessarily, before the expiration of time for
presentment, *Robson* v. *Oliver*, 10 Q. B. 704; 16 L. J. Q. B. 437; see
also *Bowes* v. *Howe*, 5 Taunt. 30; *Cumidge* v. *Allenby*, 6 B. & C. 373;
and *Sands* v. *Clarke*, 19 L. J. C. P. 84; Story on Notes, ss 500, 502;
but notice of such stoppage must be given within a reasonable time
after the holder knows of the stoppage of the bank, with an offer to
return the cheque; otherwise the holder elects to make the cheque
his own, and releases all parties except the drawer; see *Rogers* v.
Langford, 1 Cr. & M. 637. Sect. 46, sub-sect. 2 (*a*) enacts that the
fact that the holder has reason to believe that the bill will on presentment be dishonoured, does not dispense with the necessity for presentment. That section raises the question whether presentment is now
necessary in the case of the notorious stoppage of the bank on which
the cheque is drawn, and would seem to override the former law on
the subject, as laid down by the cases already cited; but whether it
does actually do so or not is doubtful, and in the absence of any
judicial decision upon it, it is not necessary to express any definite
opinion. As to cases to which that section does apply, see the notes
to that section. Like a bill of exchange, presentment of a cheque for
payment is excused, as against the drawer, by want of sufficient funds
in the banker's hands to meet the cheque at the time when the drawer
would expect the cheque to be presented, provided that the drawer
had no reason to expect that it would be paid, *Wirth* v. *Austin*, L. R.
10 C. P. 689; *Brush* v. *Barrett*, 82 N. Y. Rep. 400; but not as against
an indorser, *Mohawk Bank* v. *Broderick*, 10 Wend. 304; see also
sect. 46, sub-sect. 2 (*c*) of this Act, and the notes thereto. Notice of
dishonour to the drawer is dispensed with under similar circumstances,
as to which see sect. 50, sub-sect. 2 (c. 4) of this Act, and the notes
thereto, *Carew* v *Duckworth*, L R. 4 Ex. 313; *Bickerdike* v. *Bollman*,

S. 74.

———

Presentment of
cheques for
payment.

2 Sm. L. C. 8th Ed., 51; 1 T. R. 405. The want of funds need not be a total want of funds; want of sufficient funds to draw against is enough, the question being whether there were any such funds as the drawer might reasonably and properly draw against, with an expectation that the draft would be honoured; *Carew* v. *Duckworth, supra.* The law was similarly laid down in 1843 in an elaborate judgment by Story, J., in *In the matter of Brown,* 2 Story R. at p. 516, cited in Story on Notes, at pp. 657–660; and also in *Fletcher* v. *Pierson,* 35 Amer. Rep. 214. Again, if the drawer has funds at his banker's sufficient to meet the cheque, but knows that the bankers will not pay the cheque, he is nevertheless entitled to notice of dishonour, *Carew* v. *Duckworth,* L. R. 4 Ex. at p. 319. But the holder must present the cheque under such circumstances, sect. 46, sub-sect. 2 (a) of this Act, and the notes thereto.

(*b*). As to the meaning of a "reasonable time" see note (*d*) to sub-sect. 2 of this section. As to the meaning of "Issue," see sect. 2 of this Act and note (*l*) thereto.

(*c*) The drawer of a cheque is discharged by the fact of the cheque not being duly presented for payment only when he has sustained actual damage by the delay; e.g., by the failure of the bank on which the cheque is drawn, and then to the extent of such damage he is discharged; otherwise the holder does not lose his remedy against the drawer until barred at the end of six years, 2 Parsons on Bills, 74; *Robinson* v. *Hawksford,* 9 Q. B. 52; *Little* v. *Phœnix Bank,* 2 Hill N. Y. R. 425, *Hopkins* v. *Ware,* L. R. 4 Ex. 268, where it was held that a creditor, who takes from his debtor's agent on account of the debt the cheque of the agent, is bound to present it for payment within a reasonable time; otherwise if the delay alters the debtor's position for the worse, the debtor is discharged, although he was not a party to the cheque; see also *Alexander* v. *Burchfield,* 7 M. & G. at p. 1067; *Laws* v. *Rand,* 3 C. B. N. S. 442; 27 L. J. C. P. 76. In a note to *Serle* v. *Norton,* 2 Moo. & Rob. 404, it is said:—"It is difficult to see how a solvent drawer, on a solvent banker, can be prejudiced by delay in the presentment of a cheque... But the refusal to pay by bankers may arise from other causes than their own insolvency. The drawer of the cheque may have become insolvent, or have withdrawn his account. Another reason for the bankers refusing to pay may be the staleness of the cheque, it being understood as a rule of business with regular bankers not to pay old cheques without inquiry;" and the note goes on to add that the holder must give the drawer an opportunity of authorising his bankers to pay it. The latter part of this sub-section is new. Formerly the drawer was absolutely discharged if the banker failed (but the holder could prove for the amount of the cheque against the banker's estate). Now, by the operation of this sub-section and sub-sect. 3, the drawer is discharged only to the extent of the damage he suffers, and the holder is entitled to prove against the insolvent banker's estate, or recover from him the amount in respect of which the drawer is discharged; and this seems to have always been the law in America, Story on Notes, s. 492. For example, a cheque is drawn for £100, and not presented within a reasonable time. The banker fails, the drawer having at the time sufficient money in his hands to meet the cheque. The banker pays 10s. in the £. The drawer is only discharged as to £50, and as to that the holder can prove against the banker's estate for it, when he will get 10s. in the £ on that sum, viz., £25.

(d) The question of reasonable time may be considered as follows.— Where the person taking the cheque and the banker on whom it is drawn live in the same place, the person taking the cheque has the whole of the banking hours of the next business day within which he may present it, in order to charge the drawer if the bank fails, *Boddington* v. *Schlencker*, 4 B. & Ad at p. 759; *Robson* v. *Bennett*, 2 Taunt. 388; *Moule* v. *Brown*, 4 Bing. N. C. 266; 5 Scott, 694; 2 Parsons on Bills, 72, *Alexander* v. *Burchfield*, 7 M. & G. 1061; 3 Scott, N. R. 555, in which latter case it was decided that the holder of a cheque is bound to present it for payment not later than the day following that on which he receives it, whether the presentment is made through his bankers, or by himself. In *Bond* v. *Warden*, 14 L. J. Ch. 154, a cheque was given to the payee in the town where it was drawn and payable, but after banking hours. The payee sent it the same evening to his bankers at a town six miles away, and it was paid into his bank next morning. It was then sent by post on that day to the bank on which it was drawn, and presented on the following day, that is, two days after it was drawn. Held, a presentment in time. The rule, however, is different if the person taking the cheque and the banker on whom it is drawn do not live in the same place, for then the rule laid down in the cases is that the person taking it should send it to his banker or agent by the next business day's post, and he should present it on the next business day in order to charge the drawer if the bank fails, *Rickford* v. *Ridge*, 2 Camp. 537, *Hare* v. *Henty*, 10 C. B. N. S. 65, 30 L. J. C. P. 302; *Bailey* v. *Bodenham*, 16 C. B. N. S. 288; 33 L. J. C. P. 252; *Prideaux* v. *Criddle*, L. R. 4 Q. B. 455; *Heywood* v. *Pickering*, L. R. 9 Q. B. 428, where the cheque was on a foreign bank, and was sent direct to it by post; see also Byles on Bills, 13th Ed. 21; Chalmers on Bills, 2nd Ed., 229, Story on Notes, s. 493. As between customer and banker, where the customer sends him a cheque for presentment, the rule is the same unless circumstances exist from which a contract or duty on the part of the banker to present earlier or to defer presentment can be inferred, per Erle, C.J., in *Hare* v. *Henty*, *supra* at p. 88. In Story on Notes, s. 496, it is said that though each party to a cheque is as between himself and the party from whom he received it allowed a day to present it, the drawer and every holder is only liable on due presentment and dishonour within the time for which he would be liable if the cheque had been presented by the party immediately claiming from and under him. Where a cheque was drawn on a banker at B., cashed by a branch of the N. W. bank at M., and forwarded to the head office of the N. W. bank at K., all on the same day; but the head office did not present it for three days, the presentment was held too late to charge the drawer, the bank having failed, *Moule* v. *Brown*, 4 Bing. N. C. 266; 5 Scott, 694. If the drawer, or other party to the cheque, is discharged by delay in presentment, no action can be brought to recover the consideration given for the cheque; as, in the words of Blackburn, J., in *Heywood* v. *Pickering*, L. R. 9 Q. B. p. 431, the holder by his conduct makes the cheque his own; it is then equivalent to absolute payment. It will be noticed that the rules as to what is a reasonable time for presenting a cheque are practically the same as those as to what is reasonable time for giving notice of dishonour. See sub-sects. 12 and 13 of sect. 49 of this Act, and the notes thereto.

The subject of cheques may be further considered as follows.

OVERDUE CHEQUES.

A bill payable on demand is deemed to be overdue when it appears to have been in circulation for an unreasonable length of time; as to which see sub-section (3) of section 36, and notes (*w*) and (*v*) thereto. A cheque, however, is very often, especially when crossed, cashed by a tradesman, or paid away in the purchase of goods. It then becomes important to find out what rule, if any, has been laid down as to when a cheque is overdue, and so subject to any defect of title. The law on this point has been lately considered by Field, J., in the *London & County Banking Co.* v. *Groome*, 8 Q. B. D. 288. The following are the chief cases:—in *Down* v. *Halling*, 4 B. & C. 330; 6 D. & R 455 (which is not approved of in *Bank of Bengal* v. *Fagan*, 7 Moo. P. C. at p 72), a cheque for £50 was lost, and it was tendered five days after its date at a shop in payment for goods; the shopkeeper took it, and on the next day presented it for payment, when it was cashed; the true owner brought an action against the shopkeeper to recover the money and succeeded, the defendant having taken it when overdue, and under circumstances which ought to have excited the suspicions of a prudent man, and so, as his transferor had no title, he could get no better title. In *Rothschild* v. *Corney*, 9 B. & C. 388, two cheques had been fraudulently obtained from the drawer, and the defendants, who took them *bonâ fide* six days after date, gave cash for them to a third person who had not given value for them, presented them and received the amount; it was held, in an action by the drawer to recover back the money, that it was not true as a matter of law that a party taking a cheque at any fixed time after date does so at his peril, though the taking an overdue cheque is a circumstance which the jury may take into consideration in determining whether the defendants took the cheque under circumstances which ought to have excited the suspicions of prudent men. This last decision was followed in *London and County Banking Co.* v. *Groome*, 8 Q. B. D. 288; 51 L. J. Q. B. D. 224, 46 L. T. N. S. 60; 30 W. R. 382, where the question for the jury was considered to be whether the holder took the cheque under such circumstances as ought reasonably to have excited his suspicion, and that the lapse of time between the date of the cheque and the transfer was a circumstance to be taken into their consideration in coming to a conclusion on that question; see also *Serrell* v. *Derbyshire, &c, Railway Co.*, 9 C. B. at p. 826. A cheque does not take effect till delivery, sect. 21; so the drawer cannot, by ante-dating it, say that it is overdue; *Cowing* v. *Altman*, 27 Am. Rep. 70, following *Boehm* v. *Stirling*, 7 T. R. 423. In America it is said that a cheque found in the hands of the payee or a third person fourteen months after its date, in the absence of explanation, is discredited, and will be treated as overdue and dishonoured, whether actually presented or not, *Cowing* v. *Altman*, 27 Am. Rep 70. As to the meaning of "good faith," and as to what constitutes negligence in taking a negotiable instrument, see sect. 90.

Duties of the Banker arising out of his relation to his Customer.

"A banker is bound," says Jessel, M R., in *Hopkinson* v *Forster*, L. R. 19 Eq at p. 76, "by his contract with his customer, to honour his cheque when he has sufficient funds in hand." The relation between a banker and his customer is that the banker receives money from his customer on condition of paying it back, when asked or when drawn upon by his customer, the relation is merely one of debtor and creditor, *Foley* v. *Hill*, 2 H. L. C. at p. 43. Money in the hands of a banker is merely money lent, with the superadded obligation that it is to be paid back when called for by the draft of the customer, *Pott* v. *Clegg*, 16 M. & W. 321. So also per Cockburn, C.J, in *Goodwin* v. *Robarts*, L. R. 10 Ex. at p. 351, *Atna Bank* v. *Fourth National Bank*, 46 N. Y. Rep 82. In *Whitaker* v. *The Bank of England*, 6 C. & P. 709, Parke, B., told the jury that the real question (in an action for not paying a bill) was, whether the plaintiff had a sufficient balance at the bank at a reasonable hour before the bill was presented and dishonoured. Such then is the ordinary duty that a banker owes to his customer; and if the banker dishonours a customer's cheque without sufficient cause, the banker renders himself liable to an action by the customer, in which the jury may give substantial damages, as the injury thereby caused to the customer's credit, especially if he is a trader, must be very great, *Marzetti* v. *Williams*, 1 B. & Ad. 415; per Williams, J., in *Rolin* v. *Stewart*, 14 C B 595; *Hopkinson* v. *Forster*, L. R. 19 Eq at p. 76. This duty of the banker may be

varied by agreement, or by a course of dealing amounting to an
agreement, *Kymer* v. *Laurie*, 18 L. J. Q. B. 218 (Patteson and
Erle, J.J.); *Cumming* v. *Shand*, 5 H. & N. 95; 29 L. J. Ex. 129.
But a banker must refuse to honour a cheque when he knows that the
customer holds such funds as trustee, and that the cheque was to the
knowledge of the banker drawn to pay a debt due from him personally,
such a discharge of the debt being a misapplication of the funds, the
banker being cognizant of it, *Gray* v. *Johnston*, L. R. 2 H. L. 1. But
a mere suspicion that the customer meditates a breach of trust would
not warrant the banker in dishonouring the cheque, the banker not
being interested in the transaction; per Lord Westbury, at p. 14. A
bank cannot refuse to cash a cheque for an executor merely on the
ground that the estate is insolvent, and that the bank had a supposed
claim upon the money in its hands, *Ireland* v. *North of Scotland
Banking Co.*, Court of Sess. Cas. 4th Series, vol. 8, 215. Where a
customer has accounts at two branches of the same bank, the customer
must be taken to know the state of each account; and where his
balance at one branch is just equal to a deficiency at the other, the
branch, at which there is a balance, may refuse to honour his cheques
on account of his indebtedness at the other branch, *Garnett* v.
McKewan, L. R. 8 Ex. 10.

Payment of Cheques.

A banker can tender one shilling in bronze coins, forty shillings in
silver coins, and for any sum above 40s. and under £5, he must tender
in gold, and for £5 and upwards he can tender in gold or (by 3 & 4
Will. 4, c. 98, s. 6) in Bank of England notes, except where the
banker is the Bank of England, when, if the person wishes it, the Bank
must pay in gold, and not in notes. See 33 & 34 Vict. c. 10, s. 4.
A banker, however, usually asks the person presenting the cheque
how he will take payment, whether in notes or gold, but of course he
may accept payment in other ways, though if he does the drawer is
discharged, *Smith* v. *Ferrand*, 7 B. & C. 19; for instance, he may take
a bill of exchange, which means a good bill, *Puckford* v. *Maxwell*,
6 T. R. 52. But it must be remembered that in this latter case the
rules as to presentment for acceptance and payment laid down in
sects. 39 to 46 of this Act must be complied with in order to retain
a remedy against the banker.

As to whether a banker would be justified in paying a cheque in
part, not having sufficient funds to pay it in full, see Grant's Law of
Bankers, 4th Ed., 43, and a contrary opinion in Parsons on Bills,
vol. 2, p. 78.

Forged and Altered Cheques.

See on this subject sect. 24, and the notes thereto. Formerly a
banker paying a cheque on a forged signature could not charge his

customer with the payment; but now the rule is so far relaxed that the banker *bonâ fide* paying on a forged indorsement that is not his customer's can charge his customer's account with the payment; see below; see also *Charles* v. *Blackwell*, 2 C. P. D., at p. 157; *Arnold* v. *Cheque Bank*, 1 C. P. D. at p. 589. But a person who knows that the bank is relying on his forged signature, cannot lie by and not divulge the fact; it is then a question for the jury whether the person by doing so did not assent to it; *M'Kenzie* v. *British Linen Co.*, 6 Ap. Cas. 82; 44 L. T. N. S. 431; 29 W. R. 477. The person who presents the cheque for payment gets no title through the forgery, as to which see sect. 24 and the notes thereto. *As to the indorsement on the cheque being forged:* By 16 & 17 Vict. c. 59, s. 19, it is provided that "any draft or order drawn upon a banker for a sum of money payable to order on demand which shall, when presented for payment, purport to be indorsed by the person to whom the same shall be drawn payable, shall be a sufficient authority to such banker to pay the amount o' such draft or order to the bearer thereof; and it shall not be incumbent on such banker to prove that such indorsement, or any subsequent indorsement, was made by or under the direction or authority of the person to whom the draft or order was or is made payable, either by the drawer or any indorser thereof." This section has not been repealed. Sect. 60 substantially enacts the same, though its terms are not quite so wide as the above, see that section and the notes thereto. Of course the indorsement forged must not be the customer's indorsement, as a banker is bound to know his customer's signature; cf. *Weisser* v. *Denison*, 10 N. Y. Rep. 68. An indorsement "per procurationem," or "as agent," has been held to be within this section, *Charles* v. *Blackwell*, 1 C. P. D. 548; aff. 2 C. P. D. 151; 46 L. J. C. P. 368; 36 L. T. N. S. 195; 25 W. R. 472. This enactment does not protect any other person than the banker on whom the cheque is drawn; hence the drawer or true owner of the cheque can sue the person who has got payment of the cheque through a forged indorsement for the amount received by him, *Ogden* v. *Benas*, L R. 9 C. P 513; *Arnold* v. *Cheque Bank*, 1 C. P. D. at p. 585; *Halifax Union* v. *Wheelwright*, L. R. 10 Ex. 183; *Bobbett* v. *Pinkett*, 1 Ex. D. 368. As to altered cheques, in *Young* v. *Grote*, 4 Bing. 253, the customer signed a cheque in blank, and left it for his wife to fill in; she wrote the words "fifty pounds" so inartificially that a servant inserted the words "three hundred and" before "fifty," and got it cashed. The Court held that the bankers, having paid the £350, were entitled to credit with their customer for that amount. This decision went upon the ground that it was by the fault of the customer in the manner in which the cheque was drawn that the bank was deceived. "The principle," says the Lord Chancellor in *Orr* v. *Union Bank of Scotland*, 1 Macqueen, 513, "is a sound one, that where the customer's neglect of due caution has caused his bankers to make a payment

K

on a forged order, he shall not set up against them the invalidity of a document which he has induced them to act on as genuine." The decisions in *Young* v. *Grote, suprà,* and *Robarts* v. *Tucker,* 16 Q B. 560; 20 L. J. Q. B. 270, and *Swan* v. *North British Australasian Co.,* 2 H. & C. 175; 32 L. J. Ex. 273, which followed it, were received and followed in *Halifax Union* v. *Wheelwright,* L. R. 10 Ex. 183. See also *Baxendale* v. *Bennett,* 3 Q. B. D. 525; 47 L. J. Q. B. 624; 40 L. T. N. S. 23; 26 W. R. 899, where *Young* v. *Grote* is doubted; and 2 Parsons on Bills, 80. But it has been laid down that the negligence or want of due caution on the part of the customer must be negligence in reference to the particular transaction itself, that is, negligence in the transaction itself; it should furnish not merely an occasion, but directly lead to the loss; per Jackson, J., and Crampton, J., in *Bank of Ireland* v. *Evans' Charities,* 3 Ir. C. L. Rep. at pp. 303, 337; approved in the House of Lords, 5 H. L. C. at p. 410. See also *Arnold* v. *Cheque Bank,* 1 C. P. D. at pp. 586–588; *Baxendale* v. *Bennett, suprà.* But where a customer drew a cheque for £3, and paid it away, and the amount was altered to £200 in such a manner that no one, in the ordinary course of business, could have observed it, and the banker paid the £200 when it was presented; it was held that the banker was liable to his customer for the difference between the amount of the genuine and altered cheque, *Hall* v. *Fuller,* 5 B & C. 750; see also *Flower* v. *Shaw,* 2 C. & K. 703. As to bankers negligently paying a cancelled cheque, see *Scholey* v. *Ramsbottom,* 2 Camp. 485; *Ingham* v. *Primrose,* 7 C. B. N. S. 82; 28 L. J. C. P. 294.

In the case of a forged or altered cheque the remedy of a *bonâ fide* holder for value is confined to a right to recover the consideration for the bill as between himself and his transferor; and a similar remedy may be resorted to till the party is reached through whose fraud or laches the alteration or forgery was made, *Burchfield* v. *Moore,* 3 E. & B. 683; 23 L. J. Q. B. 261; see also sect. 55, sub-sect. 2, (*b*) and (*c*), and sect. 58, sub-sect. 3. As to alterations see further section 64 and the notes thereto. As to lost cheques, see sections 69 and 70, and the notes thereto.

Payment by Cheque—

"It is clear law," says Lord Blackburn, in *Heywood* v. *Pickering,* L. R. 10 Q B. at 431, "that a payment by cheque is *primâ facie* only a conditional payment. It does not operate as payment unless the cheque is paid, or the holder by his conduct makes the cheque his own; it is then equivalent to payment." *Cohen* v. *Hale,* 3 Q. B. D. 371. As a rule, if a person takes a cheque and does not duly present it for payment, whereby loss is sustained, he makes the cheque his own, see *Charles* v. *Blackwell,* 2 C. P. D. at p. 158; 46 L. J. C. P. 368; 36 L. T. N. S. 195; 25 W. R. 472. But a cheque is often sent by post in payment of a debt; here it is advisable for the creditor to return it if he does not wish to take it in payment, as otherwise the jury might find that he had taken it as payment, *Hough* v. *May*, 4 A. & E 954. A fraudulent cheque, however, cannot be considered as payment in any case, and therefore if given contemporaneously with and as part of any transaction, it is a question for the jury whether there was not such a fraud as would vitiate the transaction, see *Earl of Bristol* v. *Wilsmore*, 1 B. & C. 514. Payment by a negotiable security may operate as satisfaction of a debt of a larger amount, *Cumber* v. *Wane*, 1 Sm. L. C. 8th ed., 363, 366, *Sibree* v. *Tripp*, 15 M. & W. 23; and so also may payment by a cheque, *Goddard* v. *O'Brien*, 9 Q. B. D. 37 Where a debtor pays his creditor by cheque, which is lost by the latter, and the finder gets it paid by the bankers on the creditor's forged indorsement, the debtor must pay his creditor again, unless the cheque is taken as money, *Thompson* v. *Bank of British North America*, 82 N. Y. Rep. 1.

Cheques as Evidence—

Several cases have established that delivery of a cheque to a person is no evidence *per se* of a loan, or debt due by the payee to the drawer, other evidence is necessary to establish the fact of money being due, *Graham* v. *Cox*, 2 C. & K. 702; *Cary* v. *Gerrish*, 4 Esp. 9; *Mountford* v. *Harper*, 16 M. & W. 825, 16 L. J. Ex. 184; *Aubert* v. *Walsh*, 4 Taunt. 293; *Pearce* v. *Davis*, 1 Moo. & Rob. 365; 2 Parsons on Bills, 83, 84. But it may, subject to what has been already said as to payment by cheque, be very good evidence of payment, *Boswell* v. *Smith*, 6 C. & P. 60; *Mountford* v. *Harper*, 16 M. & W. 825; 16 L. J. Ex. 184; *Pearce* v. *Davis*, 1 Moo. & Rob. 365. *Egg* v. *Barnett*, 3 Esp. 196. A cheque given to a partner in a firm is strong evidence of payment for work done by the firm, *Nicoll* v. *Reid*, Cas. in Court of Sess., 4th Ser., vol. 6, 216.

Donatio mortis Causâ—

A cheque drawn by the donor on his bankers, if not presented before the donor's death, is not valid as a *donatio mortis causâ*, because the donor's death revokes the authority of the banker to pay it, see sect. 75, sub-sect. 2, and the notes thereto; see also *Austin* v. *Mead*, 15 Ch. D. 651, where all the authorities are quoted in the argument; *Tate* v. *Hilbert*, 2 Ves. Jun. 111; 4 Brown C. C. 286, where Lord Loughborough said that if a banker's cheque is paid away for value or to a creditor, it is a valid gift. In *Bromley* v. *Brunton*, L. R. 6 Eq. 275, it was held that a cheque given to a person and presented by him during the donor's lifetime, but the payment of which was wrongfully refused by the bankers, was a complete gift. See also *Moore* v. *Moore*, L. R. 18 Eq. 474. So also where a cheque was indorsed by the payee to her bankers and negotiated in the ordinary course of business during the testator's lifetime, but not presented till after his death, it was

Presentment of
cheques for
payment

held good, *Rolls* v. *Pearce,* 5 Ch. D 730; 46 L. J. Ch. 791; *Beak* v. *Beak,* L. R. 13 Eq. 489; see also 2 Parsons on Bills, 56. In *Rolls* v. *Pearce, suprà,* Malins, V.-C., made a distinction between cheques payable to bearer and those payable to order, saying that in the former case, paying it away for value is not sufficient, *sed quære,* see *Tate* v. *Hilbert,* 2 Ves. Jun., at p. 117, where the cheque was made payable to bearer. The principle of all these cases is, that a cheque is a mere order to the banker to pay a certain sum of money, and that the order is revoked by the customer's death, per Lord Romilly, in *Hewett* v. *Kaye,* L. R. 6 Eq. at p. 200; 37 L. J. Ch. 633.

Revocation
of banker's
authority

75.—The duty and authority of a banker to pay a cheque drawn on him by his customer are determined by—

(1.) Countermand of payment (*a*).

(2.) Notice of the customer's death (*b*).

(*a*) Bankers are bound to obey the orders of their customers, and hence are bound to obey an order countermanding payment of, or, as it is called, "stopping," a cheque; *Clydesdale Bank* v. *McLean,* Court of Sess. Cas., 4th Ser., vol. 10, 719, and the payee has, as we have already seen, no remedy against the banker; see note to sect. 73, note (*b* 1.).

(*b*) The death of the drawer, and notice of the fact to the banker, has always been a revocation of the banker's authority to pay the cheque. Hence, if a banker pays a cheque in ignorance of the customer's death, the payment is valid. "Bankers, having no notice of the death of a party, are entitled, when his bill becomes due, to reimburse themselves out of his funds in their hand the amount of the bill which they have before discounted," per Dallas, C. J., in *Rogerson* v. *Ladbroke,* 1 Bing. at p. 98; see note to the last preceding section under the head of "Donatio mortis causâ."

Crossed Cheques.

General and
special cross-
ings defined.

Ind Act, s. 123.

76.—(1.) Where a cheque bears across its face an addition of—

　　(*a*) The words "and Company," or any abbreviation thereof between two parallel transverse lines, either with or without the words "not negotiable," or—

Ind. Act, s. 123.

　　(*b*) Two parallel transverse lines simply, either with or without the words "not negotiable;"

that addition constitutes a crossing, and the cheque is crossed generally.

(2) Where a cheque bears across its face an addition of the name of a banker, either with or without the words " not negotiable," that addition constitutes a crossing, and the cheque is crossed specially and to that banker (*z*).

(*z*) In *Bellamy* v. *Marjoribanks*, 7 Ex. 389, it was decided that the crossing of a cheque (in that case payable to bearer) with the name of a banker did not restrict the negotiability of it to such banker, or to a banker only; but that it was a mere memorandum that the holder was to present it through some banker. Parke, B., there gave an elaborate account of the origin of crossing cheques. The legislature in 1856 passed a statute (19 & 20 Vict. c. 25) enacting that the crossing was to be a direction to the banker to pay the cheque to or through a banker. Still the crossing was held to be no part of the cheque itself (*Simmons* v. *Taylor*, 4 C. B. N. S. 463; 27 L J. C. P. 248) and so in 1858 the legislature enacted (21 & 22 Vict. c. 79) that the crossing should be deemed a material part of the cheque. It was decided, in 1875, that this statute did not affect the negotiability of a cheque; and that if a cheque is specially crossed by the payee, and indorsed by him, and stolen, and it gets into the hands of a *bonâ fide* holder for value (called in this Act a holder in due course), who pays it into his bankers, and the bank on which it is drawn pays it when presented by such holder's bankers, who are not the bankers named in the crossing, the payee cannot recover the amount as having been paid contrary to his directions, as he ceased to have any property in the cheque; and that the drawer might refuse to allow his bankers to debit him with such a payment, because the crossing would be considered his directions to his bankers to pay the cheque to the bank named in the crossing, *Smith* v. *Union Bank of London*, L. R. 10 Q. B. 291; on app. 1 Q. B. D. 31; 45 L. J. Q. B. 149; 24 W. R. 194. It has been held also that the drawer may sue the person who received the money, if the latter had no title to the cheque, as the customer may treat the payment by the banker as payment by himself, and so may recover the money back as upon a failure of consideration, *Bobbett* v. *Pinkett*, 1 Ex. D. 368; 45 L. J. Ex. 555; 24 W. R. 711. In 1876 the Crossed Cheques Act (39 & 40 Vict. c. 81) was passed, repealing the former acts as to crossed cheques, and that Act has now been repealed by this Act; but all the provisions of the repealed Act have been substantially re-enacted by this one.

77.—(1) A cheque may be crossed generally or specially by the drawer (*a*).

(2) Where a cheque is uncrossed, the holder (*b*) may cross it generally or specially.

SS. 77, 78.

Crossing by
drawer or after
issue.

Ind Act, s 125.

(3) Where a cheque is crossed generally, the holder may cross it specially.

(4) Where a cheque is crossed generally or specially, the holder may add the words "not negotiable" (*c*).

(5) Where a cheque is crossed specially, the banker to whom it is crossed may again cross it specially to another banker for collection (*d*).

(6) Where an uncrossed cheque, or a cheque crossed generally, is sent to a banker for collection, he may cross it specially to himself (*e*).

(*a*) Sect. 5 of the Crossed Cheques Act, 1876, did not give the drawer of a cheque payable to another person express power to cross a cheque, as therein provided, though probably it would have been held that he had such power. Nor does the Indian Act; see sect. 125 thereof in the appendix.

(*b*) In the Crossed Cheques Act, 1876, s. 5, the words "lawful holder" are used. As to the definition of "holder," see sect. 2, and note (*j*) thereto. As to meaning of the different crossings, see sect. 76, and the notes thereto.

(*c*) The addition of the words "not negotiable" were first authorised by the Act of 1876, see sect. 81, and the notes thereto. And it would seem that the payee or lawful holder may sue the bankers upon whom the cheque is drawn for any loss he may sustain by their paying it otherwise than according to the crossing, see sub-sect. (2) of sect. 79 of this Act, and the notes thereto. The drawer of a cheque payable to another person has not, by this section, absolute power to add the words "not negotiable;" but if he did so, it would probably be as agent of the payee, when requested by the latter to do so.

(*d*) By sect. 78 all these crossings are material parts of a cheque.

(*e*) This is not in sect. 5 of the Crossed Cheques Act, 1876, nor in the Indian Act, see sect. 125 thereof. The second crossings authorised by sub-sections 5 and 6 are the only occasions on which a cheque may be crossed twice, see sect. 79, sub-sect. 1.

Crossing a
material part
of cheque.

78.—A crossing authorised by this Act is a material part of the cheque; it shall not be lawful for any person to obliterate, or, except as authorised by this Act, to add to or alter the crossing (*a*).

(*a*) The words "except as authorised by this Act," refer to sect. 77 of this Act. As to the effect of a material alteration in a cheque, see sect 74 and notes thereto, title "Altered Cheques"; see also sect. 64 of this Act and the notes thereto.

79.—(1) Where a cheque is crossed specially to more than one banker, except when crossed to an agent for collection being a banker, the banker on whom it is drawn shall refuse payment thereof (a).

(2) Where the banker on whom a cheque is drawn which is so crossed, nevertheless pays the same, or pays a cheque crossed generally otherwise than to a banker, or if crossed specially otherwise than to the banker to whom it is crossed, or his agent for collection being a banker, he is liable to the true owner (b) of the cheque for any loss he may sustain owing to the cheque having been so paid.

Provided that where a cheque is presented for payment which does not at the time of presentment appear to be crossed, or to have had a crossing which has been obliterated, or to have been added to or altered otherwise than as authorised by this Act, the banker paying the cheque in good faith and without negligence shall not be responsible or incur any liability, nor shall the payment be questioned, by reason of the cheque having been crossed, or of the crossing having been obliterated or having been added to or altered otherwise than as authorised by this Act, and of payment having been made otherwise than to a banker, or to the banker to whom the cheque is or was crossed, or to his agent for collection being a banker, as the case may be (c).

(a) See note (e) to sect. 77.

(b) The definition of "holder in due course" given in sub-sect. (1) of sect. 29, would be applicable to the words "true owner," except that in this and the following sections, the true owner is *ex hypothesi* not the holder at the time. The word "crossed" in all these sections means lawfully crossed in accordance with the provisions of sect. 77, which see.

(c) This corresponds with the proviso to sect. 64 of this Act, as to non-apparent alterations.

80.—Where the banker on whom a crossed cheque is drawn (a) in good faith and without negligence, pays it, if crossed generally, to a banker, and if crossed specially, to the banker to whom it is crossed, or his agent for

SS. 80, 81, 82.

Protection to
banker and
drawer where
cheque is
crossed.

Ind Act, s. 128.

collection being a banker, the banker paying the cheque
(b) and, if the cheque has come into the hands of the
payee (c), the drawer shall respectively be entitled to
the same rights and be placed in the same position as if
payment of the cheque had been made to the true owner
thereof (d).

(a) The wording of the first line of this section is not very accurate,
as it would strictly only refer to a cheque that was issued crossed.
But it is submitted that it must be taken generally to include any
properly crossed cheque, no matter when crossed.

(b) The banker paying the cheque, if he complies with the provisions
of this section, runs no risk.

(c) This means if it has at any time come into the hands of the payee,
then the drawer is relieved of any liability. The drawer may be himself the payee, and if so, he runs no risk until the cheque passes out of
his hands; and even then he incurs no liability, if the provisions of
this section are complied with.

(d) As to the meaning of "true owner," see sect. 79, note (b) thereto.

Effect of cross-
ing on holder.

Ind. Act, s. 130.

81.—Where a person takes a crossed cheque which
bears on it the words "not negotiable," he shall not have
and shall not be capable of giving a better title to the
cheque than that which the person from whom he took
it had (a).

(a) See note (c) to sect. 77 of this Act. The addition of the words
"not negotiable" is very useful in transmitting cheques to bankers to
be placed to the customer's account, and every cheque so sent should
be so crossed.

Protection to
collecting
banker.

Ind Act, s 131

82.—Where a banker in good faith and without
negligence receives payment for a customer of a cheque
crossed generally or specially to himself, and the
customer has no title or a defective title thereto, the
banker shall not incur any liability to the true owner of
the cheque by reason only of having received such payment (a).

(a) By 16 & 17 Vict. c. 59, s. 19, the banker upon whom any
draft or order payable to order on demand is drawn, is protected if he
bonâ fide pays the cheque, though the indorsement is forged, and
though the forged indorsement purports on its face to be made by
an agent; see also *Charles* v. *Blackwell*, 2 C P. D. at p. 157; 46 L J.
C. P. 368, 36 L. T. N. S 195; 25 W. R. 472; but such banker is

S. 82.

Protection to collecting banker.

liable if his customer's signature is forged, *Ibid.*, 2 C. P. D., at p. 157. This protection does not extend to any other than the banker upon whom the cheque is drawn, *Ogden* v. *Benas*, L. R. 9 C. P. 513; 43 L. J. C. P. 259; *Arnold* v. *Cheque Bank*, 1 C. P. D. 578; see also note to sect. 74 of this Act under the head of "Forged Cheques." Hence the banker who merely collected the proceeds for his customer was liable to the true owner for the amount received. By this section, which is substantially the same as sect. 12 of the Crossed Cheques Act, 1876, where a cheque is crossed generally, or specially to a banker, the collecting banker is relieved of liability, leaving the law as it was before if the cheque is uncrossed. The present (82nd) section embodies the decision in *Matthiessen* v. *London and County Bank*, 5 C. P. D. 7. The "true owner" of a cheque so crossed must now look, not to the collecting banker, but to the customer, or to the person who has received payment of it. If, however, the bank has done anything more than simply collect the proceeds, and credit the customer's account with them, for example, if the bank has had the cheque indorsed to it and has thereby made, or attempted to make, itself the owner of it, the bank will be liable to the true owner for the proceeds; *ibid.*, at pp. 16, 17. It has been recently held that where a customer pays a cheque (whether crossed or not) to his bankers in order to have the amount placed to his credit, and the bankers place the amount to his credit accordingly, the bankers become immediately holders of the cheque for value, even though the customer's account is not overdrawn, *Ex parte Richdale*, 19 Ch. D. 409; 51 L. J. Ch. D. 462. A different opinion was expressed in Scotland, if the account was not overdrawn, *Clydesdale Bank* v. *McLean*, Court of Sess. Cas., 4th ser., vol. 10, 719, per Lord Shand, at p. 724. Their liability as such holders, if the cheque is crossed, is limited by this section.

PART IV.

PROMISSORY NOTES.

S. 83.

Promissory
note defined

Ind. Act, s. 4.

83.—(1.) A promissory note (*a*) is an unconditional promise (*b*) in writing made by one person to another, signed by the maker, engaging to pay, on demand (*c*) or at a fixed or determinable future time (*d*), a sum certain (*e*) in money, to, or to the order of, a specified person (*f*) or to bearer (*g*).

(2.) An instrument in the form of a note payable to maker's order is not a note within the meaning of this section, unless and until it is indorsed by the maker (*h*).

(3.) A note is not invalid by reason only that it contains also a pledge of collateral security with authority to sell or dispose thereof (*j*).

Ind Act, s 11

(4.) A note which is, or on the face of it purports to be, both made and payable within the British Islands, is an inland note (*k*). Any other note is a foreign note.

(*a*) As the different parts of this definition are very much the same as those in the definition of a bill of exchange in sect. 3, sub-sect. 1, the reader is referred to the notes to that section for additional matter.

(*b*) In *Brown* v. *De Winton*, 6 C. B. at p. 356, it is said that no precise form of words is requisite to constitute a promissory note; but it ought to have the essentials of a contract; see note (*t*) of sect. 3 of this Act. The question is whether it imports a promise, *Brooks* v. *Elkins*, 2 M. & W. 74. The promise to pay must be unconditional; if not, it is void; see sect. 3, sub-sect. 2, and the notes thereto. A promise to pay "on the death of A. B., provided he leaves us sufficient to pay the said sum, or if we shall be otherwise able to pay it," is not a note, *Roberts* v. *Peake*, 1 Burr. 323 A promise to pay £50 "at such period of time that my circumstances will admit without detriment to myself or family," is not a note, *Ex parte Tootell*, 4 Ves. 372;

Beardsley v. *Baldwin*, 2 Stra. 1151. A promise to pay, "but if the agent does not sell enough in one year, one more is granted," is not a note, *Miller* v. *Poage*, 41 Amer. Rep. 82. "At 12 months date I promise to pay Messrs. R. F. & Co. £500, to be held by them as collateral security for any moneys now owing to them by B., which they may be unable to recover on realizing the securities they now hold, and others which may be placed in their hands by him," is not a note, *Robins* v. *May*, 11 A. & E. 213; 3 Per. & D. 147; 3 Jur. 1188. A promise to pay a certain sum by instalments, but it was declared that "all installed payments thereupon from and after the decease of the plaintiff should cease," is not a note, *Worley* v. *Harrison*, 3 A. & E. 669. See *Moffatt* v. *Edwards*, Car. & M. 16; *Dixon* v. *Nuttall*, 1 C. M. & R. 307. Even if the contingency has happened, it is not a promissory note, see sect. 11, sub-sect. 2 and the notes thereto. If the event must inevitably happen, then the note is good, see sect. 11, sub-sect. 2, and the notes thereto; *Colehan* v. *Cooke*, Willes, 393, 2 Stra. 1217; *Sackett* v. *Palmer*, 25 Barb. 179. In *Richards* v. *Richards*, 2 B. & Ad. 447, at p. 454, the note was held good, as the contingency was not stated on the face of it. On the other hand, any words which amount in law to a promise to pay are sufficient, *Morris* v. *Lee* 2 Ld. Raymond, 1396, 1 Stra. 629; 8 Mod. 362. "Received of A. B. £100, which I promise to pay on demand with lawful interest," is a note, *Green* v. *Davies*, 4 B. & C. 235; *Peto* v. *Reynolds*, 9 Ex. 410; 23 L. J. Ex. 98, *Lovell* v. *Hill*, 6 C. & P. 238. "I promise to pay as per memorandum of agreement," is a note, and *primâ facie* not conditional, *Jury* v. *Barker*, E. B. & E. 459; 27 L. J. Q. B. 255. So, "borrowed of M. A., his sister, £14 in cash, as per loan, in promise of payment of which I am truly thankful for; it shall never be forgotten by me," is a good note; *Ellis* v. *Mason*, 7 Dowl. P. C. 598. So, "I have received the imperfect books, which, together with the cash overpaid on the settlement of your account, amounts to £80, which sum I will pay you within two years," is good; *Wheailey* v. *Williams*, 1 M. & W. 533, "I. O. U. £85, to be paid May 5th," is good; *Waithman* v. *Elsee*, 1 C. & K. 35; *Brooks* v. *Elkins*, 2 M. & W. 74. A mere memorandum, without any promise to pay, is not a note, *Tomkins* v. *Ashby*, 6 B. & C. 541; *Clarke* v. *Percival*, 2 B. & Ad 660, *Hyne* v. *Dewdney*, 21 L. J. Q. B. 278. For examples of promises to pay, not being promissory notes, but agreements, see *Ellis* v. *Ellis*, Gow. 216, *Leeds* v. *Lancashire*, 2 Camp. 205; *Williamson* v. *Bennett*, 2 Camp. 417; *Horne* v. *Redfearn*, 4 Bing N. C. 433; *Sibree* v. *Tripp*, 15 M. & W. 23; *Davies* v. *Wilkinson*, 10 A. & E. 98; *Jarvis* v. *Wilkins*, 7 M. & W. 410; *Drury* v. *Macaulay*, 16 M. & W. 146. See also note (y) to sect 3, sub-sect. 1. I. O. U.—An I. O. U. is neither a bill or note, but a mere acknowledgment of a debt, and as such is not negotiable; see *Curtis* v. *Richards*, 1 M. & G. 46 It does not require a stamp; see *Childers* v. *Boulnois*, D. & R. N. P. C. 8; unless

s 83 ˙
—
Promissory
note defined

it contains a promise to pay, when it becomes a promissory note, and must be stamped; see *Brooks* v. *Elkins*, 2 M. & W. 74; *Waithman* v. *Elsee*, 1 C. & K. 35. An I. O. U. is also evidence of an account stated; *Douglas* v. *Holme*, 12 A. & E. 641; *Payne* v. *Jenkins*, 4 C. & P. 324; *Curtis* v. *Richards*, 1 M. & G. 46; *Fesenmeyer* v. *Adcock*, 16 M. & W. 449; and the cases collected in the note to *Edis* v. *Bury*, 2 C. & P. at p. 560. Bank Notes.—Lastly, a word or two about bank notes. A tender in country bank notes is a good tender if the creditor only objects to the amount and not to the quality of the tender, *Polglass* v. *Oliver*, 2 Cr. & J. 15. If a country bank note be paid for valuable consideration, as in the case of a purchaser, and not in discharge of an antecedent debt, it is absolute perfect payment; but if it be paid in discharge of an antecedent debt, it is like a bill of exchange to this extent, that if the party to whom it is tendered does not deal with it by presentment without delay, as a bill of exchange or promissory note, it is payment, otherwise it is not, *M'Donnell* v. *Murray*, 9 Ir. C. L. Rep. at p. 511. In the first case it is taken at the peril of the person taking it; in the latter case it is not, *Camidge* v. *Allenby*, 6 B. & C. at p. 382. If the bank has stopped payment, the holder should return the notes to his transferor without delay, or present them to the bank as holder, Story on Notes, s. 500; *Rogers* v. *Langford*, 1 Cr. & M. 637; *Camidge* v. *Allenby*, *suprà*; *Lichfield Union* v. *Greene*, 1 H. & N. 884; 26 L. J. Ex. 140. As bank notes pass by delivery, the transferor is not liable on the instrument, but he warrants his title to it and that it is a genuine note, sect. 58. The material alteration of a bank note for a fraudulent purpose is in law a forgery, and hence, the consideration given for it can be recovered back, and the rule as to laches in giving notice of non-payment does not apply to Bank of England notes, *Leeds Bank* v. *Walker*, 11 Q. B. D. at p. 89; 52 L. J. Q. B. D. at p. 593. A bank note must in all cases be presented at the banking house before a right of action accrues against the bank, *Saunderson* v. *Bowes*, 14 East, 500; even though the bank has stopped payment, *Bowes* v. *Howe*, 5 Taunt. 30; Story on Notes, s. 500, and the note thereto. With regard to notice of dishonour, see section 49 of this Act, and the notes thereto. Bank notes though stolen become the property of any person who takes them *bonâ fide* and for value, without notice of the larceny, *Miller* v. *Race*, 1 Sm. L. C. 7th Ed., 526; *Solomons* v. *Bank of England*, 13 East, 135, n. Even though the person taking the note *bonâ fide* and for value had the means of knowledge of which he neglected to avail himself, *e.g.*, where he could have discovered from certain advertisements that it was a stolen note, he can recover, *Raphael* v. *Bank of England*, 17 C. B. 161; 25 L. J. C. P. 33; cf. *Bank of Bengal* v. *Fagan*, 7 Moore P. C. C. at p. 72; see sect. 90, *post*. It has been seen that upon the loss of a negotiable instrument the Court or a Judge can order that the party liable shall not set up such loss as a defence, provided an indemnity is given; see sect. 70 of this Act and the notes thereto; and 17 & 18 Vict. c. 125, s. 87; this only applies to the High Court of Justice; *Noble* v. *Bank of England*, 2 H. & C. 355; 33 L. J. Ex. 81. It is presumed that section 70 of this Act applies only to the High Court. However, the true owner can get a fresh note under sect. 69 of this Act, and then, if necessary, sue on it in the County Court. These sections (69 and 70) apply to bank notes, *M'Donnell* v. *Murray*, 9 Ir. C. L. Rep. 495; *Redmayne* v. *Burton*, 2 L. T. N. S. 324; *Smith* v. *Mundy*, 3 E. & E. 22; 29 L. J. Q. B. 172, where it was held that, where halves of notes are sent by post, the property in them does not pass till the second halves are sent, and the sender may recover back the first halves if he has not sent the second; the transaction being merely inchoate and conditional, to be completed on the arrival of the second half. If half the note is lost, the owner of the other half, being the rightful owner of the whole, can recover on it, either on giving an indemnity, or without giving an indemnity, on the ground that the mere fact of taking a half note implies notice of something wrong, and the taker would take it subject to all the equities attaching to it in the hands of the person transferring it; per Willes, J., in *Redmayne* v. *Burton*, 2 L. T. N. S. 324. A material alteration in a bank note avoids it; see sect. 64 of this Act, and the notes thereto. It has been decided in the case of *Suffell* v. *Bank of England*, 9 Q. B. D. 555; 51 L. J. Q. B. D. 401; 47 L. T. N. S. 146; 80 W. R. 932, that the alteration of the number on a Bank of England note is a material alteration, so as to prevent a *bonâ-fide* holder for value from recovering on it. The decision turned upon the question, whether the alteration was a material one; not meaning thereby one that affected the contract, but an alteration of the instrument in a material way. As a Bank of England note differs from an ordinary note, it being part of the currency of the country, the number is of most material importance in enabling the note to be traced, not only by the Bank, but also by any holder. Hence it was held that an alteration in the number was a material alteration. See also *Leeds Bank* v. *Walker*, 11 Q. B. D. 84; 52 L. J. Q. B. D. 590, where it was decided by Denman, J., that sect. 64 of this Act does not apply to Bank of England notes, and that *Suffell's* case is still law. A person who gives change for a Bank of England note, that turns out to have been materially altered, can recover the money given for it, *Leeds Bank* v. *Walker*, *supra*. As to the power of Banking Companies to issue notes, see Grant's Law of Bankers, 4th ed., pp. 328, *et seq.*

(c) A note payable at sight is payable on demand, see sect. 10 of this Act, and the notes thereto. As to the words engaging to pay, see the last note. Days of grace are not allowed on a note payable on demand, sect. 14 of this Act and the notes thereto. See also *Brown* v. *Harraden*, 4 T. R. 148; *Smith* v. *Kendal*, 6 T. R. 123; 1 Esp. 231. A note may be made payable by instalments, and days of grace are allowed on the falling due of each instalment, *Oridge* v. *Sherborne*, 11 M. & W. 374; 12 L. J. Ex. 313. A note payable on demand with interest is payable immediately, *Norton* v. *Ellam*, 2 M. & W. 461.

(*d*) The time when the event is to happen upon which the note becomes payable may be uncertain, provided it must happen; see sect. 11, sub-sect. 2, and the notes thereto. A note payable on death is good, *Colehan* v. *Cooke*, Willes, 393; see also note (*b*) hereto.

(*e*) As to what is a "sum certain," see sect. 9 of this Act and the notes thereto, and note (*p*) to sect. 3 of this Act.

(*f*) See sect. 7, and sub-sect. (2) of sect. 5 of this Act, and the notes thereto. As to the meaning of the words "specified person," see note (*n*) to sect. 3, and also sub-sect. (1) of sect. 7 of this Act and the notes thereto.

(*g*) By 3 & 4 Anne, c. 9, notes were made negotiable; that statute is repealed by this Act.

(*h*) The reason of this is that no man can make a contract with himself; there ought to be two parties to it, a promisor and a promisee. An instrument payable to the maker's order is an incomplete instrument, being in the nature of a conditional engagement, in case he should afterwards indorse the note, to pay it to the person to whom by such indorsement he should direct it to be paid. Such an instrument, if indorsed to J. S. or order, imports a promise to pay to J. S. or order the money therein mentioned. And if the maker of such a note indorses it in blank and circulates it, he must be considered as engaging to pay the amount to the bearer; see the judgment in *Brown* v. *De Winton*, 6 C. B. at pp. 356, 359; also *Gay* v. *Lander*, 6 C. B. at p. 361; *Hooper* v. *Williams*, 2 Ex. 13. See also sect. 8, sub-sects. 3 & 4. By sect. 5, sub-sect. 2, of this Act, where in a bill drawer and drawee are the same person, the holder may treat the instrument, at his option, as a bill or note: in strictness such an instrument is a note, *Willans* v. *Ayers*, 3 Ap. Cas. 133, at p. 142; 37 L. T. N. S. 732 Where an instrument is ambiguous, the holder may treat it as a bill or note, *Edis* v. *Bury*, 6 B. & C. 433. *Lloyd* v. *Oliver*, 18 Q. B. 471. A note, it appears, could not formerly have been made by a man to himself without adding "or order;" Byles on Bills, 13th Ed., 6. This was because a bill or note payable to a particular person, without more, was not negotiable. This has been altered by sub-sect. 4 of sect. 8 of this Act, which see, such a note now being payable to order. As to a promissory note that is negotiated back to a prior party already liable on it, see sect. 37 of this Act and the notes thereto.

(*j*) For instance, "I promise to pay H. £500; and I have lodged with H. the counterpart leases, signed by D. and others, as a collateral security for the said £500 and interest;" *Fancourt* v. *Thorne*, 9 Q. B. 312; *Wise* v. *Charlton*, 4 A. & E. 786; 6 N. & M. 364. In Massachusetts it has been held that where in the margin of a note is

written, "Given as collateral security with agreement," such a note   SS. 83, 84, 85.
is not negotiable, *Costelo* v. *Crowell*, 127 Mass. Rep. 293.

Promissory note defined.

(*k*) By sect. 4, sub-sect. 1, of this Act, an inland bill is defined to be
"a bill which is or on the face of it purports to be both drawn and payable
within the British Islands, or drawn within the British Islands upon
some person resident therein." It will be seen that the second part of
this last definition has nothing to correspond with it in the definition of
an inland promissory note. For instance, a note made within the British
Islands, and payable to a person resident therein, but at some place
abroad, would be a foreign note; whereas a bill drawn within the
British Islands upon a person resident therein, but accepted payable
abroad and not elsewhere, would be an inland bill. However, unless
the fact of its being payable abroad appears on its face, the holder may
treat the note as an inland one; see sub-sect. 2 of sect. 4 of this Act,
and the notes thereto. As to the meaning of the words "British
Islands," see sub-sect. 1 of sect. 4 of this Act.

84.—A promissory note is inchoate and incomplete   *Delivery necessary.*
until delivery thereof to the payee or bearer (*a*).   Ind. Act, s 20

(*a*) As to inchoate instruments, see sect. 20 of this Act, and the
notes thereto. And as to the meaning of "delivery," see sects. 2 and
21 of this Act, and the notes thereto.

85.—(1.) A promissory note may be made by two or   *Joint and several notes.*
more makers, and they may be liable thereon jointly, or
jointly and severally according to its tenour.

(2.) Where a note runs "I promise to pay," and is
signed by two or more persons, it is deemed to be their
joint and several note (*a*).

(*a*) A note, "I promise to pay," signed by more than one person has
always been held to be a joint and several note; *Clerk* v. *Blackstock*,
Holt's N. P. C. 474; *Monson* v. *Drakeley*, 16 Am. R. 74.; *Chalmers*
on Bills, 2nd ed., 216; Story on Notes, s. 57. A note ran: "I promise
to pay bearer on demand £5. For C., M., P., and I., (signed) M.'
The parties were in partnership as bankers. Held, a joint promise
only by the partnership; Parke, B., saying that the person who signed
for the firm made but one promise, and two promises cannot be made
out of one; *Ex parte Buckley*, 14 M. & W. 469; 14 L. J. Ex. 341.
A note, "I, A., promise to pay B. or his order £50, with interest at
six months' notice, (signed) A., or else C.," is not a note by C, it
being an absolute undertaking by A.; but as against C, it is conditional on A. not paying it, *Ferris* v. *Bond*, 4 B. & Ald. 679. A
note signed by more than one person, and beginning "We promise to
pay," is a joint note only, *Byles on Bills* (13th Ed.), 7; *Parsons on
Bills*, vol. 1., 247. A note, which appears on its face to be the

separate note of A. only, cannot be sued on as the joint note of A. and B., though given to secure a debt for which A. and B. are jointly liable; it being treated as a separate note for a joint debt; *Siffkin* v. *Walker*, 2 Camp. 308; "We promise jointly or severally to pay," is a joint and several note, *Rees* v. *Abbott*, Cowp. 832. Where the note is joint, the judgment against one maker is a bar to an action against any of the others; *King* v. *Hoare*, 13 M. & W. at p. 505. A joint and several obligation at common law must be deemed to consist of separate obligations, and the defendant (one of the co-obligors) is *primâ facie* separately liable; per Brett, L J., in *Beckett* v. *Addyman*, 9 Q B. D. at p. 791; *Beecham* v. *Smith*, E. B. & E. 442; 27 L. J. Q. B. 257, *Owen* v. *Wilkinson*, 5 C. B. N. S. 526; 28 L. J. C. P. 3, where Crowder, J., said that the payee might have sued the plaintiff separately on his several note; see also *Beaumont* v. *Greathead*, 2 C. B. 494. Where in the case of a joint and several note, one maker is in reality the principal, and the others are sureties, if this was not known to the parties taking the note, they cannot be affected by it, *York Banking Co.* v. *Bainbridge*, 43 L. T. N S. 732. But where the person receiving it knows at the time of taking the note that one only is principal, and the others are merely sureties for him, he is bound by that fact, *Hollier* v. *Eyre*, 9 Cl. & F. at pp. 45, 51; *Pooley* v. *Harradine*, 7 E. & B. 431; 26 L. J. Q. B. 156; *Mutual Loan Fund* v. *Sudlow*, 5 C. B. N. S 449; 28 L. J. C. P. 108; *Taylor* v. *Burgess*, 5 H. & N. 1; 29 L. J. Ex. 7; *Greenough* v. *M'Clelland*, 2 E. & E 424; 30 L. J. Q. B. 15. This was not formerly so at law, unless the creditor assented to treat them as sureties only, *Manley* v. *Boycot*, 2 E. & B. 46; *Strong* v. *Foster*, 17 C. B. at p. 214, 218, 224; in this last case, however, there was an equitable plea, but the Court thought (wrongly as it is now decided) that the rule at law and in equity was the same. By the Common Law Procedure Act, 1854, a plea on equitable grounds, embodying the law as laid down in equity, was allowed; and now by sect. 25, sub-sect. 11, of the Judicature Act, 1873, the equitable rule will prevail. See the American cases as to joint makers of a note being principal and sureties discussed in *M'Closkey* v. *Indianopolis Union*, 33 American Rep 76. Where a note is signed by the maker and two others as sureties, and issued, and then another person signs his name beneath these three names without the knowledge of the sureties, he is presumed to have signed as co-surety, and is liable to contribution, *Monson* v. *Drakeley*, 16 Amer. Rep. 74. In America it has been held that where a joint and several note is signed by three persons as makers, and to the signature of the last is added the words "as surety," the presumption is that he is surety for the other two, but this may be rebutted; *Sayles* v. *Sims*, 73 New York Rep. 551. Where the question arises between the makers, parol evidence has always been admissible to shew in what relation they stood to each other,

Williams, J , saying " that if the relation of surety subsists, he is entitled to contribution, and we are entiled to disregard the form of the instrument," *Reynolds* v. *Wheeler*, 10 C. B. N. S. at p. 566; 30 L J. C. P. 350. And in *Macdonald* v. *Murray*, 8 Ap. Cas. 733, it was held that though the liabilities *inter se* of successive indorsers must generally be determined by the ordinary principle of a prior indorser indemnifying a subsequent one, yet the whole circumstances may be looked to for the purpose of ascertaining the true relation, and so indorsers who successively indorsed as sureties for the maker of a note were entitled to equal contribution *inter se* See also *Holmes* v. *Durkee*, 1 Cababe & Ellis N. P. Rep. 21. Where a note is re-indorsed to a previous indorser or to the payee, he has, as a rule, no remedy against the intermediate indorsers, because he would himself be liable to them by reason of his antecedent indorsement; sect. 37 of this Act; but where the holder would not be liable by reason of his antecedent indorsement, he may sue such intermediate indorser; sect. 37 of this Act and the notes thereto. An instance of this would be where the defendant indorsed the note as surety for the maker back to the payee (the plaintiff), parol evidence being admissible to prove that the defendant indorsed the note to make himself liable as surety, *Wilkinson* v. *Unwin*, 7 Q. B. D. 636, 50 L. J. Q. B. D. 338, where the previous cases are reviewed and followed. Joint makers of a note, being joint debtors, are entitled to contribution among themselves. " I think it is established by the case of *Dering* v. *Lord Winchelsea*, 2 B. & P. 270, and the observations of Lord Eldon in *Craythorne* v. *Swinburne*, 14 Ves. 165, and Lord Redesdale in *Stirling* v. *Forrester*, 3 Bli. 575, that where a creditor has a right to come upon more than one person or fund for the payment of a debt, there is an equity that each shall bear no more than his due proportion," *Duncan, Fox & Co.* v. *North & South Wales Bank*, 6 Ap. Cas. at p. 19.

A joint maker who is only a surety is entitled, on paying the debt, to the securities that the creditor possesses at the time the debt is paid, as against the principal. The indorser of a bill or note is in the nature of a surety for the acceptor or maker, and having paid the bill or note, is entitled to the benefit of any securities deposited with the holder, whether at the time of his indorsement he knew of the deposit of those securities or not, *Duncan, Fox, & Co.* v *North and South Wales Bank*, 6 Ap. Cas. 1; 50 L. J. Ch. 355; 43 L. T. N. S. 706; 29 W. R. 763. One co-surety cannot claim any greater benefit than his co-sureties from having taken a security from the principal debtor, even though he only consented to be a surety upon the terms of having the security, *Steel* v. *Dixon*, 17 Ch. D. 825. See also *In re Arcedeckne*, 24 Ch D. 709 Until a surety has paid more than his own proportion of the debt, he cannot call upon his co-sureties for contribution, *Ex parte Snowdon*, 17 Ch D. 44, *Davies* v *Humphreys*, 6 M. & W 153

86.—(1.) Where a note payable on demand has been indorsed, it must be presented for payment within a reasonable time of the indorsement. If it be not so presented the indorser is discharged (*a*).

(2.) In determining what is a reasonable time, regard shall be had to the nature of the instrument, the usage of trade, and the facts of the particular case (*b*).

(3.) Where a note payable on demand is negotiated, it is not deemed to be overdue for the purpose of affecting the holder with defects of title of which he had no notice, by reason that it appears that a reasonable time for presenting it for payment has elapsed since its issue (*c*).

(*a*) In order to charge the indorsers, a note must be duly presented for payment. If it is not payable on demand, it must be presented on the day it falls due; see sub-sect. (1) of sect. 45 of this Act, and the notes thereto. Where it is payable on demand and indorsed, then by this section it must be presented for payment within a reasonable time of the indorsement to render the indorser liable. A note payable on demand, however, is often intended as a continuing security, and need not be presented immediately, *Chartered Bank* v. *Dickson*, L. R. 3 P. C. 574; *Brooks* v. *Mitchell*, 9 M. & W. 15; see note (*b*) to this section. A note was payable "on demand after date" at a bank with interest "after maturity;" held, that it was not intended as a continuing security, and that not having been presented for payment for three years and a half from its date, the indorser was discharged, *Crim* v. *Starkweather*, 88 N. Y. Rep. 339. So too a note taken two years and three months after date, *Niver* v. *Best*, 10 Barb. 369.

As the maker of a note by sub-sect. (2) of sect. 89 of this Act corresponds with the acceptor of a bill, he is not discharged by the note not being duly presented for payment, see sub-sect. (1) of sect. 45 of this Act, and the notes thereto. The first indorser corresponds with the drawer of a bill. Bearing this in mind, the rules as to presentment for payment of a bill, laid down in sect. 45, are applicable to notes Where a person guarantees the payment of a note if not "duly honoured and paid" by the maker, he is liable on his guarantee if the note is not paid when due, without any presentment to the maker, and he is not entitled to notice of its dishonour; *Walton* v. *Mascall*, 13 M. & W. 452; 2 D. & L. 410; *Carter* v. *White*, 28 Sol. Journal, 123.

(*b*) If a note is made payable on demand, the time, at which payment thereof must be demanded, must depend upon the circumstances of each particular case, and no general rule can be laid down, Story on Notes, 2nd ed., s. 207. It may well be, therefore, that a "reasonable time for presentation" would in the case of a note receive a more liberal construction than in the case of bills or cheques; see Byles on Bills (13th Ed.), 213; *Chartered Bank* v. *Dickson*, L. R. 3 P. C. 574; *Brooks* v. *Mitchell*, 9 M. & W. 15; see also note (a) to this section.

(c) As a general rule any one receiving a negotiable instrument after it is due is presumed to have taken it upon the credit of the person from whom he received it, and subject to all the objections and equities to which it was liable in the hands of that person; *Taylor* v. *Mather*, 3 T. R. 83, n.; see also sub-sect. (2) of sect. 36 of this Act, and the notes thereto. This sub-section constitutes an exception to this rule, and is in accordance with the decision of *Brooks* v *Mitchell*, 9 M & W. 15, where the note was indorsed a number of years after its date, and no interest had been paid on it for several years before its indorsement to the indorsee, who sued upon it; and it was held that the note could not be considered overdue. But if it has been dishonoured, and that appears on its face or is known to the indorsee, suspicion attaches to the note, *Brown* v. *Davies*, 3 T. R. 80 (where the maker was allowed to give evidence that the note was paid as between him and the payee from whom the indorsee received it).

87.—(1.) Where a promissory note is in the body of it made payable at a particular place, it must be presented for payment at that place in order to render the maker liable (a). In any other case, presentment for payment is not necessary in order to render the maker liable (b).

(2.) Presentment for payment is necessary in order to render the indorser of a note liable (c).

(3.) Where the note is in the body of it made payable at a particular place, presentment at that place is necessary in order to render an indorser liable (d); but when a place of payment is indicated by way of memorandum only, presentment at that place is sufficient to render the indorser liable, but a presentment to the maker elsewhere, if sufficient in other respects, shall also suffice (e).

(a) Notes differ from bills in this, that if a bill is accepted payable at a particular place, without adding such words as "and not elsewhere," the bill need not be presented for payment either at the place named, or at any other place, in order to render the acceptor liable; see sect. 52 of this Act and the notes thereto. This, so far as bills are concerned, was first settled by statute 1 & 2 Geo. 4, c. 78, in consequence of a decision of the House of Lords in *Rowe* v. *Young*, 2 B. & B. 165; 2 Bligh, 391. This statute was held not to apply to notes, *Emblin* v. *Dartnell*, 12 M. & W. 831. Therefore, as before this Act, if a note is,

SS 87, 88.
―――
Presentment
of note for
payment.

in the body of it, made payable at a particular place, it is necessary to present it there, in order to render the maker (or indorser, sub-sect. 3) liable; *Saunderson* v. *Bowes*, 14 East, 500; *Sands* v. *Clarke*, 8 C. B. 751; *Quinn* v. *Fitzgerald*, 1 Ir C. L. Rep. 552; *Van der Donckt* v. *Thellusson*, 8 C. B. 812; 19 L J. C. P. 12, where the place of payment was in the body of the note, but separated by a full point, *Trecothick* v *Edwin*, 1 Stark. 468; *Roche* v. *Campbell*, 3 Camp. 247. But if the place of payment is not in the body of the note, but is indicated by way of memorandum, this is not an essential part of the contract, and presentment at that place is not necessary in order to render the maker liable, *Williams* v. *Waring*, 10 B. & C 2; 5 M. & R. 9; *Trecothick* v. *Edwin*, 1 Stark. 468. If a country bank-note is made payable both in London and in the country, the holder has a right to present it at either place, *Beeching* v. *Gower*, Holt's N. P. C. 313.

(*b*) *Walton* v. *Mascall*, 13 M. & W. at pp. 457, 458. If the note is not presented for payment, or demand of payment made, and if the maker paid on action brought, the Court would probably deprive the plaintiff of his costs, *M'Intosh* v. *Haydon*, Ry. & M. 362 Now under Order LXV. of the Rules of the Supreme Court, 1883, the plaintiff under such circumstances may be ordered to pay the defendant's costs.

(*c*) This means due presentment in all cases in accordance with sects. 45 & 46 of this Act as modified by this section. As to what is a reasonable time within which to present a note, see sect. 86 of this Act, and the notes thereto.

(*d*) This has always been the law; see note (*a*) hereto. The same rule applies to bills; see sub-sect. (4) of sect. 45 of this Act.

(*e*) See *Saunderson* v. *Judge*, 2 H. Bl. 510.

Liability of
maker.
Ind. Act, s. 32.

88.—The maker of a promissory note by making it—

(1.) Engages that he will pay it according to its tenour (*a*).

Ind. Act, ss
120 & 121.

(2.) Is precluded from denying to a holder in due course the existence of the payee and his then capacity to indorse (*b*).

(*a*) The maker of a note is primarily liable on it, and in this way stands in the same position as the acceptor of a bill, see sub-sect. (1) of sect. 89 of this Act, and the notes thereto, the acceptor of a bill engaging to pay according to the tenour of his acceptance; see sect. 54, subs. 1, and the notes thereto.

(*b*) In the case of *Drayton* v. *Dale*, 2 B & C. 299, which was an action by the indorsee against the maker of a note, Bayley, J., said:—" The defendant, by making such a note, intimates to all persons that he considers Clarke (the payee) capable of making an order sufficient to transfer the property in the note. It is a general principle, applicable to all negotiable securities, that a person shall not dispute the power of another to indorse such an instrument, when he asserts by the instrument which he issues to the world that the other has such power. . . . . It appears to me that as the defendant, by the form of his note, has stated that he will pay to Clarke's order he cannot now allege Clarke's inability to make an order as a ground of defence to this action" This was a case of the payee becoming bankrupt, and indorsing the note after his bankruptcy.

89.—(1.) Subject to the provisions in this Part, and except as by this section provided, the provisions of this Act relating to bills of exchange apply, with the necessary modifications, to promissory notes.

(2.) In applying those provisions, the maker of a note shall be deemed to correspond with the acceptor of a bill, and the first indorser of a note shall be deemed to correspond with the drawer of an accepted bill payable to drawer's order (z)

(3.) The following provisions (y) as to bills do not apply to notes; namely, provisions relating to—

(a) Presentment for acceptance;

(b) Acceptance ,

(c) Acceptance *suprà* protest;

(d) Bills in a set.

(4.) Where a foreign note is dishonoured, protest thereof is unnecessary (x).

(z) *Gwinnell* v. *Herbert*, 5 A & E. at p. 440. It follows from this that, though each indorser of a bill is in the nature of a new drawer to subsequent parties, each indorser of a note is not in the position of a new maker, because if each indorser became a new maker, he would be liable in the first instance, *Gwinnell* v *Herbert*, *suprà*.

(y) Besides the provisions mentioned in sub-sect. 3 of this section, the following other provisions not applicable to notes are the most important:—The provisions contained in sub-sect. (3) of sect. 86 (which see). Part of the provisions of sub-sect. (1) of sect. 52; for by sect. 87, sub-sect. 1, where a note is in the body of it made payable at a particular place, it must be presented at that place in order to render the maker liable. In the case of a bill, the acceptance in such a form would be general, (see sub-sect (2) (c) of sect. 19), and presentment for payment is not necessary in order to render the acceptor liable, see sub-sect. (1) of sect. 52 of this Act, and the notes thereto.

(x) So decided in *Bonar* v. *Mitchell*, 19 L. J. Ex. 302.

PART V.

SUPPLEMENTARY.

90.—A thing is deemed to be done in good faith (*a*) within the meaning of this Act, where it is, in fact, done honestly; whether it is done negligently or not (*b*).

(*a*) The words " good faith " occur in this Act in sect. 12; sect. 29, sub-sect. 1, b.; sect. 30, sub-sect. 2; sect. 59, sub-sect. 1, sect. 60; sect. 79, sub-sect. 2; sect. 80; sect 82.

(*b*) This point was decided in *Raphael* v. *Bank of England*, 17 C.B. 161; 25 L. J. C. P. 33; and in *The Bank of Bengal* v. *Macleod*, 7 Moore P. C. C at p. 72 (dissenting from *Gill* v. *Cubitt*, 3 B. & C 466, and *Down* v. *Halling*, 4 B. & C. 330, on this point); *Brown* v. *Spofford*, 5 Otto, Sup. Ct. U. S, 474, at p. 478. The negligence here mentioned must stop short of that alluded to by Parke, B., in *May* v. *Chapman*, 16 M. & W. 355, where he says:—" I agree that ' notice and knowledge' mean not merely express notice, but knowledge, or the means of knowledge to which the party wilfully shuts his eyes;" *Willis* v. *Bank of England*, 4 A. & E. at p. 32; *Swan* v. *North British Company*, 2 H. & C. at p. 185. Such " wilful shutting of the eyes " would probably not come within this section. Gross negligence may be evidence of *mala fides*; but is not the same thing, per Lord Denman, in *Goodman* v. *Harvey*, 4 A. & E. at p 876; also in *Jones* v. *Gordon*, 2 Ap. Cas. at pp. 625, 626, 628, 635. See also *Ormsbee* v. *Howe*, 41 Amer. Rep. 841.

91.—(1) When by this Act any instrument or writing is required to be signed by any person, it is not necessary that he should sign it with his own hand, but it is sufficient if his signature is written thereon by some other person by or under his authority (*a*).

(2) In the case of a corporation, where, by this Act, any instrument or writing is required to be signed, it is sufficient if the instrument or writing be sealed with the corporate seal.

4

But nothing in this section shall be construed as requiring the bill or note of a corporation to be under seal (*b*).

SS. 91, 92, 93.
Signature.

(*a*) As to the appointment and powers of an agent see sect. 24, note (*b*). In *Lord* v. *Hall*, 8 C. B. 627, it was held to be a question of fact whether a person who had authority to draw, accept, and indorse bills cannot select a third person to write the name of the principal.

(*b*) As to the power of a corporation or company in relation to bills and notes, see sect. 22, note (*c*). By this sub-section a seal without signature is now sufficient. Therefore, it appears that now the bill or note of a corporation may be either signed, or sealed without any signature.

92. Where the time limited for doing any act or thing is less than three days, in reckoning time, non-business days are excluded.

Computation of time

"Non-business" days for the purposes of this Act mean
(*a*) Sunday, Good Friday, Christmas Day :
(*b*) A bank holiday under the Bank Holidays Act, 1871, or acts amending it :
(*c*) A day appointed by Royal proclamation as a public fast or thanksgiving day.
Any other day is a business day (*z*).

(*z*) The definition of non-business days in this section applies to all the purposes of this Act. This section does not affect the days of grace, as it only applies to time, when such time is less than three days. As to the rule, when the last day of grace falls on one of the days above-mentioned, see sect. 14 of this Act and the notes thereto.

93. For the purposes of this Act, where a bill or note is required to be protested within a specified time or before some further proceeding is taken, it is sufficient that the bill has been noted for protest before the expiration of the specified time or the taking of the proceeding; and the formal protest may be extended at any time thereafter as of the date of the noting (*a*).

When noting equivalent to protest.

(*a*) Noting a bill is in reality only the initial step in the protest, per Buller, J., in *Leftley* v. *Mills*, 4 T. R. at p. 175. As to the meaning of "noting" a bill, see note (*z*) to section 51, and as to the meaning of "protest," see note (*y*) to section 51 of this Act.

When noting equivalent to protest

It has been decided that a protest may be drawn up and completed at any time, either before or after the commencement of an action on the bill, *Chaters* v. *Bell*, 4 Esp. 48; *Geralopulo* v. *Wieler*, 10 C. B. 690; 20 L. J. C. P. 105; or during the trial, Bull. N. P. 7th Edit. 272; *Orr* v. *Maginnis*, 7 East, 361; Byles on Bills, 13th Ed. 262. The protest may be extended as of the date of the noting, and ante-dated accordingly; see sub-section 4 of sect. 51 of this Act.

Protest when notary not accessible.

94. Where a dishonoured bill or note is authorised or required to be protested, and the services of a notary cannot be obtained at the place where the bill is dishonoured, any householder or substantial resident of the place may, in the presence of two witnesses, give a certificate signed by them, attesting the dishonour of the bill, and the certificate shall in all respects operate as if it were a formal protest of the bill.

The form given in schedule 1 to this Act may be used with necessary modifications, and if used shall be sufficient (*a*).

(*a*) Bayley on Bills, 6th Ed., p. 263, Parsons on Notes, vol. 1, pp. 633, 634. As to the meaning of "protest," and as to who a notary is, see note (*y*) to section 51.

In America, it seems that the witnesses need not subscribe their names; Parsons, p. 633, note *n*.

In France, by the Code de Commerce, all protests must be made by two notaries, or by one notary and two witnesses, or by a bailiff and two witnesses; Art. 173; Chalmers on Bills, 2nd ed., 151.

Dividend warrants may be crossed.

95. The provisions of this Act as to crossed cheques shall apply to a warrant for payment of dividend.

Repeal

96. The enactments mentioned in the second schedule to this Act are hereby repealed as from the commencement of this Act to the extent in that schedule mentioned

Provided that such repeal shall not affect anything done or suffered, or any right, title, or interest acquired or accrued before the commencement of this Act, or any legal proceeding or remedy in respect of any such thing, right, title, or interest.

Savings

97.—(1.) The rules in bankruptcy relating to bills of

exchange, promissory notes, and cheques, shall continue to apply thereto notwithstanding anything in this Act contained (*z*).

(2.) The rules of Common Law, including the law-merchant, save in so far as they are inconsistent with the express provisions of this Act, shall continue to apply to bills of exchange, promissory notes, and cheques.

(3.) Nothing in this Act or in any repeal effected thereby shall affect—

(*a*) The provisions of the Stamp Act, 1870, or Acts amending it, or any law or enactment for the time being in force relating to the revenue (*y*):

(*b*) The provisions of the Companies Act, 1862, or Acts amending it, or any Act relating to joint stock banks or companies (*x*):

(*c*) The provisions of any Act relating to or confirming the privileges of the Bank of England or the Bank of Ireland respectively (*v*):

(*d*) The validity of any usage relating to dividend warrants, or the indorsements thereof (*u*).

S 97.

Savings.

33 & 34 Vict c 97.

25 & 26 Vict. c 89

(*z*) Though the law of bankruptcy is outside the scope of this treatise, still a few of the leading principles are here set out. Under the Bankruptcy Act, 1883, ss. 44, 168, if the lawful holder of a bill becomes bankrupt, the title thereto vests in his trustee in bankruptcy.

As to proof on a bill of exchange, it can, says Lord Selborne in *Ex parte Macredie*, L. R. 8 Ch. Ap. at p. 537; 42 L. J. Bank. 90, only be admitted for that sum for which an action could have been maintained had there been no bankruptcy. The rights of the parties are the same as if no bankruptcy had happened. Hence, the rules as to notice of dishonour apply; but if the bill or note is dishonoured after the bankruptcy, notice may be given either to the bankrupt or to his trustee; sect. 49, sub-sect. 10, of this Act, *Ex parte Baker*, 4 Ch. D. 795; 46 L. J. Bank. 60; 36 L. T. N. S. 339, 25 W. R. 454. Proof will not be allowed in respect of an acceptance in blank at the date of the receiving order, even though the transaction is *bonâ fide*; *Ex parte Hayward*, L. R. 6 Ch. Ap. 546; 40 L. J. Bank. 49; 24 L. T. N. S 782, 19 W. R. 833. Proof will also be allowed of the usual expenses, such as protesting, re-exchange, posting and telegraphic messages, *Prehn v. Bank of Liverpool*, L. R. 5 Ex. 92; 39 L. J. Ex. 41; *Ex parte Banco de Lima*, 7 Ch. D. 637; 47 L. J. Ch. 67; 37 L. T. N. S. 599; 26 W. R. 232. Interest from the date of the bill being due to the date of the receiving order at 4 per cent. per annum, where no interest is expressly reserved, may be proved for; Bankruptcy Act, 1883, sch. 2, r. 20. A creditor cannot prove his debt upon a bill or note without specifying it in the schedule to his affidavit; Bank Act, 1883, sch. 2, r. 2; form 52. See, however, *Ex parte Jacobs,* L. R. 17 Eq. 575; 43 L. J. Bank. 46; 22 W. R. 439; nor can he receive a dividend without exhibiting the bill or note to the trustee, and the amount of the dividend paid must be indorsed on it; Bankruptcy Rules, 1883, r. 176. There is one advantage that a holder gets in bankruptcy; he need not wait until the bill or note is due, but may prove upon it before it is due; Bankruptcy Act, 1883, s. 37, sub-s. 3; but in such a case interest at the rate of 5 per cent. per annum from the declaration of the dividend to the time at which the bill or note would have become payable must be deducted; Bankruptcy Act, 1883, sch. 2, r. 21. If a creditor has negotiated the bills or notes, he will not be allowed to prove against the acceptor's estate, as he is no longer the holder, and so no action would lie at law; *Ex parte Macredie,* L. R. 8 Ch. Ap. 535, 28 L. T. N. S. 827; 21 W. R. 535 The drawer of a bill is under no obligation to direct the drawee not to pay it, if the payee has become bankrupt before the bill matures, *Ex parte Richdale,* 19 Ch. D. 409; 51 L. J. Ch. D. 462. A vote in respect of a current bill is not to be allowed, unless the creditor is willing to treat the liability of every person liable thereon antecedently to the debtor as a security in his hands, and to estimate the value thereof, and to deduct it from his proof, though only for the purposes of voting; Bank. Act, 1883, sch. 1, r. 11.

(*y*) The material parts of the Stamp Act are set out in the Appendix.

(*x*) By s. 47 of the Companies Act, 1862 (25 & 26 Vict. c. 89), "a promissory note or bill of exchange shall be deemed to have been made, accepted, or indorsed on behalf of any company under this Act, if made, accepted, or indorsed in the name of the company by any person acting under the authority of the company, or if made, accepted, or indorsed by or on behalf or on account of the company by any person acting under the authority of the company." See the cases under this section collected in Buckley on the Companies Acts, 3rd ed. 138. As to the power of a company to issue bills, see s. 22 of this Act, note (*c*). See further sect. 26 of this Act, and the notes thereto. By sects. 41 and 42 of the Companies Act, 1862, the word "limited" must be written on the bill or note, if the Company is limited. The person neglecting to do so may be made personally liable thereon, *Penrose* v. *Martyr,* E. B. & E. 499; 28 L. J. Q B. 28. Sect. 95 of the Companies Act, 1862, gives the official liquidator power to draw, &c., bills and notes, with the sanction of the Court; *Orders of November,* 1862, O. 48.

(*v*) As to the Acts affecting the Banks of England and Ireland, see Grant's Law of Bankers, 4th ed, chapters 34, 35, 36, & 37, pp. 305 *et seq*

(*u*) By the National Debt Act, 1870 (33 & 34 Vict. c. 71), sects. 20, 21, the Banks of England and Ireland may by arrangement pay dividends on stock by sending warrants through the post, such warrant being deemed a cheque; and where a stockholder requests his dividends to be sent by post, the posting of a letter containing the dividend warrant to the address given by him to the Bank is equivalent to the delivery of the warrant to the stockholder himself.

98. Nothing in this Act or in any repeal effected thereby shall extend or restrict, or in any way alter or affect, the law and practice in Scotland in regard to summary diligence (*a*).

Saving of summary diligence in Scotland.

(*a*) Summary diligence is a mode of obtaining the summary enforcement of a bill or note, without an action. Upon dishonour, a protest of the bill for non-payment or non-acceptance, or of the note for non-payment, is made, and registered with the bill or note prefixed, upon which a charge to pay is made (1 & 2 Vict c. 114), and execution may then issue on default of payment; 12 Geo. 3, c. 72, ss. 41, 42, see Bell's Commentaries on the Laws of Scotland, 7th Ed., vol. 1, pp 4, 413; Thompson on Bills, 2nd Ed , ch. 7.

99. Where any Act or document refers to any enactment repealed by this Act, the Act or document shall be construed, and shall operate, as if it referred to the corresponding provisions of this Act.

Construction with other Acts, &c.

100. In any judicial proceeding in Scotland, any fact relating to a bill of exchange, bank cheque, or promissory note, which is relevant to any question of liability thereon, may be proved by parole evidence : Provided that this enactment shall not in any way affect the existing law and practice whereby the party who is, according to the tenour of any bill of exchange, bank cheque, or promissory note, debtor to the holder in the amount thereof, may be required, as a condition of obtaining a sist of diligence, or suspension of a charge, or threatened charge, to make such consignation, or to find such caution as the Court or judge before whom the cause is depending may require (*a*).

Parole evidence allowed in certain judicial proceedings in Scotland

This section shall not apply to any case where the bill

of exchange, bank cheque, or promissory note, has undergone the sesennial prescription (b).

(a) When in the case of summary diligence any question requires to be settled upon a bill or note, the Lord Ordinary stays the diligence, or suspends the charge, until the question is determined. A bond of caution resembles the English contract of suretyship. When summary diligence is stayed, it is on condition of a cautionary obligation being lodged in court. Consignation is the deposit of a sum of money, which is the subject of dispute, in the hands of a third party.

(b) Sesennial prescription corresponds to the English Statute of Limitations, barring an action on a bill or note after six years. It was introduced by 12 Geo. 3, c. 72.

SCHEDULES.

FIRST SCHEDULE

Form of protest which may be used when the services of a notary cannot   Section 94
be obtained.

KNOW all men that I, *A. B.* [householder], of   in the County
of   , in the United Kingdom, at the request of *C. D.*, there
being no notary public available, did on the   day of
188   at   demand payment [or acceptance] of the bill of
exchange hereunder written, from *E. F.*, to which demand he made
answer [state answer, if any]; wherefore I now, in the presence of *G. H.*
and *J. K.*, do protest the said bill of exchange.

(Signed) *A. B.*

G. H. }
J. K. } *Witnesses.*

N.B.—The bill itself should be annexed, or a copy of the bill, and all
that is written thereon should be underwritten.

SECOND SCHEDULE.

ENACTMENTS REPEALED.

Title of Act and extent of Repeal.	Session and Chapter
An Act for the better payment of Inland Bills of Exchange.	9 Will. 3, c. 17.
An Act for giving like remedy upon Promissory Notes as is now used upon Bills of Exchange, and for the better payment of Inland Bills of Exchange.	3 & 4 Anne c. 8 (*a*).
An Act for further restraining the negotiation of Promissory Notes and Inland Bills of Exchange under a Limited sum within that part of Great Britain called England.	17 Geo. 3, c. 30.
An Act for the better observance of Good Friday in certain cases therein mentioned.	39 & 40 Geo. 3, c. 42.

(*a*) Chapter 8 is evidently a mistake for chapter 9.

Title of Act and extent of Repeal.	Session and Chapter
An Act to restrain the Negotiation of Promissory Notes and Inland Bills of Exchange under a limited sum in England.	48 Geo. 3, c. 88.
An Act to regulate Acceptances of Bills of Exchange.	1 & 2 Geo. 4, c. 78
An Act for declaring the law in relation to Bills of Exchange and Promissory Notes becoming payable on Good Friday or Christmas Day.	7 & 8 Geo. 4, c 15.
An Act to repeal certain Acts, and to consolidate and amend the laws relating to Bills of Exchange and Promissory Notes in Ireland, in part; that is to say, Sections two, four, seven, eight, nine, ten, eleven.	9 Geo 4, c 24 (*b*)
An Act for regulating the protesting for non-payment of Bills of Exchange drawn payable at a place not being the place of the residence of the drawee or drawees of the same.	2 & 3 Will. 4, c 98
An Act for declaring the law as to the day on which it is requisite to present for payment to Acceptor, or Acceptors *suprà* protest for honour, or to the Referee or Referees, in case of need, Bills of Exchange which have been dishonoured.	6 & 7 Will. 4, c 58
An Act to regulate the issue of bank notes in Ireland, and to regulate the repayment of certain sums advanced by the Governor and Company of the Bank of Ireland for the public service, in part; that is to say, Section twenty-four.	8 & 9 Vict c 37, in part.
The Mercantile Law Amendment Act, 1856, in part; that is to say, Sections six and seven.	19 & 20 Vict c 97, in part
An Act for granting to Her Majesty certain duties of stamps, and to amend the laws relating to the stamp duties, in part; that is to say, Section nineteen.	23 & 24 Vict. c. 111, in part.
An Act to abolish days of grace in the case of Bills of Exchange and Promissory Notes payable at sight or on presentation	34 & 35 Vict. c. 74
The Crossed Cheques Act, 1876.	39 & 40 Vict. c. 81.
The Bills of Exchange Act, 1878.	41 & 42 Vict c. 13.

(*a*) The words, "in part," seem to be here omitted by mistake

ENACTMENT REPEALED AS TO SCOTLAND.

Title of Act and extent of Repeal.	Session and Chapter.
The Mercantile Law (Scotland) Amendment Act, 1856, in part, that is to say, Sections ten, eleven, twelve, thirteen, fourteen, fifteen, and sixteen.	19 & 20 Vict. c. 60, in part.

APPENDIX.

The Stamp Act, 1870.

(33 & 34 *Vict. c.* 97.)

SECT. 97, SUB-SECT. 3, OF THE BILLS OF EXCHANGE ACT, 1882,
SAVES THE STAMP ACTS.

An Act for granting certain Stamp Duties in lieu of
duties of the same kind now payable under various
Acts, and consolidating and amending provisions
relating thereto.

[*10th August,* 1870.]

SS. 7, 11, 15.

How instruments are to be written and stamped.

7.—(1.) Every instrument written upon stamped material is to be
written in such manner, and every instrument partly or wholly written
before being stamped is to be so stamped, that the stamp may appear
on the face of the instrument, and cannot be used for or applied to any
other instrument written upon the same piece of material.

(2) If more than one instrument be written upon the same piece of
material, every one of such instruments is to be separately and dis-
tinctly stamped with the duty with which it is chargeable.

Money in foreign or colonial currency to be valued

11.—Where an instrument is chargeable with *ad valorem* duty in
respect of any money in foreign or Colonial currency, such duty shall
be calculated on the value of such money in British currency according
to the current rate of exchange on the day of the date of the instrument.

Terms upon which instruments may be stamped after execution

15.—(1.) Except where express provision to the contrary is made
by this or any other Act, any unstamped or insufficiently stamped
instrument may be stamped after the execution thereof on payment of
the unpaid duty and a penalty of ten pounds, and also by way of
further penalty, where the unpaid duty exceeds ten pounds of interest
on such duty, at the rate of five pounds per centum per annum, from
the day upon which the instrument was first executed up to the time
when such interest is equal in amount to the unpaid duty.

And the payment of any penalty or penalties is to be denoted on the
instrument by a particular stamp.

(2) Provided as follows :

   (*a*) Any unstamped or insufficiently stamped instrument, which has been first executed at any place out of the United Kingdom, may be stamped at any time within two months after it has been first received in the United Kingdom, on payment of the unpaid duty only :

   (*b*) The Commissioners may, if they think fit, at any time within twelve months after the first execution of any instrument, remit the penalty or penalties, or any part thereof.

17.—Save and except as aforesaid, no instrument executed in any part of the United Kingdom, or relating, wheresoever executed, to any property situate, or to any matter or thing done or to be done, in any part of the United Kingdom, shall, except in criminal proceedings, be pleaded or given in evidence, or admitted to be good, useful, or available in law or equity, unless it is duly stamped in accordance with the law in force at the time when it was first executed.

23.—Except where express provision is made to the contrary, all duties are to be denoted by impressed stamps only.

24.—(1.) An instrument, the duty upon which is required, or permitted by law, to be denoted by an adhesive stamp, is not to be deemed duly stamped (*a*) with an adhesive stamp unless the person required by law to cancel such adhesive stamp cancels the same by writing on or across the stamp his name or initials, or the name or initials of his firm, together with the true date of his so writing, so that the stamp may be effectually cancelled (*b*), and rendered incapable of being used for any other instrument, or unless it is otherwise proved that the stamp appearing on the instrument was affixed thereto at the proper time.

(2.) Every person who, being required by law to cancel an adhesive stamp, wilfully neglects or refuses duly and effectually to do so in manner aforesaid, shall forfeit the sum of ten pounds (*c*).

(*a*) The presumption is in favour of the bills having been duly stamped at the proper time, *Bradlaugh* v. *De Rin*, L. R. 3 C. P. 286 See sect. 54, note (*a*) post.

(*b*) *The cancellation may be done by a stamping machine; the stamp may be cancelled at any time before verdict, even in open court*, Viale *v.* Michael, 30 *L. T. N. S.* 463. *See* Pooley *v.* Brown, 11 *C B N. S.* 566; 31 *L J. C. P.* 134, cited in sect. 54, post.

(*c*) *By the Revenue, &c., Act, 1882 (45 & 46 Vict. c. 72), it is further enacted:*

Sect. 14. (1.) Where two or more adhesive stamps are used to denote a stamp duty upon an instrument, such instrument is not to be deemed duly stamped unless the person upon whom the duty of cancellation is by law imposed cancels each or every stamp by writing on or across

SS. 24, 45, 46, 47, 48.
——
General direction as to the cancellation of adhesive stamps

the same his name or initials, or the name or initials of his firm, together with the true date of his so writing, so that both or all and every of the stamps may be effectually cancelled and rendered incapable of being used for any other instrument, or for any postal purpose, or unless it is otherwise proved that the stamps appearing on the instrument were affixed thereto at the proper time.

(2.) If any person contravenes this section, he shall incur the penalty imposed by sect. 24 of the Stamp Act, 1870.

Interpretation of terms

45.—The term " banker " means and includes any corporation, society, partnership, and persons, and every individual person carrying on the business of banking in the United Kingdom.

The term " bank note " means and includes :

(1.) Any bill of exchange or promissory note issued by any banker, other than the Governor and Company of the Bank of England, for the payment of money not exceeding one hundred pounds to the bearer on demand :

(2.) Any bill of exchange or promissory note so issued which entitles or is intended to entitle the bearer or holder thereof, without indorsement, or without any further or other indorsement than may be thereon at the time of the issuing thereof, to the payment of money not exceeding one hundred pounds on demand, whether the same be so expressed or not, and in whatever form, and by whomsoever such bill or note is drawn or made.

Bank notes may be re-issued

46.—A bank note issued duly stamped, or issued unstamped by a banker duly licensed or otherwise authorised to issue unstamped bank notes, may be from time to time re-issued without being liable to any stamp duty by reason of such re-issuing.

Penalty for issuing an unstamped bank note, £50.

47.—(1.) If any banker, not being duly licensed or otherwise authorised to issue unstamped bank notes, issues, or causes or permits to be issued, any bank note not being duly stamped, he shall forfeit the sum of fifty pounds.

For receiving, £20.

(2.) If any person receives or takes any such bank note in payment or as a security, knowing the same to have been issued unstamped contrary to law, he shall forfeit the sum of twenty pounds.

Interpretation of term " bill of exchange "

48.—(1.) The term " bill of exchange " for the purposes of this Act includes also draft, order, cheque (a), and letter of credit, and any document or writing (except a bank note) entitling or purporting to entitle any person, whether named therein or not, to payment by any other person of, or to draw upon any other person for, any sum of money therein mentioned.

(2) An order for the payment of any sum of money by a bill of exchange or promissory note, or for the delivery of any bill of exchange or promissory note in satisfaction of any sum of money, or for the

payment of any sum of money out of any particular fund which may or may not be available, or upon any condition or contingency which may or may not be performed or happen, is to be deemed for the purposes of this Act a bill of exchange for the payment of money on demand (b)

(3.) An order for the payment of any sum of money weekly, monthly, or at any other stated periods, and also any order for the payment by any person at any time after the date thereof of any sum of money, and sent or delivered by the person making the same to the person by whom the payment is to be made, and not to the person to whom the payment is to be made, or to any person on his behalf, is to be deemed for the purposes of this Act a bill of exchange for the payment of money on demand.

(a) *A cheque may be post-dated; Bills of Exchange Act, 1882, sect. 13, sub-sect. 2. A cheque with a penny stamp, post-dated, is admissible in evidence in an action brought by the holder, though he took it with knowledge of the post-dating;* Gatty v. Fry, 2 *Ex. D.* 265; 46 *L J Ex.* 605; 36 *L. T. N. S.* 182; 25 W. R. 305.

(b) *A letter in these words:* "*I hereby assign to R. & Son the sum of £40, or any other sum now due, or that may hereafter become due in respect of the steam launch,*" &c., *has been held to be an assignment of a debt, and not an order for the payment of money within this section,* Buck v. Robson, 3 *Q. B. D.* 686; 48 *L J. Q. B.* 250; 39 *L. T N S* 325; 26 *W. R.* 804; see also *Brice* v. *Bannister*, 3 Q. B. D 569, where it appears to have been assumed on all hands that subject to the disputed question as to how far the defendant was entitled to set off the advances subsequently made by him to the assignor, the effect of the instrument was as between the builder and the defendant to all intents and purposes an assignment of the debt. *Buck v. Robson* was followed in *Fisher* v *Calvert*, 27 W. R. 301, per Jessel, M.R., over-ruling, *Ex parte Shellard, In re Adams*, L. R. 17 Eq 109; 22 W. R. 152.

49. (1.) The term "promissory note" means and includes any document or writing (except a bank note) containing a promise to pay any sum of money.

(2) A note promising the payment of any sum of money out of any particular fund which may or may not be available, or upon any condition or contingency which may or may not be performed or happen, is to be deemed for the purposes of this Act a promissory note for the said sum of money (a).

(a) "I, D., promise to pay Y. on his signing a lease of the Castle Hotel £150," is a note within this section, and cannot be stamped, by s. 53, after execution as an agreement, *Yeo* v *Dawe*, 32 W. R. 203.

50. The fixed duty of one penny on a bill of exchange for the payment of money on demand may be denoted by an adhesive stamp, which is to be cancelled by the person by whom the bill is signed before he delivers it out of his hands, custody, or power

Margin notes:
SS. 48, 49, 50, 51
Interpretation of term "bill of exchange."
Interpretation of term 'promissory note"
The fixed duty may be denoted by adhesive stamp

M 2

Ad valorem duties to be denoted in certain cases by adhesive stamps

51. (1.) The *ad valorem* duties upon bills of exchange and promissory notes drawn or made out of the United Kingdom are to be denoted by adhesive stamps.

(2.) Every person into whose hands any such bill or note comes in the United Kingdom before it is stamped shall, before he presents for payment, or indorses, transfers, or in any manner negotiates, or pays such bill or note, affix thereto a proper adhesive stamp or proper adhesive stamps of sufficient amount, and cancel every stamp so affixed thereto.

(3.) Provided as follows:

Provisoes for the protection of bonâ fide holders.

(*a*) If at the time when any such bill or note comes into the hands of any *bonâ fide* holder thereof there is affixed thereto an adhesive stamp effectually obliterated, and purporting and appearing to be duly cancelled, such stamp shall, so far as relates to such holder, be deemed to be duly cancelled, although it may not appear to have been so affixed or cancelled by the proper person.

(*b*) If at the time when any such bill or note comes into the hands of any *bonâ fide* holder thereof there is affixed thereto an adhesive stamp not duly cancelled, it shall be competent for such holder to cancel such stamp as if he were the person by whom it was affixed, and upon his so doing such bill or note shall be deemed duly stamped, and as valid and available as if the stamp had been duly cancelled by the person by whom it was affixed.

Not to relieve any other person.

(4.) But neither of the foregoing provisoes is to relieve any person from any penalty incurred by him for not cancelling any adhesive stamp.

Bills and notes purporting to be drawn, &c, abroad, to be deemed to have been so drawn, &c.

52. A bill of exchange or promissory note purporting to be drawn or made out of the United Kingdom is, for the purposes of this Act, to be deemed to have been so drawn or made, although it may in fact have been drawn or made within the United Kingdom.

Terms upon which bills and notes may be stamped after execution.

53. (1.) Where a bill of exchange or promissory note has been written on material bearing an impressed stamp of sufficient amount but of improper denomination, it may be stamped with the proper stamp on payment of the duty, and a penalty of forty shillings if the bill or note be not then payable according to its tenour, and of ten pounds if the same be so payable.

(2.) Except as aforesaid, no bill of exchange or promissory note shall be stamped with an impressed stamp after execution thereof.

Penalty for issuing, &c, any unstamped bill or note, £10; and the bill or note to be unavailable.

54. (1.) Every person who issues, indorses, transfers, negotiates, presents for payment, or pays any bill of exchange or promissory note liable to duty and not being duly stamped (*a*), shall forfeit the sum of ten pounds, and the person who takes or receives from any other person any such bill or note not being duly stamped, either in payment or as a security, or by purchase or otherwise, shall not be entitled to recover thereon, or to make the same available for any purpose whatever (*b*).

(2.) Provided that if any bill of exchange for the payment of money on demand, liable only to the duty of one penny, is presented for payment unstamped, the person to whom it is so presented may affix thereto a proper adhesive stamp, and cancel the same, as if he had been the drawer of the bill, and may, upon so doing, pay the sum in the said bill mentioned, and charge the duty in account against the person by whom the bill was drawn, or deduct such duty from the said sum, and such bill is, so far as respects the duty, to be deemed good and valid.

SS 54, 55.
——
Proviso as to
fixed duty;

(3.) But the foregoing proviso is not to relieve any person from any penalty he may have incurred in relation to such bill.

not to relieve
from penalty

(a) *" Duly stamped " here means, as regards a foreign bill, simply stamped, and not stamped and cancelled as in sect.* 24; *Marc* v. *Rouy,* 31 L. T. N. S. 372.

(b) The purchaser of foreign bills, of which the stamps were never cancelled, though both parties were ignorant of the defect, cannot recover from the seller the price paid for them, *Pooley* v. *Brown,* 11 C. B. N. S 566 ; 31 L. J. C. P. 134.

55. When a bill of exchange is drawn in a set according to the custom of merchants, and one of the set is duly stamped, the other or others of the set shall, unless issued or in some manner negotiated apart from such duly stamped bill, be exempt from duty ; and upon proof of the loss or destruction of a duly stamped bill forming one of a set, any other bill of the set which has not been issued or in any manner negotiated apart from such lost or destroyed bill may, although unstamped, be admitted in evidence to prove the contents of such lost or destroyed bill.

One bill only
out of a set
need be
stamped.

SCHEDULE

Bank Note—			s.	d.
For money not exceeding £1 . .	.		0	5
Exceeding £1 and not exceeding £2	.		0	10
„ £2 „ „ £5 .	.		1	3
„ £5 „ „ £10 .	. .		1	9
„ £10 „ „ £20	.		2	0
„ £20 „ „ £30 .	. . .		3	0
„ £30 „ „ £50 .	.		5	0
„ £50 „ „ £100 .			8	6
Bill of Exchange—				
Payable on demand . . .	.		0	1

Bill of Exchange of any other kind whatsoever (except a Bank Note) and Promissory Note of any kind whatsoever (except a Bank Note), drawn, or expressed to be payable, or actually paid, or indorsed,

or in any manner negotiated in the United
Kingdom:

	s.	d.
Where the amount or value of the money for which the bill or note is drawn or made does not exceed £5	0	1
Exceeds £5 and does not exceed £10	0	2
" £10 " " £25 . . .	0	3
" £25 " " £50 . . .	0	6
" £50 " " £75 . . .	0	9
" £75 " " £100 . . .	1	0
" £100—		
for every £100, and also for any fractional part of £100, of such amount or value . . .	1	0

Exemptions.

(1.) Bill or note issued by the Governor and Company of the Bank of England or Bank of Ireland.

(2.) Draft or order drawn by any banker in the United Kingdom upon any other banker in the United Kingdom, not payable to bearer or to order, and used solely for the purpose of settling or clearing any account between such bankers.

(3.) Letter written by a banker in the United Kingdom to any other banker in the United Kingdom, directing the payment of any sum of money, the same not being payable to bearer or to order, and such letter not being sent or delivered to the person to whom payment is to be made, or to any person on his behalf.

(4.) Letter of credit granted in the United Kingdom authorising drafts to be drawn out of the United Kingdom payable in the United Kingdom.

(5.) Draft or order drawn by the Accountant General of the Court of Chancery in England or Ireland.

(6.) Warrant or order for the payment of any annuity granted by the Commissioners for the Reduction of the National Debt, or for the payment of any dividend or interest on any share in the Government or Parliamentary stocks or funds.

(7.) Bill drawn by the Lords Commissioners of the Admiralty, or by any person under their authority, under the authority of any Act of Parliament upon and payable by the Accountant General of the Navy (a)

(8.) Bill drawn (according to a form prescribed by Her Majesty's orders by any person duly authorised to draw the same) upon and payable out of any public account for any pay or allowance of the army or other expenditure connected therewith

(9.) Coupon or warrant for interest attached to and issued with any security

(*a*) *The words " under the authority of any Act of Parliament" were repealed by sect 7 of 35 & 36 Vict. c. 20, which has itself been repealed by the Statute Law Revision Act, 1883, but such last-mentioned repeal does not revive the above words.*

In addition to the above exemptions, the Revenue, &c., Act, 1882, (45 & 46 Vict. c. 72), enacts as follows:—

Sect. 9.—No stamp duty shall be chargeable upon the following instruments (that is to say):

Draft or order drawn upon any banker in the United Kingdom by an officer of a public department of the State for the payment of money out of a public account.

Receipt given by an officer of a public department of the State for money paid by way of imprest or advance, or in adjustment of an account, where he derives no personal benefit therefrom.

STATUTE OF LIMITATIONS.

The following are a few of the principal points as to the Statute of Limitations (21 Jac. 1, c. 16) with respect to bills and notes.

The limitation is six years, and the statute begins to run on a bill or note from the time that a right of action first accrued to the party.

Therefore on a bill or note payable on demand or at sight, the statute runs from the date of the instrument, *Christie* v. *Fonsick*, Sel. N. P., 13th edit, 301, *De Lavalette* v. *Wendt*, 75 N. Y. Rep. 579, if payable after sight, from presentment, *Holmes* v. *Kerrison*, 2 Taunt. 323; if payable a certain time after sight, or demand, or notice, or date, then from the expiration of that time after sight (*Sturdy* v. *Henderson*, 4 B & Ald. 592), or after demand (*Thorpe* v. *Booth*, Ry. & M. 388), or after notice (*Clayton* v. *Gosling*, 5 B. & C 360; 8 D. & R. 110), or after date (*Wittersheim* v. *Lady Carlisle*, 1 H. Bl. 631).

A note was given in 1857 promising to pay £150 three months after demand, no interest being reserved. Receipts for interest were indorsed by the payee on the note in 1857 and 1858. It was held that payment of interest implied a demand, and that the statute ran from such payment, *In re Rutherford*, 14 Ch D. 687; 49 L J. Ch. 654; 43 L T N. S. 105; 28 W. R 802.

The statute runs as against each indorser from the date of notice of dishonour.

Where a loan is made by cheque, the statute begins to run from the time of the payment of the cheque by the drawer's bankers, and not from the date of the cheque, *Garden* v. *Bruce*, L. R. 3 C. P. 300.

When a bill of exchange or a promissory note has been once so delivered on account of part of a debt as to raise an implication of a promise to pay the balance, the statute is answered as from the time of such delivery, whatever afterwards becomes of the bill or note, *Turney* v. *Dodwell*, 3 E. & B. 136; 23 L. J. Q. B. 137.

In *Morris* v. *Richards*, 45 L. T. N. S. 210, the last day of grace in a note fell on Sunday, June 14th, 1874; the holder commenced an action against the maker on June 14th, 1880; held, that the claim was barred, as the note became due on June 13th, 1874.

An absolute acknowledgment in writing of the debt (9 Geo. 4, c 14, s. 1), or part payment of principal, or payment of interest, within six years of the commencement of the action, takes the case out of the statute.

L., in 1846, promised to pay, three months after date, to *B.*, or *C.*, his wife, £500. *B.* died in 1863, leaving *C.* surviving. There was an indorsement on the note in *L.*'s handwriting of his name and the year 1866. *C.* died in 1868. Held, that this indorsement was a sufficient acknowledgment to exclude the statute, *Bourdin* v. *Greenwood*, L. R. 13 Eq. 281; 41 L. J. Ch. 73; 25 L. T. N. S. 782; 20 W. R. 166.

Where the drawer of a cheque has no funds to meet it, the cheque is due immediately without presentment, and the statute of limitations begins to run from its date; *Brush* v. *Barrett*, 82 N. Y. Rep. 400.

Money deposited at a banker's is money lent, and the statute runs in the same way as in the case of a loan, *Pott* v. *Clegg*, 16 M. & W. 321.

NOTE.—*The sections quoted in the margin of this Act refer to the corresponding sections of the English Act and to some of the notes thereto.*

NEGOTIABLE INSTRUMENT ACT (INDIA) 1881.

ACT No. XXVI. OF 1881.

PASSED BY THE GOVERNOR GENERAL OF INDIA IN COUNCIL.

(*Received the assent of the Governor General on the 9th December, 1881.*)

AN ACT to define and amend the law relating to Promissory Notes, Bills of Exchange and Cheques.

Whereas it is expedient to define and amend the law relating to promissory notes, bills of exchange and cheques; it is hereby enacted as follows :— *Preamble*

CHAPTER I.

PRELIMINARY   SS 1, 2, 3

1. This Act may be called "The Negotiable Instruments Act, 1881." *Short title.*

It extends to the whole of British India; but nothing herein contained affects the Indian Paper Currency Act, 1871, section 21, or affects any local usage relating to any instrument in an oriental language. Provided that such usages may be excluded by any words in the body of the instrument, which indicate an intention that the legal relations of the parties thereto shall be governed by this Act, and it shall come into force on the first day of March, 1882. *Local extent Saving of usages relating to hundís, &c*

Commencement.

2. On and from that day the enactments specified in the shedule hereto annexed shall be repealed to the extent mentioned in the third column thereof *Repeal of enactments*

3. In this Act— *Interpretation-clause*
   "Banker" includes also persons or a corporation or company acting as bankers; and *"Banker" Eng Act, s 2*

"Notary public."

"Notary public" includes also any person appointed by the Governor-General in Council to perform the functions of a notary public under this Act.

CHAPTER II.

OF NOTES, BILLS AND CHEQUES.

"Promissory note."

Eng. Act, s 83 (1).

4. A "promissory note" is an instrument in writing (not being a bank note or a currency note) containing an unconditional undertaking, signed by the maker, to pay a certain sum of money only to, or to the order of, a certain person, or to the bearer of the instrument.

Illustrations.

A signs instruments in the following terms :—

(*a*) "I promise to pay B or order Rs. 500."

(*b*) "I acknowledge myself to be indebted to B in Rs. 1,000, to be paid on demand, for value received."

(*c*) "Mr. B, I O U Rs. 1,000."

(*d*) "I promise to pay B Rs. 500 and all other sums which shall be due to him "

(*e*) "I promise to pay B Rs. 500, first deducting thereout any money which he may owe me "

(*f*) "I promise to pay B Rs. 500 seven days after my marriage with C."

(*g*) "I promise to pay B Rs. 500 on D's death, provided D leaves me enough to pay that sum."

(*h*) "I promise to pay B Rs. 500 and to deliver to him my black horse on 1st January next."

The instruments respectively marked (*a*) and (*b*) are promissory notes. The instruments respectively marked (*c*), (*d*), (*e*), (*f*), (*g*) and (*h*) are not promissory notes.

"Bill of exchange."

s 3 (1).

5. A "bill of exchange" is an instrument in writing containing an unconditional order, signed by the maker, directing a certain person to pay a certain sum of money only to, or to the order of, a certain person or to the bearer of the instrument.

s. 11 (2).

A promise or order to pay is not "conditional," within the meaning of this section and section four, by reason of the time for payment of the amount or any instalment thereof being expressed to be on the lapse of a certain period after the occurrence of a specified event which, according to the ordinary expectation of mankind, is certain to happen, although the time of its happening may be uncertain.

s 9 (1).

The sum payable may be "certain," within the meaning of this section and section four, although it includes future interest or is payable at an indicated rate of exchange, or is according to the course of exchange, and although the instrument provides that, on default of payment of an instalment, the balance unpaid shall become due.

The person to whom it is clear that the direction is given or that payment is to be made may be a "certain person," within the meaning of this section and section four, although he is mis-named or designated by description only. Eng. Act, ss, 6, 7.

6. A "cheque" is a bill of exchange drawn on a specified banker and not expressed to be payable otherwise than on demand. "Cheque." s 73

7. The maker of a bill of exchange or cheque is called the "drawer;" the person thereby directed to pay is called the "drawee." "Drawer" "Drawee." s. 3, notes (v) & (s).

When in the bill or in any indorsement thereon the name of any person is given in addition to the drawee to be resorted to in case of need, such person is called a "drawee in case of need." "Drawee in case of need." s. 15.

After the drawee of a bill has signed his assent upon the bill, or, if there are more parts thereof than one, upon one of such parts, and delivered the same, or given notice of such signing to the holder or to some person on his behalf, he is called the "acceptor." "Acceptor" ss 2, 17.

When acceptance is refused and the bill is protested for non-acceptance, and any person accepts it *supra protest* for honour of the drawer or of any one of the indorsers, such person is called an "acceptor for honour." "Acceptor for honour." s. 65.

The person named in the instrument, to whom or to whose order the money is by the instrument directed to be paid, is called the "payee." "Payee." s. 3, note (n).

8. The "holder" of a promissory note, bill of exchange or cheque means any person entitled in his own name to the possession thereof and to receive or recover the amount due thereon from the parties thereto. "Holder." s. 2

Where the note, bill or cheque is lost or destroyed, its holder is the person so entitled at the time of such loss or destruction.

9. "Holder in due course" means any person who for consideration became the possessor of a promissory note, bill of exchange or cheque if payable to bearer, "Holder in due course" s. 29.

or the payee or the indorsee thereof, if payable to, or to the order of, a payee,

before the amount mentioned in it became payable, and without having sufficient cause to believe that any defect existed in the title of the person from whom he derived his title.

10. "Payment in due course" means payment in accordance with the apparent tenor of the instrument in good faith and without negligence to any person in possession thereof under circumstances which do not afford a reasonable ground for believing that he is not entitled to receive payment of the amount therein mentioned. "Payment in due course" s. 59 (1)

Inland instrument.

Eng. Act, ss. 4, 83 (4).

11. A promissory note, bill of exchange or cheque drawn or made in British India, and made payable in, or drawn upon any person resident in, British India shall be deemed to be an inland instrument.

Foreign instrument.

ss. 4, 83 (4).

12. Any such instrument not so drawn, made or made payable shall be deemed to be a foreign instrument.

"Negotiable instrument."

s. 8

13. A "negotiable instrument" means a promissory note, bill of exchange or cheque expressed to be payable to a specified person or his order, or to the order of a specified person, or to the bearer thereof, or to a specified person or the bearer thereof.

Negotiation.

s. 31 (1)

14. When a promissory note, bill of exchange or cheque is transferred to any person, so as to constitute that person the holder thereof, the instrument is said to be negotiated.

Indorsement.

s. 32.

15. When the maker or holder of a negotiable instrument signs the same, otherwise than as such maker, for the purpose of negotiation, on the back or face thereof or on a slip of paper annexed thereto, or so signs for the same purpose a stamped paper intended to be completed as a negotiable instrument, he is said to indorse the same, and is called the "indorser."

Indorsement "in blank" and "in full."

"Indorsee."

ss. 32 (6), 34 (1) (2).

16. If the indorser signs his name only, the indorsement is said to be "in blank," and if he adds a direction to pay the amount mentioned in the instrument to, or to the order of, a specified person, the indorsement is said to be "in full;" and the person so specified is called the "indorsee" of the instrument.

Ambiguous instruments. s. 3, note (*l*), s. 5 (2), s. 83, note (*h*) Where amount is stated differently in figures and words. s. 9 (2). Instruments payable on demand. s. 10 (1). Inchoate stamped instruments.

s 20

17. Where an instrument may be construed either as a promissory note or bill of exchange, the holder may at his election treat it as either, and the instrument shall be thenceforward treated accordingly.

18. If the amount undertaken or ordered to be paid is stated differently in figures and in words, the amount stated in words shall be the amount undertaken or ordered to be paid.

19. A promissory note or bill of exchange, in which no time for payment is specified, and a cheque, are payable on demand.

20. Where one person signs and delivers to another a paper stamped in accordance with the law relating to negotiable instruments then in force in British India, and either wholly blank or having written thereon an incomplete negotiable instrument, he thereby gives *primâ facie* authority to the holder thereof to make or complete, as the case may be, upon it a negotiable instrument, for any amount specified therein and not exceeding the amount covered by the stamp. The person so signing shall be liable upon such instrument, in the capacity in which he signed the same, to any holder in due course for such amount : provided that no person other than a holder in due course shall recover from the person delivering the instrument anything in excess of the amount intended by him to be paid thereunder.

21. In a promissory note or bill of exchange the expressions "at sight" and "on presentment" mean on demand. The expression "after sight" means, in a promissory note, after presentment for sight, and in a bill of exchange, after acceptance, or noting for non-acceptance, or protest for non-acceptance.

"At sight"
"On present-
ment."
"After sight"
Eng. Act, ss. 10
(1), 11 (1).

22. The maturity of a promissory note or bill of exchange is the date at which it falls due

Every promissory note or bill of exchange which is not expressed to be payable on demand, at sight or on presentment, is at maturity on the third day after the day on which it is expressed to be payable.

"Maturity."

Days of grace
s. 14 (1).

23. In calculating the date at which a promissory note or bill of exchange, made payable a stated number of months after date or after sight, or after a certain event, is at maturity, the period stated shall be held to terminate on the day of the month which corresponds with the day on which the instrument is dated, or presented for acceptance or sight, or noted for non-acceptance, or protested for non-acceptance, or the event happens, or, where the instrument is a bill of exchange made payable a stated number of months after sight and has been accepted for honour, with the day on which it was so accepted. If the month in which the period would terminate has no corresponding day, the period shall be held to terminate on the last day of such month.

Calculating
maturity of
bill or note
payable so
many months
after date or
sight.
s 14 (2) (3) (4)

Illustrations.

(*a*) A negotiable instrument, dated 29th January, 1878, is made payable at one month after date. The instrument is at maturity on the third day after the 28th February, 1878.

(*b*) A negotiable instrument, dated 30th August, 1878, is made payable three months after date. The instrument is at maturity on the 3rd December, 1878.

(*c*) A promissory note or bill of exchange, dated 31st August, 1878, is made payable three months after date. The instrument is at maturity on the 3rd December, 1878.

24. In calculating the date at which a promissory note or bill of exchange made payable a certain number of days after date or after sight or after a certain event is at maturity, the day of the date, or of presentment for acceptance or sight, or of protest for non-acceptance, or on which the event happens, shall be excluded.

Calculating
maturity of
bill or note
payable so
many days
after date or
sight
s 14 (2).

25. When the day on which a promissory note or bill of exchange is at maturity is a public holiday, the instrument shall be deemed to be due on the next preceding business day.

When day of
maturity is a
holiday.
s. 14 (1a).

Explanation.—The expression "public holiday" includes Sundays;

New Year's day, Christmas day: if either of such days falls on a Sunday, the next following Monday: Good-Friday; and any other day declared by the Local Government, by notification in the official Gazette, to be a public holiday.

CHAPTER III.

Parties to Notes, Bills and Cheques.

Capacity to make, &c., promissory notes, &c.
Eng. Act, s 22 (1).
Minor.
s. 22 (2).
s 22 (1)

26. Every person capable of contracting, according to the law to which he is subject, may bind himself and be bound by the making, drawing, acceptance, indorsement, delivery and negotiation of a promissory note, bill of exchange or cheque.

A minor may draw, indorse, deliver and negotiate such instruments so as to bind all parties except himself.

Nothing herein contained shall be deemed to empower a corporation to make, indorse or accept such instruments except in cases in which, under the law for the time being in force, they are so empowered

Agency
s. 91.

s. 24, note (b).

s 24, note (b).

27. Every person capable of binding himself or of being bound, as mentioned in section twenty-six, may so bind himself or be bound by a duly authorized agent acting in his name.

A general authority to transact business and to receive and discharge debts does not confer upon an agent the power of accepting or indorsing bills of exchange so as to bind his principal.

An authority to draw bills of exchange does not of itself import an authority to indorse.

Liability of agent signing.
s. 26 (1).

28. An agent who signs his name to a promissory note, bill of exchange or cheque without indicating thereon that he signs as agent, or that he does not intend thereby to incur personal responsibility, is liable personally on the instrument, except to those who induced him to sign upon the belief that the principal only would be held liable.

Liability of legal representative signing.
s 26 (1)

29. A legal representative of a deceased person who signs his name to a promissory note, bill of exchange or cheque is liable personally thereon unless he expressly limits his liability to the extent of the assets received by him as such.

Liability of drawer.
s 55 (1)

30. The drawer of a bill of exchange or cheque is bound, in case of dishonour by the drawee or acceptor thereof, to compensate the holder, provided due notice of dishonour has been given to, or received by, the drawer as hereinafter provided.

Liability of drawee of cheque
s 74, note.

31. The drawee of a cheque having sufficient funds of the drawer in his hands properly applicable to the payment of such cheque must pay the cheque when duly required so to do, and in default of such payment, must compensate the drawer for any loss or damage caused by such default.

32. In the absence of a contract to the contrary, the maker of a promissory note and the acceptor before maturity of a bill of exchange are bound to pay the amount thereof at maturity according to the apparent tenor of the note or acceptance respectively, and the acceptor of a bill of exchange at or after maturity is bound to pay the amount thereof to the holder on demand.

In default of such payment as aforesaid, such maker or acceptor is bound to compensate any party to the note or bill for any loss or damage sustained by him and caused by such default.

Liability of maker of note and acceptor of bill. Eng Act, ss 54, 88

33. No person except the drawee of a bill of exchange, or all or some of several drawees, or a person named therein as a drawee in case of need, or an acceptor for honour, can bind himself by an acceptance.

Only drawee can be acceptor except in need or for honour. s. 6 (2), note b.

34. Where there are several drawees of a bill of exchange who are not partners, each of them can accept it for himself, but none of them can accept it for another without his authority.

Acceptance by several drawees not partners ss 6 (2), 41 (1b)

35. In the absence of a contract to the contrary, whoever indorses and delivers a negotiable instrument before maturity, without, in such indorsement, expressly excluding or making conditional his own liability, is bound thereby to every subsequent holder, in case of dishonour by the drawee, acceptor or maker, to compensate such holder for any loss or damage caused to him by such dishonour, provided due notice of dishonour has been given to, or received by, such indorser as hereinafter provided.

Every indorser after dishonour is liable as upon an instrument payable on demand.

Liability of indorser. s. 55 (2a)

36. Every prior party to a negotiable instrument is liable thereon to a holder in due course until the instrument is duly satisfied.

Liability of prior parties to holder in due course. s. 29 (3).

37. The maker of a promissory note or cheque, the drawer of a bill of exchange until acceptance, and the acceptor are, in the absence of a contract to the contrary, respectively liable thereon as principal debtors, and the other parties thereto are liable thereon as sureties for the maker, drawer or acceptor, as the case may be.

Maker, drawer and acceptor principals ss 54, 88, note (a), 85, note (a).

38. As between the parties so liable as sureties, each prior party is, in the absence of a contract to the contrary, also liable thereon as a principal debtor in respect of each subsequent party.

Prior party a principal in respect of each subsequent party. s 55.

Illustration.

A draws a bill payable to his own order on B, who accepts. A afterwards indorses the bill to C, C to D, and D to E. As between E and

B, B is the principal debtor, and A, C and D are his sureties. As between E and A, A is the principal debtor, and C and D are his sureties. As between E and C, C is the principal debtor and D is his surety.

Suretyship

39. When the holder of an accepted bill of exchange enters into any contract with the acceptor which, under section 134 or 135 of the Indian Contract Act, 1872, would discharge the other parties, the holder may expressly reserve his right to charge the other parties, and in such case they are not discharged.

Discharge of indorser's liability.
Eng. Act, ss. 62, 63 (2)

40. Where the holder of a negotiable instrument, without the consent of the indorser, destroys or impairs the indorser's remedy against a prior party, the indorser is discharged from liability to the holder to the same extent as if the instrument had been paid at maturity.

Illustration.

A is the holder of a bill of exchange made payable to the order of B, which contains the following indorsements in blank :—

First indorsement, "B."
Second indorsement, "Peter Williams."
Third indorsement, "Wright & Co."
Fourth indorsement, "John Rozario."

This bill A puts in suit against John Rozario and strikes out, without John Rozario's consent, the indorsements by Peter Williams and Wright & Co. A is not entitled to recover anything from John Rozario.

Acceptor bound, although indorsement forged.
s 54(2),note(*t*).
Acceptance of bill drawn in fictitious name
s. 54 (2 *b*).

41. An acceptor of a bill of exchange already indorsed is not relieved from liability by reason that such indorsement is forged, if he knew or had reason to believe the indorsement to be forged when he accepted the bill.

42. An acceptor of a bill of exchange drawn in a fictitious name and payable to the drawer's order is not, by reason that such name is fictitious, relieved from liability to any holder in due course claiming under an indorsement by the same hand as the drawer's signature, and purporting to be made by the drawer.

Negotiable instrument made, &c., without consideration.
s. 28 (2).
ss. 27 (2), 28, 29 (3).

43. A negotiable instrument made, drawn, accepted, indorsed or transferred without consideration, or for a consideration which fails, creates no obligation of payment between the parties to the transaction. But if any such party has transferred the instrument with or without indorsement to a holder for consideration, such holder, and every subsequent holder deriving title from him, may recover the amount due on such instrument from the transferor for consideration or any prior party thereto.

Exception I.—No party for whose accommodation a negotiable instrument has been made, drawn, accepted or indorsed can, if he have paid the amount thereof, recover thereon such amount from any person who became a party to such instrument for his accommodation.

Exception II.—No party to the instrument who has induced any other party to make, draw, accept, indorse or transfer the same to him for a consideration which he has failed to pay or perform in full shall recover thereon an amount exceeding the value of the consideration (if any) which he has actually paid or performed.

44. When the consideration for which a person signed a promissory note, bill of exchange or cheque consisted of money, and was originally absent in part or has subsequently failed in part, the sum which a holder standing in immediate relation with such signer is entitled to receive from him is proportionally reduced.

Explanation.—The drawer of a bill of exchange stands in immediate relation with the acceptor. The maker of a promissory note, bill of exchange or cheque stands in immediate relation with the payee, and the indorser with his indorsee. Other signers may by agreement stand in immediate relation with a holder.

Partial absence or failure of money-consideration.

Illustration.

A draws a bill on B for Rs. 500 payable to the order of A. B accepts the bill, but subsequently dishonours it by non-payment. A sues B on the bill. B proves that it was accepted for value as to Rs 400, and as an accommodation to the plaintiff as to the residue. A can only recover Rs. 400.

45. Where a part of the consideration for which a person signed a promissory note, bill of exchange or cheque, though not consisting of money, is ascertainable in money without collateral enquiry, and there has been a failure of that part, the sum which a holder standing in immediate relation with such signer is entitled to receive from him is proportionally reduced.

Partial failure of consideration not consisting of money

CHAPTER IV.

Of Negotiation.

46. The making, acceptance or indorsement of a promissory note, bill of exchange or cheque is completed by delivery, actual or constructive.

As between parties standing in immediate relation, delivery to be effectual must be made by the party making, accepting or indorsing the instrument, or by a person authorized by him in that behalf.

As between such parties and any holder of the instrument other than

Delivery

Eng Act, s. 21 (1).

s. 21 (2a)

s. 21 (2b).

N

a holder in due course, it may be shown that the instrument was delivered conditionally or for a special purpose only, and not for the purpose of transferring absolutely the property therein.

Eng. Act, s. 31 (2)

A promissory note, bill of exchange or cheque payable to bearer is negotiable by the delivery thereof.

s. 31 (3).

A promissory note, bill of exchange or cheque payable to order is negotiable by the holder by indorsement and delivery thereof.

Negotiation by delivery.
s. 31 (2).

47. Subject to the provisions of section fifty-eight, a promissory note, bill of exchange or cheque payable to bearer is negotiable by delivery thereof.

s 29 (2) (3).

Exception.—A promissory note, bill of exchange or cheque delivered on condition that it is not to take effect except in a certain event, is not negotiable (except in the hands of a holder for value without notice of the condition) unless such event happens.

Illustrations.

(*a*) A, the holder of a negotiable instrument payable to bearer, delivers it to B's agent to keep for B. The instrument has been negotiated.

(*b*) A, the holder of a negotiable instrument payable to bearer, which is in the hands of A's banker, who is at the time the banker of B, directs the banker to transfer the instrument to B's credit in the banker's account with B. The banker does so, and accordingly now possesses the instrument as B's agent. The instrument has been negotiated, and B has become the holder of it.

Negotiation by indorsement.
s. 31 (3).

48. Subject to the provisions of section fifty-eight, a promissory note, bill of exchange or cheque payable to the order of a specified person, or to a specified person or order, is negotiable by the holder by indorsement and delivery thereof.

Conversion of indorsement in blank into indorsement in full.
s. 34 (4).

49. The holder of a negotiable instrument indorsed in blank may, without signing his own name, by writing above the indorser's signature a direction to pay to any other person as indorsee, convert the indorsement in blank into an indorsement in full; and the holder does not thereby incur the responsibility of an indorser.

Effect of indorsement.
s. 31 (1).

s. 35.

50. The indorsement of a negotiable instrument followed by delivery transfers to the indorsee the property therein with the right of further negotiation; but the indorsement may, by express words, restrict or exclude such right, or may merely constitute the indorsee an agent to indorse the instrument, or to receive its contents for the indorser, or for some other specified person.

Illustrations.

B signs the following indorsements on different negotiable instruments payable to bearer :—

(*a*) " Pay the contents to C only."

(*b*) " Pay C for my use."

(*c*) " Pay C or order for the account of B."

(*d*) " The within must be credited to C."

These indorsements exclude the right of further negotiation by C.

(*e*) " Pay C."

(*f*) " Pay C value in account with the Oriental Bank."

(*g*) " Pay the contents to C, being part of the consideration in a certain deed of assignment executed by C to the indorser and others."

These indorsements do not exclude the right of further negotiation by C.

51. Every sole maker, drawer, payee or indorsee, or all of several joint makers, drawers, payees or indorsees, of a negotiable instrument may, if the negotiability of such instrument has not been restricted or excluded as mentioned in section fifty, indorse and negotiate the same

Explanation.—Nothing in this section enables a maker or drawer to indorse or negotiate an instrument, unless he is in lawful possession or is holder thereof; or enables a payee or indorsee to indorse or negotiate an instrument, unless he is holder thereof.

Who may negotiate

Illustration.

A bill is drawn payable to A or order. A indorses it to B, the indorsement not containing the words " or order " or any equivalent words. B may negotiate the instrument.

52. The indorser of a negotiable instrument may, by express words in the indorsement, exclude his own liability thereon, or make such liability or the right of the indorsee to receive the amount due thereon depend upon the happening of a specified event, although such event may never happen.

Where an indorser so excludes his liability and afterwards becomes the holder of the instrument, all intermediate indorsers are liable to him.

Indorser who excludes his own liability or makes it conditional. Eng. Act, s. 32 (6) s. 33.

Illustrations.

(*a*) The indorser of a negotiable instrument signs his name, adding the words—

" Without recourse."

Upon this indorsement he incurs no liability.

(*b*) A is the payee and holder of a negotiable instrument. Excluding personal liability by an indorsement " without recourse," he transfers the instrument to B, and B indorses it to C, who indorses it to A. A is not only reinstated in his former rights, but has the rights of an indorsee against B and C.

Holder deriving title from holder in due course.
Eng. Act, s. 29 (3).
Instrument indorsed in blank.
s. 8 (3).
Conversion of indorsement in blank into indorsement in full
s. 32 note (*h*), s. 34 (4).
Indorsement for part of sum due.
s. 32 (2).
Legal representative cannot by delivery only negotiate instrument indorsed by deceased.
Instrument obtained by unlawful means or for unlawful consideration
ss. 29, 38.

53. A holder of a negotiable instrument who derives title from a holder in due course has the rights thereon of that holder in due course.

54. Subject to the provisions hereinafter contained as to crossed cheques, a negotiable instrument indorsed in blank is payable to the bearers thereof even although originally payable to order.

55. If a negotiable instrument, after having been indorsed in blank, is indorsed in full, the amount of it cannot be claimed from the indorser in full, except by the person to whom it has been indorsed in full, or by one who derives title through such person.

56. No writing on a negotiable instrument is valid for the purpose of negotiation if such writing purports to transfer only a part of the amount appearing to be due on the instrument; but where such amount has been partly paid, a note to that effect may be indorsed on the instrument, which may then be negotiated for the balance

57. The legal representative of a deceased person cannot negotiate by delivery only a promissory note, bill of exchange or cheque payable to order and indorsed by the deceased but not delivered.

58. When a negotiable instrument has been lost, or has been obtained from any maker, acceptor or holder thereof by means of an offence or fraud, or for an unlawful consideration, no possessor or indorsee who claims through the person who found or so obtained the instrument is entitled to receive the amount due thereon from such maker, acceptor or holder, or from any party prior to such holder, unless such possessor or indorsee is, or some person through whom he claims was, a holder thereof in due course.

Instrument acquired after dishonour or when overdue
s 36 (2) (5).
Accommodation note or bill.
s. 36, note (*x*).

59. The holder of a negotiable instrument, who has acquired it after dishonour, whether by non-acceptance or non-payment, with notice thereof, or after maturity, has only, as against the other parties, the rights thereon of his transferor:

Provided that any person who, in good faith and for consideration, becomes the holder, after maturity, of a promissory note or bill of exchange made, drawn or accepted without consideration, for the purpose of enabling some party thereto to raise money thereon, may recover the amount of the note or bill from any prior party.

Illustration.

The acceptor of a bill of exchange, when he accepted it, deposited with the drawer certain goods as a collateral security for the payment of the bill, with power to the drawer to sell the goods and apply the proceeds in discharge of the bill if it were not paid at maturity. The bill not having been paid at maturity, the drawer sold the goods and retained the proceeds, but indorsed the bill to A. A's title is subject to the same objection as the drawer's title.

60. A negotiable instrument may be negotiated (except by the maker, drawee or acceptor after maturity) until payment or satisfaction thereof by the maker, drawee or acceptor at or after maturity, but not after such payment or satisfaction.

Instrument negotiable till payment or satisfaction. Eng. Act, s. 36 (1).

CHAPTER V.

Of Presentment.

61. A bill of exchange payable after sight must, if no time or place is specified therein for presentment, be presented to the drawee thereof for acceptance, if he can, after reasonable search, be found, by a person entitled to demand acceptance, within a reasonable time after it is drawn, and in business hours on a business day. In default of such presentment, no party thereto is liable thereon to the person making such default.

Presentment for acceptance. ss. 39 (1), 40, 41 (1a).

If the drawee cannot, after reasonable search, be found, the bill is dishonoured.

s 41 (2 b).

If a bill is directed to the drawee at a particular place, it must be presented at that place; and if at the due date for presentment he cannot, after reasonable search, be found there, the bill is dishonoured.

ss 39 (2), 41 (2b).

62. A promissory note, payable at a certain period after sight, must be presented to the maker thereof for sight (if he can after reasonable search be found) by a person entitled to demand payment, within a reasonable time after it is made and in business hours on a business day. In default of such presentment, no party thereto is liable thereon to the person making such default.

Presentment of promissory note for sight.

63. The holder must, if so required by the drawee of a bill of exchange presented to him for acceptance, allow the drawee twenty-four hours (exclusive of public holidays) to consider whether he will accept it.

Drawee's time for deliberation. s. 42, note.

64. Promissory notes, bills of exchange and cheques must be presented for payment to the maker, acceptor or drawee thereof respectively, by or on behalf of the holder as hereinafter provided. In default of such presentment, the other parties thereto are not liable thereon to such holder.

Presentment for payment. s. 45.

Exception.—Where a promissory note is payable on demand and is not payable at a specified place, no presentment is necessary in order to charge the maker thereof.

ss. 86, note (a), 87 (1)

65. Presentment for payment must be made during the usual hours of business, and, if at a banker's, within banking hours.

66. A promissory note or bill of exchange, made payable at a specified period after date or sight thereof, must be presented for payment at maturity.

67. A promissory note payable by instalments must be presented for payment on the third day after the date fixed for payment of each instalment, and non-payment on such presentment has the same effect as non-payment of a note at maturity.

68. A promissory note, bill of exchange or cheque made, drawn or accepted payable at a specified place and not elsewhere must, in order to charge any party thereto, be presented for payment at that place.

69. A promissory note or bill of exchange made, drawn or accepted payable at a specified place must, in order to charge the maker or drawer thereof, be presented for payment at that place.

70. A promissory note or bill of exchange, not made payable as mentioned in sections sixty-eight and sixty-nine, must be presented for payment at the place of business (if any), or at the usual residence, of the maker, drawee or acceptor thereof, as the case may be.

71. If the maker, drawee or acceptor of a negotiable instrument has no known place of business or fixed residence, and no place is specified in the instrument for presentment for acceptance or payment, such presentment may be made to him in person wherever he can be found.

72. A cheque must, in order to charge the drawer, be presented at the bank upon which it is drawn before the relation between the drawer and his banker has been altered to the prejudice of the drawer.

73. A cheque must, in order to charge any person except the drawer, be presented within a reasonable time after delivery thereof by such person.

74. Subject to the provisions of section thirty-one, a negotiable instrument payable on demand must be presented for payment within a reasonable time after it is received by the holder.

75. Presentment for acceptance or payment may be made to the duly authorized agent of the drawee, maker or acceptor, as the case may be, or, where the drawee, maker or acceptor has died, to his legal representative, or, where he has been declared an insolvent, to his assignee.

76. No presentment for payment is necessary, and the instrument is dishonoured at the due date for presentment, in any of the following cases:—

(*a*) if the maker, drawee or acceptor intentionally prevents the presentment of the instrument, or, if the instrument being payable at his place of business, he closes such place on a business day during the usual business hours, or,

Eng. Act, ss. 46 (2), note (y). 45 (5).

if the instrument being payable at some other specified place, neither he nor any person authorized to pay it attends at such place during the usual business hours, or,

s. 45 (5).

if the instrument not being payable at any specified place, he cannot after due search be found;

s. 45 (4d) note.

(b) as against any party sought to be charged therewith, if he has engaged to pay notwithstanding non-presentment,

s. 46 (2c).

(c) as against any party if, after maturity, with knowledge that the instrument has not been presented—

s. 46 (2c).

he makes a part payment on account of the amount due on the instrument,

or promises to pay the amount due thereon in whole or in part,

or otherwise waives his right to take advantage of any default in presentment for payment;

(d) as against the drawer, if the drawer could not suffer damage from the want of such presentment.

s. 46 (2c).

77. When a bill of exchange, accepted payable at a specified bank, has been duly presented there for payment and dishonoured, if the banker so negligently or improperly keeps, deals with or delivers back such bill as to cause loss to the holder, he must compensate the holder for such loss.

Liability of banker for negligently dealing with bill presented for payment.

CHAPTER VI.

OF PAYMENT AND INTEREST.

78. Subject to the provisions of section eighty-two, clause (c), payment of the amount due on a promissory note, bill of exchange or cheque must, in order to discharge the maker or acceptor, be made to the holder of the instrument.

To whom payment should be made. Eng. Act, s. 59 (1).

79. When interest at a specified rate is expressly made payable on a promissory note or bill of exchange, interest shall be calculated at the rate specified, on the amount of the principal money due thereon, from the date of the instrument, until tender or realization of such amount, or until such date after the institution of a suit to recover such amount as the Court directs.

Interest when rate specified. s. 57, note (s).

80. When no rate of interest is specified in the instrument, interest on the amount due thereon shall, except in cases provided for by the Code of Civil Procedure, section 532, be calculated at the rate of six per centum per annum, from the date at which the same ought to have been paid by the party charged, until tender or realization of the

Interest when no rate specified s. 57 (1b).

amount due thereon, or until such date after, the institution of a suit to recover such amount as the Court directs.

Explanation.—When the party charged is the indorser of an instrument dishonoured by non-payment, he is liable to pay interest only from the time that he receives notice of the dishonour.

Delivery of instrument on payment, or indemnity in case of loss. Eng. Act, ss. 52 (4), 70.

81. Any person liable to pay, and called upon by the holder thereof to pay, the amount due on a promissory note, bill of exchange or cheque is before payment entitled to have it shown, and is on payment entitled to have it delivered up, to him, or, if the instrument is lost or cannot be produced, to be indemnified against any further claim thereon against him.

CHAPTER VII.

OF DISCHARGE FROM LIABILITY ON NOTES, BILLS AND CHEQUES.

Discharge from liability—

by cancellation; s. 63.

by release; s. 62.

by payment; s. 59.

82. The maker, acceptor or indorser respectively of a negotiable instrument is discharged from liability thereon—

(*a*) to a holder thereof who cancels such acceptor's or indorser's name with intent to discharge him, and to all parties claiming under such holder;

(*b*) to a holder thereof who otherwise discharges such maker, acceptor or indorser, and to all parties deriving title under such holder after notice of such discharge;

(*c*) to all parties thereto, if the instrument is payable to bearer, or has been indorsed in blank, and such maker, acceptor or indorser makes payment in due course of the amount due thereon.

Discharge by allowing drawee more than twenty-four hours to accept. s. 42. When cheque not duly presented and drawer damaged thereby. s. 74 Cheque payable to order. s. 60. Parties not consenting discharged by qualified or limited acceptance. s. 42.

83. If the holder of a bill of exchange allows the drawee more than twenty-four hours, exclusive of public holidays, to consider whether he will accept the same, all previous parties not consenting to such allowance are thereby discharged from liability to such holder.

84. When the holder of a cheque fails to present it for payment within a reasonable time, and the drawer thereof sustains loss or damage from such failure, he is discharged from liability to the holder.

85. Where a cheque payable to order purports to be indorsed by or on behalf of the payee, the drawee is discharged by payment in due course.

86. If the holder of a bill of exchange acquiesces in a qualified acceptance, or one limited to part of the sum mentioned in the bill, or which substitutes a different place or time for payment, or which, where the drawees are not partners, is not signed by all the drawees, all previous parties whose consent is not obtained to such acceptance are discharged as against the holder and those claiming under him, unless on notice given by the holder they assent to such acceptance.

Explanation.—An acceptance is qualified— Eng. Act, s 19 (2)

(*a*) where it is conditional, declaring the payment to be dependent on the happening of an event therein stated ;

(*b*) where it undertakes the payment of part only of the sum ordered to be paid ;

(*c*) where, no place of payment being specified on the order, it undertakes the payment at a specified place, and not otherwise or elsewhere ; or where, a place of payment being specified in the order, it undertakes the payment at some other place, and not otherwise or elsewhere ;

(*d*) where it undertakes the payment at a time other than that at which under the order it would be legally due.

87. Any material alteration of a negotiable instrument renders the same void as against any one who is a party thereto at the time of making such alteration and does not consent thereto, unless it was made in order to carry out the common intention of the original parties ; Effect of material alteration s. 64.

and any such alteration, if made by an indorsee, discharges his indorser from all liability to him in respect of the consideration thereof. Alteration by indorsee.

The provisions of this section are subject to those of sections twenty, forty-nine, eighty-six and one hundred and twenty-five.

88. An acceptor or indorser of a negotiable instrument is bound by his acceptance or indorsement notwithstanding any previous alteration of the instrument. Acceptor or indorser bound notwithstanding previous alteration. s. 64.

89. Where a promissory note, bill of exchange or cheque has been materially altered but does not appear to have been so altered, Payment of instrument on which alteration is not apparent. ss. 64 (1), 79 (2).

or where a cheque is presented for payment which does not at the time of presentation appear to be crossed or to have had a crossing which has been obliterated,

payment thereof by a person or banker liable to pay, and paying the same according to the apparent tenor thereof at the time of payment and otherwise in due course, shall discharge such person or banker from all liability thereon; and such payment shall not be questioned by reason of the instrument having been altered, or the cheque crossed.

90. If a bill of exchange which has been negotiated is, at or after maturity, held by the acceptor in his own right, all rights of action thereon are extinguished. Extinguishment of rights of action on bill in acceptor's hands. s 61.

CHAPTER VIII.

OF NOTICE OF DISHONOUR.

Dishonour by non-accept-ance. s. 43.

91. A bill of exchange is said to be dishonoured by non-acceptance when the drawee, or one of several drawees not being partners, makes default in acceptance upon being duly required to accept the bill, or where presentment is excused and the bill is not accepted.

s. 41 (2a).

Where the drawee is incompetent to contract, or the acceptance is qualified, the bill may be treated as dishonoured.

Dishonour by non-payment. s. 47.

92. A promissory note, bill of exchange or cheque is said to be dishonoured by non-payment when the maker of the note, acceptor of the bill or drawee of the cheque makes default in payment upon being duly required to pay the same.

By and to whom notice should be given. s. 48.

93. When a promissory note, bill of exchange or cheque is dishonoured by non-acceptance or non-payment, the holder thereof, or some party thereto who remains liable thereon, must give notice that the instrument has been so dishonoured to all other parties whom the holder seeks to make severally liable thereon, and to some one of several parties whom he seeks to make jointly liable thereon.

Nothing in this section renders it necessary to give notice to the maker of the dishonoured promissory note, or the drawee or acceptor of the dishonoured bill of exchange or cheque.

Mode in which notice may be given. s. 49.

94. Notice of dishonour may be given to a duly authorized agent of the person to whom it is required to be given, or, where he has died, to his legal representative, or, where he has been declared an insolvent, to his assignee, may be oral or written; may, if written, be sent by post; and may be in any form; but it must inform the party to whom it is given, either in express terms or by reasonable intendment, that the instrument has been dishonoured, and in what way, and that he will be held liable thereon; and it must be given within a reasonable time after dishonour, at the place of business or (in case such party has no place of business) at the residence of the party for whom it is intended.

If the notice is duly directed and sent by post and miscarries, such miscarriage does not render the notice invalid.

Party receiv-ing must trans-mit notice of dishonour. s. 49 (14).

95. Any party receiving notice of dishonour must, in order to render any prior party liable to himself, give notice of dishonour to such party within a reasonable time, unless such party otherwise receives due notice as provided by section ninety-three.

Agent for presentment. s. 49 (13).

96. When the instrument is deposited with an agent for present-ment, the agent is entitled to the same time to give notice to his principal as if he were the holder giving notice of dishonour, and the principal is entitled to a further like period to give notice of dishonour.

97. When the party to whom notice of dishonour is despatched is dead, but the party despatching the notice is ignorant of his death, the notice is sufficient.

98. No notice of dishonour is necessary—

(*a*) when it is dispensed with by the party entitled thereto;

(*b*) in order to charge the drawer, when he has countermanded payment;

(*c*) when the party charged could not suffer damage for want of notice:

(*d*) when the party entitled to notice cannot after due search be found; or the party bound to give notice is, for any other reason, unable without any fault of his own to give it;

(*e*) to charge the drawers, when the acceptor is also a drawer,

(*f*) in the case of a promissory note which is not negotiable;

(*g*) when the party entitled to notice, knowing the facts, promises unconditionally to pay the amount due on the instrument

---

CHAPTER IX.

Of Noting and Protest.

99. When a promissory note or bill of exchange has been dishonoured by non-acceptance or non-payment, the holder may cause such dishonour to be noted by a notary public upon the instrument, or upon a paper attached thereto, or partly upon each.

Such note must be made within a reasonable time after dishonour, and must specify the date of dishonour, the reason, if any, assigned for such dishonour, or, if the instrument has not been expressly dishonoured, the reason why the holder treats it as dishonoured, and the notary's charges.

100. When a promissory note or bill of exchange has been dishonoured by non-acceptance or non-payment, the holder may, within a reasonable time, cause such dishonour to be noted and certified by a notary public. Such certificate is called a protest.

When the acceptor of a bill of exchange has become insolvent, or his credit has been publicly impeached, before the maturity of the bill, the holder may, within a reasonable time, cause a notary public to demand better security of the acceptor, and on its being refused may, within a reasonable time, cause such facts to be noted and certified as aforesaid. Such certificate is called a protest for better security.

101. A protest under section one hundred must contain—

(*a*) either the instrument itself, or a literal transcript of the instrument and of everything written or printed thereupon;

(*b*) the name of the person for whom and against whom the instrument has been protested;

(*c*) a statement that payment or acceptance, or better security, as the case may be, has been demanded of such person by the notary public; the terms of his answer, if any, or a statement that he gave no answer, or that he could not be found;

(*d*) when the note or bill has been dishonoured, the place and time of dishonour, and, when better security has been refused, the place and time of refusal;

Eng. Act, ss. 65, note (*t*), 68 (3) (4).

(*e*) the subscription of the notary public making the protest;

(*f*) in the event of an acceptance for honour or of a payment for honour, the name of the person by whom, of the person for whom, and the manner in which, such acceptance or payment was offered and effected.

Notice of protest.

102. When a promissory note or bill of exchange is required by law to be protested, notice of such protest must be given instead of notice of dishonour, in the same manner and subject to the same conditions; but the notice may be given by the notary public who makes the protest.

Protest for non-payment after dishonour by non-acceptance. s. 51 (6*b*).

103. All bills of exchange drawn payable at some other place than the place mentioned as the residence of the drawee, and which are dishonoured by non-acceptance, may, without further presentment to the drawee, be protested for non-payment, in the place specified for payment, unless paid before or at maturity.

Protest of foreign bills. s. 51 (2).

104. Foreign bills of exchange must be protested for dishonour when such protest is required by the law of the place where they are drawn.

CHAPTER X.

Of Reasonable Time.

Reasonable time. ss 40 (3), 45 (2), 49 (12), 51 (4), 92

105. In determining what is a reasonable time for presentment for acceptance or payment, for giving notice of dishonour and for noting, regard shall be had to the nature of the instrument and the usual course of dealing with respect to similar instruments; and, in calculating such time, public holidays shall be excluded.

Reasonable time of giving notice of dishonour. s. 49 (12).

106. If the holder and the party to whom notice of dishonour is given carry on business or live (as the case may be) in different places, such notice is given within a reasonable time if it is despatched by the next post or on the day next after the day of dishonour.

If the said parties carry on business or live in the same place, such notice is given within a reasonable time if it is despatched in time to reach its destination on the day next after the day of dishonour.

107. A party receiving notice of dishonour, who seeks to enforce his right against a prior party, transmits the notice within a reasonable time if he transmits it within the same time after its receipt as he would have had to give notice if he had been the holder.

Reasonable time for transmitting such such notice. Eng Act, s. 49 (14)

CHAPTER XI.

Of Acceptance and Payment for Honour and Reference in Case of Need.

108. When a bill of exchange has been noted or protested for non-acceptance or for better security, any person not being a party already liable thereon may, with the consent of the holder, by writing on the bill, accept the same for the honour of any party thereto.

Acceptance for honour. s. 65

Unless the person who intends to accept *supra protest* first declares in the presence of a notary that he does it for honour, and has such declaration duly recorded in the notarial register at the time, his acceptance shall be a nullity.

109. A person desiring to accept for honour must, in the presence of a notary public, subscribe the bill with his own hand, and declare that he accepts under protest the protested bill for the honour of the drawer or of a particular indorser whom he names, or generally for honour; and such declaration must be recorded by the notary in his register.

How acceptance for honour must be made.

110. Where the acceptor does not express for whose honour it is made, it shall be deemed to be made for the honour of the drawer.

Acceptance not specifying for whose honour it is made. s. 65 (4)

111. An acceptor for honour binds himself to all parties subsequent to the party for whose honour he accepts to pay the amount of the bill if the drawee do not; and such party and all prior parties are liable in respective capacities to compensate the acceptor for honour for all loss or damage sustained by him in consequence of such acceptance.

Liability of acceptor for honour. s. 66.

But an acceptor for honour is not liable to the holder of the bill unless it is presented, or (in case the address given by such acceptor on the bill is a place other than the place where the bill is made payable) forwarded for presentment, not later than the day next after the day of its maturity.

s. 67.

112. An acceptor for honour cannot be charged unless the bill has at its maturity been presented to the drawee for payment, and has been dishonoured by him, and noted or protested for such dishonour.

When acceptor for honour may be charged. s. 66 (1).

113. When a bill of exchange has been noted or protested for non-payment, any person may pay the same for the honour of any party liable to pay the same, provided that the person so paying has previously declared before a notary public the party for whose honour

Payment for honour. s. 68 (1) (3) (4).

he pays, and that such declaration has been recorded by such notary public.

Right of payer for honour. Eng. Act, s. 68 (5).

114. Any person so paying is entitled to all the rights, in respect of the bill, of the holder at the time of such payment, and may recover from the party for whose honour he pays all sums so paid, with interest thereon and with all expenses properly incurred in making such payment.

Drawee in case of need.

115. Where a drawee in case of need is named in a bill of exchange, or in any indorsement thereon, the bill is not dishonoured until it has been dishonoured by such drawee.

Acceptance and payment without protest.

116. A drawee in case of need may accept and pay the bill of exchange without previous protest.

CHAPTER XII.

OF COMPENSATION.

Rules as to compensation.

117. The compensation payable in case of dishonour of a promissory note, bill of exchange or cheque, by any party liable to the holder or any indorsee, shall (except in cases provided for by the Code of Civil Procedure, section 532) be determined by the following rules :—

Eng. Act, s. 57 (1).

(*a*) the holder is entitled to the amount due upon the instrument, together with the expenses properly incurred in presenting, noting and protesting it;

s. 57 (2).

(*b*) when the person charged resides at a place different from that at which the instrument was payable, the holder is entitled to receive such sum at the current rate of exchange between the two places;

s. 57 (1b).

(*c*) an indorser who, being liable, has paid the amount due on the same is entitled to the amount so paid with interest at six per centum per annum from the date of payment until tender or realization thereof, together with all expenses caused by the dishonour and payment;

s. 57 (2).

(*d*) when the person charged and such indorser reside at different places, the indorser is entitled to receive such sum at the current rate of exchange between the two places;

s. 57, note (p).

(*e*) the party entitled to compensation may draw a bill upon the party liable to compensate him, payable at sight or on demand, for the amount due to him, together with all expenses properly incurred by him. Such bill must be accompanied by the instrument dishonoured and the protest thereof (if any). If such bill is dishonoured, the party dishonouring the same is liable to make compensation thereof in the same manner as in the case of the original bill.

CHAPTER XIII.

SPECIAL RULES OF EVIDENCE.

118. Until the contrary is proved, the following presumptions shall be made :— *(Presumptions as to negotiable instruments of consideration; Eng. Act, s. 30 (1).)*

(a) that every negotiable instrument was made or drawn for consideration, and that every such instrument, when it has been accepted, indorsed, negotiated or transferred was accepted, indorsed, negotiated or transferred for consideration;

(b) that every negotiable instrument bearing a date was made or drawn on such date; *(as to date; s. 13 (1).)*

(c) that every accepted bill of exchange was accepted within a reasonable time after its date and before its maturity; *(as to time of acceptance;)*

(d) that every transfer of a negotiable instrument was made before its maturity; *(as to time of transfer; s. 36 (4).)*

(e) that the indorsements appearing upon a negotiable instrument were made in the order in which they appear thereon; *(as to order of indorsements; s. 32 (5).)*

(f) that a lost promissory note, bill of exchange or cheque was duly stamped; *(as to stamp;)*

(g) that the holder of a negotiable instrument is a holder in due course: provided that, where the instrument has been obtained from its lawful owner, or from any person in lawful custody thereof, by means of an offence or fraud, or has been obtained from the maker or acceptor thereof by means of an offence or fraud, or for unlawful consideration, the burthen of proving that the holder is a holder in due course lies upon him. *(that holder is a holder in due course. s. 30 (2).)*

119. In a suit upon an instrument which has been dishonoured, the Court shall, on proof of the protest, presume the fact of dishonour, unless and until such fact is disproved. *(Presumption on proof of protest.)*

120. No maker of a promissory note, and no drawer of a bill of exchange or cheque, and no acceptor of a bill of exchange for the honour of the drawer shall, in a suit thereon by a holder in due course, be permitted to deny the validity of the instrument as originally made or drawn. *(Estoppel against denying original validity of instrument. ss. 88 (1), 55 (1a), 66 (1).)*

121. No maker of a promissory note and no acceptor of a bill of exchange payable to, or to order of, a specified person shall, in a suit thereon by a holder in due course, be permitted to deny the payee's capacity, at the date of the note or bill, to indorse the same. *(Estoppel against denying capacity of payee to indorse. ss. 88 (2), 54 (2c).)*

122. No indorser of a negotiable instrument shall, in a suit thereon by a subsequent holder, be permitted to deny the signature or capacity to contract of any prior party to the instrument. *(Estoppel against denying signature or capacity of prior party. s. 55 (2b).)*

CHAPTER XIV.

OF CROSSED CHEQUES.

Cheque crossed generally.
Eng. Act, s. 76 (1).

123. Where a cheque bears across its face an addition of the words "and company" or any abbreviation thereof, between two parallel transverse lines, or of two parallel transverse lines simply, either with or without the words "not negotiable," that addition shall be deemed a crossing, and the cheque shall be deemed to be crossed generally.

Cheque crossed specially.
s. 76 (2).

124. Where a cheque bears across its face an addition of the name of a banker, either with or without the words "not negotiable," that addition shall be deemed a crossing, and the cheque shall be deemed to be crossed specially, and to be crossed to that banker.

Crossing after issue.
s 77 (2).
s. 77 (3)

125. Where a cheque is uncrossed, the holder may cross it generally or specially.

Where a cheque is crossed generally, the holder may cross it specially.

s. 77 (4).

Where a cheque is crossed generally or specially, the holder may add the words "not negotiable."

s. 77 (5).

Where a cheque is crossed specially, the banker to whom it is crossed may again cross it specially to another banker, his agent, for collection.

Payment of cheque crossed generally.
s. 79 (2).
Payment of cheque crossed specially.

126. Where a cheque is crossed generally, the banker on whom it is drawn shall not pay it otherwise than to a banker.

Where a cheque is crossed specially, the banker on whom it is drawn shall not pay it otherwise than to the banker to whom it is crossed, or his agent for collection.

Payment of cheque crossed specially more than once.
s. 79 (1)

127. Where a cheque is crossed specially to more than one banker, except when crossed to an agent for the purpose of collection, the banker on whom it is drawn shall refuse payment thereof.

Payment in due course of crossed cheque.
s. 80.

128. Where the banker on whom a crossed cheque is drawn has paid the same in due course, the banker paying the cheque, and (in case such cheque has come to the hands of the payee) the drawer thereof, shall respectively be entitled to the same rights, and be placed in the same position in all respects as they would respectively be entitled to and placed in if the amount of the cheque had been paid to and received by the true owner thereof.

Payment of crossed cheque out of due course.
s. 79 (2).

129. Any banker paying a cheque crossed generally otherwise than to a banker, or a cheque crossed specially otherwise than to the banker to whom the same is crossed, or his agent for collection, being a banker, shall be liable to the true owner of the cheque for any loss he may sustain owing to the cheque having been so paid.

Cheque bearing "not negotiable."
s. 81.

130. A person taking a cheque crossed generally or specially, bearing in either case the words "not negotiable," shall not have, and shall not be capable of giving, a better title to the cheque than that which the person from whom he took it had.

131. A banker who has in good faith and without negligence received payment for a customer of a cheque crossed generally or specially to himself shall not, in case the title to the cheque proves defective, incur any liability to the true owner of the cheque by reason only of having received such payment.

Non-liability of banker receiving payment of cheque. Eng. Act, s. 82

CHAPTER XV.

OF BILLS IN SETS.

132. Bills of exchange may be drawn in parts, each part being numbered and containing a provision that it shall continue payable only so long as the others remain unpaid. All the parts together make a set; but the whole set constitutes only one bill, and is extinguished when one of the parts, if a separate bill, would be extinguished.

Set of bills. s. 71 (1), (6)

Exception.—When a person accepts or indorses different parts of the bill in favour of different persons, he and the subsequent indorsers of each part are liable on such part as if it were a separate bill.

s. 71 (2), (4).

133. As between holders in due course of different parts of the same set, he who first acquired title to his part is entitled to the other parts and the money represented by the bill.

Holder of first acquired part entitled to all. s. 71 (3)

CHAPTER XVI.

OF INTERNATIONAL LAW.

134. In the absence of a contract to the contrary, the liability of the maker or drawer of a foreign promissory note, bill of exchange or cheque is regulated in all essential matters by the law of the place where he made the instrument, and the respective liabilities of the acceptor and indorser by the law of the place where the instrument is made payable.

Law governing liability of maker, acceptor or indorser of foreign instrument. s. 72.

Illustration.

A bill of exchange was drawn by A in California, where the rate of interest is 25 per cent., and accepted by B, payable in Washington, where the rate of interest is 6 per cent. The bill is endorsed in British India, and is dishonoured. An action on the bill is brought against B in British India. He is liable to pay interest at the rate of six per cent. only; but if A is charged as drawer, A is liable to pay interest at the rate of 25 per cent.

Law of place of payment governs dishonour. Eng. Act, s. 72 (3).

135. Where a promissory note, bill of exchange or cheque is made payable in a different place from that in which it is made or indorsed, the law of the place where it is made payable determines what constitutes dishonour and what notice of dishonour is sufficient.

Illustration.

A bill of exchange drawn and indorsed in British India, but accepted payable in France, is dishonoured. The indorsee causes it to be protested for such dishonour, and gives notice thereof in accordance with the law of France, though not in accordance with the rules herein contained in respect of bills which are not foreign. The notice is sufficient.

Instrument made, &c., out of British India, but in accordance with its law. s. 72 (1 *b*)

136. If a negotiable instrument is made, drawn accepted or indorsed out of British India, but in accordance with the law of British India, the circumstance that any agreement evidenced by such instrument is invalid according to the law of the country wherein it was entered into does not invalidate any subsequent acceptance or indorsement made thereon in British India.

Presumption as to foreign law.

137. The law of any foreign country regarding promissory notes, bills of exchange and cheques shall be presumed to be the same as that of British India, unless and until the contrary is proved.

[SCHEDULE.

SCHEDULE.

(a)—Statutes.

Year and chapter	Title.	Extent of repeal.
9 Wm III , c. 17	An Act for the better payment of Inland Bills of Exchange.	The whole.
3 & 4 Anne, c. 8	An Act for giving like remedy upon promissory notes as is now used upon Bills of Exchange, and for the better payment of Inland Bills of Exchange.	The whole

(b)—Acts of the Governor General in Council.

Number and year.	Title	Extent of repeal.
VI of 1840 ...	An Act for the amendment of the law concerning the negotiation of Bills of Exchange.	The whole.
V of 1866 ...	An Act to amend in certain respects the Commercial law of British India.	Sections 11, 12, and 13.
XV. of 1874 ...	The Laws Local Extent Act, 1874.	The first schedule, so far as relates to Act VI of 1840 and Act V of 1866, sections 11, 12 and 13

INDEX.

USANCE,
    meaning of, 22
    foreign bills commonly drawn at, 22

VALUE,
    meaning of, 6, 8
    presumed, 55
    " value received " not necessary in a bill or note, 9, 16

VARYING ACCEPTANCE. *See Qualified Acceptance.*

VOID BILLS, 36–39, 53, 54

WAIVER,
    of presentment, 76, 78
    of notice of dishonour, 85, 86
    of protest, 89
    discharge of bill by, 103, 104

WARRANTY *See Estoppel.*

WIFE. *See Married Woman.*

WRITING,
    includes printing, 6

Lightning Source UK Ltd.
Milton Keynes UK
UKHW031836190321
380653UK00008B/1409